THE
BOSTON RED SOX
TRIVIA BOOK

THE
BOSTON RED SOX
TRIVIA BOOK

David S. Neft,
Bob Carroll, and
Richard M. Cohen

ST. MARTIN'S PRESS   NEW YORK

Special thanks to Michael Neft
for compiling the players' lifetime
totals for the Boston Red Sox.

Editor: George Witte
Production Editor: Mara Lurie
Copyeditor: Bruce Cleary
Design: Judy Christensen

Library of Congress Cataloging-in-Publication Data

Neft, David S.
    The Boston Red Sox trivia book/David S. Neft, Bob Carroll, and
Richard M. Cohen.
        p. cm.
    ISBN 0-312-08712-8
    1. Boston Red Sox (Baseball team)—Miscellanea. I. Carroll, Bob.
II. Cohen, Richard M., 1948–   III. Title.
GV875.B62N44   1993
796.357'64'0974461—dc20   92-44102
                                                    CIP

10 9 8 7 6 5 4 3 2

Books are available in quantity for promotional or premium use. Write to Director of Special Sales, St. Martin's Press, 175 Fifth Avenue, New York, N.Y. 10010, for information on discounts and terms, or call toll-free (800) 221-7945. In New York, call (212) 674-5151 (ext. 645).

Contents

1
TEAM HISTORY

Pilgrims' Progress, 1901–1909

Originally, they weren't the Red Sox, nor were they supposed to be in Boston.

In 1900 Ban Johnson, the energetic president of what had been a smartly run baseball minor league in the Midwest, changed his circuit's name from the "Western League" to the "American League," a clear signal that he envisioned a wider stage for his organization. Still claiming only minor status, Johnson moved the St. Paul team to Chicago to compete against the entrenched National League club there. The ex-Minnesotans did very well indeed in the Windy City, winning the 1900 pennant and encouraging Johnson to go to Phase Two.

As of 1901, Johnson proclaimed, his A.L. would consider itself a major league. The eight circuit teams would include Chicago, Cleveland, Detroit, Milwaukee and Buffalo from the previous season. New teams would be placed in Washington and Baltimore, both of which had formerly hosted National League clubs. Another newcomer would start up in Philadelphia, face to face with the N.L.'s Phillies. He hoped that by impinging on National League territory only in Chicago and Philadelphia, his American League could stay at peace with the older league.

Those hopes were quickly dashed. The National League immediately made it clear that it considered itself at war with Johnson and his "Americans" and would do its best to crush the upstarts. So be it, decided Johnson. In that case, there was no reason to go in for half a loaf. Buffalo was out; the A.L. would open in Boston, in competition with the National League club that had ruled the roost there since 1876.

Bankrolling the new Boston team was one Charles W. Somers.

3

Almost as much as Johnson himself, Somers was responsible for the birth of the new league. A coal, lumber, and shipping millionaire, he was the American League's "angel," putting his money into the Cleveland, Chicago, and Philadelphia franchises as well as Boston. Such multiple ownership is patently illegal today, but in those distant days it was common.

At first, the team went by several different names, none of them official. "Puritans," "Somersets" (in honor of the owner), "Plymouth Rocks," and the generic "Americans" were tried, but "Pilgrims" eventually got the nod. If nothing else, it was appropriate in view of the team's journey east from Buffalo.

The newborn Pilgrims found a place to erect a ballpark at the Huntington Avenue Grounds, which is today the site of Northeastern University's indoor-athletics building. In those days of wooden stands, the creation of a brand-new baseball park did not require nearly the time or money that it does today.

Nor did finding players to fill the new uniforms. With war declared, the American Leaguers saw no impediment to signing scads of National League players, which they accomplished by the honorable means of offering the players more money. The N.L. had painted itself into a corner by establishing a salary cap of $2,500 per season for its players. As long as there was no competition, the cap worked to the N.L.'s advantage. But as soon as players had somewhere else to go at higher pay, they went.

The Pilgrims were particularly fortunate in that the owners of the established Boston N.L. team—later called the Braves but at that time known as the Beaneaters—were unusually tightfisted even by the standards of the day. Even Boston fans thought the Beaneaters were underpaid, and thus their loyalty was easily won when many of their heroes jumped to better contracts with the Pilgrims.

John "Buck" Freeman, a powerful-hitting outfielder–first baseman, and pitcher Ted Lewis were two Beaneaters who succumbed to the Puritans' siren song. Lewis won 16 games for his new team in 1901.

The most important ex-Beaneater was Jimmy Collins, regarded at the time as the best third baseman in the world. Jimmy was a consistent .300 hitter who hit with good power for that deadball era, but he really put all others to shame in the field. Sure of glove and arm, he invented and perfected the technique of racing in, fielding bunts barehanded, and firing the ball unerringly to the appropriate base. The way baseball was played in those days, with everyone scrambling for a run, Collins's ability to quash an opponent's bunting attack made him the cornerstone of his team's defense. He signed with the Pilgrims for $4,000, taking on the manager's duties as well as the third basing. Even more important to the team's success was the signing of pitcher Denton "Cy" Young. The man for whom the modern outstanding-pitcher award is named was unhappy pitching in the heat of St. Louis and jumped at the chance to earn more money in Boston's more temperate climate. With Young winning a league-leading 33 games, and Collins, first baseman Buck Freeman, and center fielder Chick Stahl providing the batting power, the first edition of the Pilgrims stayed in the 1901 pennant race to the end, finally finishing a creditable second to Chicago. The Beaneaters sank to fifth, abandoned by many players and even more fans. From that first season, when the Pilgrims nearly doubled the Beaneaters' attendance, Boston was an "American League city." The "other" Boston team, which soon became the Braves, seldom approached their A.L. foes in attendance during the ensuing years, and after more than fifty years of lingering death, they moved on to Milwaukee in 1953.

After slipping to third in 1902, the Pilgrims sprinted to the pennant in 1903, finishing 14½ games in front of second-place Philadelphia. Collins hit .304 and outfielder Patsy Dougherty led the team at .331. Moved to the outfield, Freeman led the league with 13 home runs and 104 RBI. The pitching was magnificent: Young, Long Tom Hughes, and Bill Dinneen all were 20-game winners.

In the interim, the National and American Leagues had patched up their quarrel and agreed to mutually exist without stealing players from each other. It was a compromise that amounted to total victory for the American League. Part of Ban Johnson's winning strategy had been to take on the N.L. in its own backyard. In 1902, he moved the Milwaukee team to St. Louis to contend with the Cardinals. After the season, he made his major move, shifting Baltimore to New York, where the Giants were ensconced. The National League, realizing that its Pittsburgh Pirates were next on Johnson's list, sued for peace.

Pittsburgh won its third straight N.L. pennant in 1903. Pirate owner Barney Dreyfuss thought it would be a capital idea to renew the World Series that had been such a crowd-pleaser in the 1880s when the National League contended with the then-major American Association. He made his proposal to Henry J. Killilea, who'd taken over Pilgrims ownership from Somers. The challenge was accepted and the first modern World Series was on.

Unfortunately for Pittsburgh, by the time the teams took the field at the Huntington Grounds for Game One, the Pirates were down to one healthy pitcher. But for a while, that looked like enough. Control-artist Charles "Deacon" Phillippe bested Young, 7–3, in the opener, and came back to outduel Hughes, 4–2, in Game Three. Then, after a two-day travel break, he won over Dinneen, 5–4, at Pittsburgh. The Pirates led three games to one, but they still needed two more wins, the Series being set as best of nine. Young and Dinneen won the next two games to tie the Series. Phillippe returned in Game Seven, but this time Young had the better of him, 7–3. The teams returned to Boston. After another two-day break, Collins sent Bill Dinneen to the mound, and Pittsburgh countered with Phillippe once more. When Dinneen pitched a four-hit shutout for his third win of the Series, Boston had a World Championship. And the upstart American League had proved itself the equal of the National.

Killilea sold the team before the 1904 season to retired general Charles Henry Taylor, owner of the *Boston Globe*. The general turned the team over to his son, John I. Taylor, in hope that the new toy would wean the young playboy away from his single-minded pursuit of wine, women, and song.

Defending the world champion's crown proved more difficult than winning it. Not even Young could match the numbers put up by Jack Chesbro of New York in 1904. "Happy Jack," one of the early spitballers, won 41 games! Had there been a Cy Young Award, he'd have won it hands down. For most of the year, Chesbro and his unbeatable spitter kept New York ahead of Boston in the standings. But Collins's champs came on late.

The pennant was on the line on October 10, when the two contenders met for a doubleheader at New York's Hilltop Park. New York needed a sweep. Naturally, Chesbro started for New York in the first game. He was still pitching in the ninth inning with the game tied 2–2, a man on third, and two outs. At that moment, one of his spitters sailed high over his catcher's head. In one brief second, Chesbro's wild pitch allowed the winning run for Boston, lost the pennant for New York, and damned the man who'd set the all-time American League record for victories forever as a "goat."

There was no World Series in 1904. John T. Brush, owner of the pennant-winning New York Giants, refused to let his team sully itself in competition with the still-hated American League. Giants manager John McGraw stoutly backed Brush's decision although he was perhaps the only other man on the planet who felt that way. At the root of the Brush-McGraw brush-off was the strong showing New York's American League team had made in 1904. For most of the season, it looked like both pennants would fall to New York teams, and it was the thought of legitimizing his city rival with a World Series appearance that most offended Brush. By the time Boston took the A.L. crown, Brush and McGraw were so often and so vehemently on record as opposing a World Series that they couldn't back down.

Boston couldn't claim another World Championship for 1904, but it got a lot of mileage out of juxtaposing the names of Brush and McGraw with such phrases as "dirty cowards." That was some consolation for the down days to come in the next few years.

The Pilgrims grew very old very fast. In 1905 they dipped to fourth place. The next year, they tumbled all the way to last. Manager Collins and owner Taylor saw eye to eye on almost nothing, and toward the end of the season, outfielder Chick Stahl replaced Collins as manager.

It was a job Stahl hadn't sought and, as a close friend of Collins, didn't want. But that hardly explains his actions during spring training in 1908. A doctor in one of the towns on the way north gave Stahl a prescription for carbolic acid to be mixed with water and rubbed on a stone bruise Chick had acquired in one of the spring games. Unaccountably, on March 28, Stahl drank a glass of the stuff and died within minutes. Officially, it was called a suicide, although no one could explain why the religious, happily married Stahl should even contemplate ending his life.

John I. Taylor had renamed his team the "Red Sox" for 1907, apparently hoping to divert fans' attention from the last-place finish of the Pilgrims of 1906. The original National League team of the 1870s had been called the "Red Stockings" and had won several pennants under that banner. Whether Pilgrims or Red Sox, the team was destined for the bottom of the standings, despite Cy Young's 22 pitching victories. Counting Stahl, Taylor employed five different managers in the process of finishing seventh in 1907.

Cy Young enjoyed the final 20-win season of his long and illustrious career in helping the Red Sox up to fifth in 1908. In February of the next year, his contract was traded to Cleveland. In his eight Red Sox seasons, he'd won 193 games—which is still the team record. Included among all those wins was a 1905 gem, the first perfect game to be tossed in the twentieth century.

Better days were on the horizon for the Red Sox, however. Their future was to be found in a number of youngsters who appeared in only a handful of games at season's end. These included an 18-year-old fireballing right-hander called "Smokey Joe" Wood, a smooth-fielding third baseman named Larry Gardner, a lantern-jawed catcher named Bill Carrigan whose pugnacious nickname was "Rough," and a ground-covering centerfielder from Texas who answered to the handle Tris Speaker. In 1909 when the Sox moved up to third, Carrigan, Speaker, and Wood became regulars, Gardner was ready to blossom, and strong-armed right fielder Harry Hooper arrived on the scene. These and a few other players would lead the Red Sox to their greatest heights during the next decade.

AS GOOD AS HIS WORD

Cy Young's favorite catcher was Lou Criger, a backstop with a weak bat but defensive skills that more than made up for his lack of batting prowess. When Ty Cobb came to the American League and began running wild on the bases, Criger was his nemesis. Lou's snap throws cut the "Georgia Peach" down with regularity.

Finally, Cobb had had enough. One day he informed Criger that the next time he got on base, he intended to steal all the way around to home. Sure enough, Cobb reached first early in the game and immediately set sail for second. Despite his being forewarned, Criger's throw arrived too late.

As Cobb dusted himself off, he yelled in to the catcher, "And now, you old ice wagon, I'm on my way to third." Lou put all he had into his throw, but Ty slid into third base safely. "And now," Cobb announced, "I'm coming home!" And on the next pitch, he did.

Safe, signaled the umpire. "I'll be damned," said Criger. And, from then on, Cobb ran against Criger just as effectively as he ran on every other catcher in the league.

THANK HEAVEN HE GOT HERE LATE

In the midst of the 1902 season, Connie Mack purchased the contract of minor-leaguer Danny Murphy for his Philadelphia Athletics. Murphy was scheduled to join the team in Boston on July 2, but through some mix-up did not arrive until the second inning was underway. Anxious to test his new acquisition under fire, Mack inserted him into the game immediately. What Connie saw must have made his eyes bug out.

Against three Boston pitchers including Cy Young in a 22–9 massacre, Murphy, the latecomer, went six for six! One of his safeties was a grand-slam home run.

CY VS. RUBE

During his 22 major-league seasons, Cy Young won an astonishing 511 games, but one of his most famous appearances ended in a loss in 1905. For the second game of a July 4, morning-afternoon doubleheader, the thirty-eight-year-old Young took the mound against Philadelphia's great-but-eccentric lefty, "Rube" Waddell. Boston nicked Waddell for two runs in the first inning, and Philadelphia tied it with a home run in the sixth. After that, both hurlers held the opposition scoreless as the innings mounted. After nineteen frames, the score was still knotted.

In the 20th inning, an error helped the A's tally twice, and Waddell held Boston in check in the bottom half to gain the win. Although he was touched for 18 hits (to Waddell's 15), Young negotiated his twenty innings without allowing a walk. "I don't walk anybody in twenty innings, and I still lose!" he exclaimed in amazement.

For Waddell, the victory involved a bonus. In later years when he was short on cash and credit, he was able to trade the baseball he "beat ol' Cy with" for a round of drinks. It's said that eventually no fewer than two dozen different Philadelphia bartenders owned the "authentic" ball.

"TESSIE"

During the 1903 World Series, Boston's "Royal Rooters" nearly drove Pittsburgh players and fans (and anyone else who wasn't a Royal Rooter) crazy by endlessly singing "Tessie," a popular song of the day. Here are the words, for anyone who happens to remember the tune:

Tessie, you make me feel so badly,
Why don't you turn around,
Tessie, you know I love you madly,
Babe, my heart weighs about a pound;

Don't blame me if I ever doubt you,
You know I wouldn't live without you,
Tessie, you are the only, only, only.

Diligent research has failed to uncover any connection between the lyrics and baseball, but apparently that mattered not a whit to loyal Boston fans.

The Best of Times, 1910–1918

The Red Sox spent 1910 and 1911 loitering in the middle of the American League pack. The cream of Ban Johnson's circuit was in Philadelphia, where Connie Mack's Athletics had too much pitching to be kept from pennants. The staff of Eddie Plank, Jack Coombs, Chief Bender, and Cy Morgan consistently held the opposition to a minimum of runs. Mack always said that pitching was 80 percent of baseball, and certainly that was true during the deadball era when hits were hard to come by and home runs were as rare as Swiss admirals.

But while they lingered with the also-rans, the Red Sox were not idle. They were putting their ducks in place for the big push.

In 1910, Duffy Lewis joined Speaker and Hooper to form what some still consider the greatest outfield of all time. Speaker was by far the best hitter of the three, lashing out line drives with monotonous regularity, but Lewis usually checked in with a batting average around .300, and Hooper was a reliable leadoff man. On defense, they put all others to shame, chasing down fly-ball outs that were sure hits in other outfields. Lewis was outstanding in left, and Hooper, with a cannon for an arm, was even better in right. Once again, though, it was Speaker in center who was nonpareil. "Spoke" played an extremely shallow center field which made him sure-death on flares and bloops. Moreover, he was often able to race in, scoop up an apparent base hit, and throw for a force-out at second base. As shallow as he set up, he was still able to get back for long flies that would have gone over the heads of other fielders playing at normal depth. Speaker still is usually ranked in the top echelon of all the center fielders in the long history of baseball.

The infield boasted strong hitting at the corners once Larry Gardner settled in at third base. The .300-hitting first baseman was Jake

11

Stahl, brother to the late Chick. In 1912, Jake was named Red Sox manager. To this date, they are still the only two brothers to have managed the same team.

Jake was a lucky manager. The team he took over in 1912 was on the brink of success, and, as an omen, it had a brand-new ballpark in which to show off its charms. Fenway Park opened that year and has provided a friendly home for the Red Sox ever since.

The greatest source of luck for Stahl was "Smokey Joe" Wood. At the ripe old age of twenty-two, Wood, who had been threatening greatness for four seasons, suddenly put all his considerable skills together and became the best pitcher in baseball. For several years that honor had been reserved for Walter Johnson of the otherwise-undistinguished Washington Senators. Johnson slipped not at all in 1912. In fact, at one point, he set a new American League record by rattling off 16 straight wins. Yet, as the season wore on, it was Wood who came to the fore as a more certain bet when he pitched. Fans argued endlessly over which right-hander had the more potent fastball. Johnson himself said, "There's no man alive can throw the ball harder than Smokey Joe Wood."

Eventually, Wood had a winning streak of his own going. On September 6, he went for his fourteenth consecutive victory. Facing him was Johnson. An overflow crowd estimated to be around 30,000 packed into Fenway in anticipation of the pitching duel of the year. Johnson was magnificent, allowing only a single run on back-to-back, two-out doubles by Speaker and Lewis in the sixth inning. Wood was even better. He gave up one less run to register number 14 in a row. He reached 16 and a share of the record before finally being beaten by Detroit in late September.

Smokey Joe finished with a gawdy 34–5 record. No Red Sox hurler has ever won more in a season.

Wood's great season keyed the BoSox to 105 victories and a first-place finish by a healthy 14 games. Their World Series opponents were John McGraw's Giants, the same crew that had beat the Red Sox in 1904.

Wood got the Red Sox off and winging with a 4–3 win in the opener. Game Two was called because of darkness after eleven innings, and the Giants won Game Three. But Smokey Joe came back to put Boston in front again with a 3–1 victory the next day. The Sox stretched their lead to three games to one in the fifth game as Hugh Bedient outdueled Giant ace Christy Mathewson with a three-hitter.

The Giants won a second game but had to face Wood the next day. For once, Smokey Joe got smoked, as New York pounded him for 6 first-inning runs and tied the Series three games apiece.

It was Bedient vs. Mathewson in the final game, and the Giants led 1–0 until the Red Sox tied the score with a run in the bottom of the seventh. Joe Wood relieved Bedient in the eighth and shut out the Giants for two innings. But Mathewson was equally impenetrable, and the game went into the tenth.

New York squeezed out a run in the top of the inning. Mathewson was only three outs away from a World Championship. He promptly got pinch hitter Clyde Engle to lift an easy fly . . . which center fielder Fred Snodgrass dropped! Engle was perhaps the only one in Fenway Park who didn't gasp in amazement at the muff; he was too busy hustling to second base.

Harry Hooper smashed a liner that could have, should have tied the game, but now Snodgrass made an impossible catch to save the day. Temporarily. Engle tagged and went to third. Mathewson, whose control was legendary, then walked Boston second baseman Steve Yerkes, the potential winning run.

Speaker was next up, but Boston fans groaned when he popped a routine foul fly down the first-base line. New York first baseman Fred Merkle had it all the way, but for some reason Mathewson kept yelling for his catcher Chief Meyers to take it. Merkle backed off; Meyers couldn't make the play. *Plop!* The ball fell safely in foul territory.

One reprieve was enough for Speaker, who singled to score Engle with the tying run and send Yerkes to third. McGraw ordered Duffy Lewis intentionally passed, bringing up Larry Gardner. The BoSox third sacker needed to put the ball in the air, and that's just what he did. His long fly was the second out of the inning, but that's all there were to be as Yerkes raced gleefully home to make Boston the champions.

Jake Stahl's luck didn't continue into 1913. It ended when Joe Wood came down with a sore arm. Although Joe could occasionally pitch effectively on guile alone, the fastball that had put terror in the hearts of A.L. batters was gone forever. Late in the season, Rough Carrigan replaced Stahl as manager and began rebuilding the pitching staff from the ground up.

For one brief season—1914—Boston's "other" team actually outshone the Red Sox. Under Manager George Stallings, the Braves made a "miracle" stretch run from last place to the National League pennant and then shocked the Philadelphia Athletics by taking the World Series in four straight games. It was a one-shot moment of glory, for the Braves immediately slid back into the doldrums.

Meanwhile, Rough Carrigan tinkered with his pitching staff. In 1915, he was ready. For starters, he had right-handers Rube Foster and Ernie Shore, who won 20 and 19, respectively. Joe Wood sore-armed his way to 14 victories and managed to lead the league in ERA. Dutch Leonard was a crackerjack lefty, but the *wunderkind* of the staff was a big twenty-year-old left-hander with a world of talent named George Ruth. They called him "Babe." His 18–5 record made him the league's win-loss percentage leader. Surprisingly, the kid could hit pretty well, too. In fact, his 4 home runs were twice as many as anyone else on the team had hit.

After losing the 1914 World Series to the "Miracle Braves," Connie Mack had been forced by economics to break up his great team. Boston benefited by acquiring Jack Barry, a smooth gloveman, from what had been called the Athletics' "$10,000 Infield," and Herb Pennock, a young left-handed pitcher. Carrigan's Red Sox team had its strongest competition from the hard-hitting Tigers of Ty Cobb, but, as usual, pitching prevailed. Boston finished 2½ games ahead of Detroit.

The BoSox's World Series opponents were the Philadelphia Phillies, who had gotten there primarily on the arm of Grover Alexander. Alex was arguably one of the half-dozen greatest pitchers of all time, but in this series he was one great against a great staff. After Alexander won the opening game, Foster, Leonard, Shore, and Foster again won the next four. Another World Championship banner flew at Fenway, although the Series wasn't played there. The Red Sox had opted to play their home share of Series games at brand-new and bigger Braves Field.

When the Red Sox set out to defend their championship in 1916, something was missing, and it was Tris Speaker. Spoke had been paid royally the previous two years to keep him from jumping to the Federal League, an upstart aggregation that tried in 1914–1915 to become a third major league. When the Feds folded, Speaker saw no reason why he should make less money. Red Sox owner (and, by now, real-estate magnate) Joseph J. Lannin disagreed. One thing led to another, and the next thing Spoke knew, he was traded to Cleveland, where he went on to justify his salary by leading the American League in hitting for 1916.

Joe Wood also had money squabbles and held out for the whole year, but the rest of the staff returned intact. Carl Mays, an underarm thrower who'd been in the bullpen most of 1915, blossomed into an 18-game winner in 1916.

The White Sox, who'd also benefited from Connie Mack's fire sale by acquiring the great second baseman Eddie Collins, chased the Red Sox down to the wire but fell two games short.

Surprise winners in the National League were Brooklyn's Dodgers, a feisty team but no match for the Red Sox. Again playing their home games at Braves Field, Boston blew them away in 5 games. The only loss came in Game Three at the hands of Jack Coombs, another one of Connie Mack's ex-A's. The gem of the Series was Game Two. Babe Ruth hooked up with Brooklyn's Sherry Smith in a 14-inning duel won by Boston 2–1.

Lannin decided to go out on top by selling his World Champions before another season rolled around. The buyer was Harry Frazee, a New Yorker well known for producing Broadway shows of varied critical esteem. In one sense, he turned out to be the most significant owner in Red Sox history: not for who he signed but for who he sold.

After winning his second straight World Series, Manager Rough Carrigan also retired from the scene, choosing to follow a career in banking. Rough had been a good catcher, but when he turned his mind to managing, he approached greatness, at least in the estimation of many of the men who played for him. Jack Barry took over and perhaps received more blame than he deserved for the BoSox second-place finish in 1917. The main knock against him was that he wasn't Carrigan. In truth, the White Sox were not to be outdone. Their pitching matched Boston's in brilliance, and their hitting, with Collins, Shoeless Joe Jackson, and Hap Felsch, gave them a big edge.

Barry wasn't around to manage in 1918, but not because he was fired. Jack, like many major-league players that year, joined the service. There was a world war going on "Over There." The government issued a "work or fight" ultimatum, meaning that able-bodied American males could choose between working in some war-essential industry or carrying a gun. Baseball carried on as best it could, chopping the 1918 regular season off at September 1, to allow its employees to decide among patriotic careers.

Replacing Barry at the Red Sox helm was Ed Barrow, an experienced major- and minor-league manager whose greatest claim to fame up to then was that he'd discovered Honus Wagner many years before. Barrow eventually earned entrance into the Baseball Hall of Fame, primarily for serving as New York Yankee president and guiding hand during the dynasty years of the 1920s and '30s. But something he did in Boston in 1918 helped get him to Cooperstown, too, although at first a lot of people thought he was crazy.

Barrow, in surveying his Red Sox, looked out in left field and saw not Duffy Lewis, who was in the army, but instead a gaping hole. Had Lewis been on station as usual, perhaps Barrow would never have considered his next move. Not many people would try to fill an outfield hole with the best pitcher on his staff—twice a 20-game winner, no less! Admittedly the pitcher had shown some ability with a bat, but the name of the game, remember, was pitching. At least 80 percent. Undaunted by baseball's accumulated wisdom, Manager Barrow sent Babe Ruth to left field.

As every fan knows, the position switch turned out to be one of the most unqualified successes in baseball history. Babe's booming bat would eventually change the way baseball was played, and Ruth himself would become an American icon. The bulk of Ruth's glory would be achieved in a city to the south of Boston (and under the aegis of Ed Barrow!), but his 1918 accomplishment of a league-high eleven home runs helped the Red Sox win yet another pennant. When not shagging flies, the Babe found time to win 13 games on the mound, but this was to be his final season as a double-figure winner.

The World Series of 1918, played in the first two weeks of September, matched the BoSox against the Chicago Cubs. Ruth hit no homers but he pitched a 1–0 shutout in the opener and won the fourth game 3–2. Carl Mays also won a pair of games, both by 2–1 scores, and that was all the Red Sox needed to hoist their fifth World Championship banner.

It was a wonderful time to be a Red Sox fan. In the American League's first eighteen years of existence, the Red Sox had taken fully one-third of the pennants. Even more impressive was their perfect performance in World Series competition—five for five! The Red Sox jinx was undreamed of then. And with world peace restored, BoSox fans saw no reason why the success of their favorites should not continue unabated.

They should have asked Harry Frazee about that.

A "SHORE" THING

As a pitcher, young Babe Ruth had marvelous control of his pitches. His self-control, however, left a lot to be desired. On June 23, 1917, he opened a game against Washington by walking the leadoff man. This, he decided, was the fault of the umpire's poor eyesight, and he proceeded to say so loudly and profanely. The umpire in question suggested a shower might cool Ruth's temper. Actually, he ordered it by tossing the Babe from the game.

In came Ernie Shore, who'd expected a day off. When Ernie was ready to pitch, the runner on first decided to steal second, but he'd overestimated his speed and was thrown out. Shore then retired the next 26 batters without incident, and has been regarded ever since as having pitched a legitimate but most unusual perfect game.

BEFORE THE BABE DID IT

Everyone knows Babe Ruth started as a pitcher and then became an outfielder, but how many remember Joe Wood did it first? Wood's switch wasn't dictated by his bat, however, but by his sore arm. After sitting out the 1916 season, Joe contacted his old Boston buddy Tris Speaker, who was now in Cleveland, about making a comeback. He pitched in five games for the Indians in 1917, but the arm was definitely gone.

But 1918 saw a lot of star players in the service or occupied in war work. Wood, who'd always been a pretty good hitter, made the Indians as an outfielder and hit .296 in 119 games. He went on to play four more years with the Tribe, including the World Championship season of 1920. His career batting average was a highly respectable .283.

DROP ANOTHER ONE, FRED!

Fred Snodgrass's place in history as "goat" of the 1912 World Series is secure. Everybody remembers his muff of an easy fly and forgets his great catch of Harry Hooper's drive on the next play. Manager John McGraw never blamed Snodgrass. After the season, he showed it in the most obvious way. He raised Fred's salary.

The Worst of Times, 1919–1932

In 1925, Harry Frazee—by then the ex-owner of the Red Sox—had a monster Broadway hit in the musical *No, No, Nanette*. At one point, there were five road companies crisscrossing the country singing "Tip-Toe Through the Tulips" and raking in the dollars for Harry. Had *Nanette* been written only a half-dozen years earlier, Red Sox fans might have been spared a ton of grief.

Unfortunately, during the time when Frazee owned the Sox, his productions on Broadway were bigger bombs than had ever been dropped in what was called "The Great War." Harry was able to pay off his various actors, musicians, scene designers, stage hands, costumers, and so on by selling off in bits and pieces the one valuable commodity he held—namely, the Red Sox players. In doing so, he kept himself viable for his ultimate triumph with *No, No, Nanette*, but he also destroyed baseball at Fenway Park for more than a decade.

He didn't plan it that way, of course. In fact, in his pennant-winning season of 1918, he actually went out and got a valuable player, first baseman Stuffy McInnis, and put him in a Red Sox uniform to help make the pennant possible.

However, before the 1919 season began, something prophetic happened. What with so many good players returning from the service, Harry decided he had more than he needed to stay on top. It so happened that Harry's Broadway office was only a few doors away from the office of one Jacob Ruppert, the owner of the New York Yankees, an American League team that had never won a pennant and seldom come close. Jake had the money; Harry had the players. Before you could say, "fifteen thousand dollars and four minor leaguers," Duffy Lewis, Ernie Shore, and Dutch Leonard were in Yankee pinstripes. It wasn't the deal of the century. The Yankees got scant value.

Lewis and Shore were nearing the end of their careers, and Leonard was quickly sent on to Detroit when he and Ruppert argued over his wages. Nor was Boston mortally wounded by losing the three. But in the theatrical terms of Frazee's world, the trade was "an ominous offstage rumble."

Frazee quickly found that though he had many good players returning, so did everyone else. The Red Sox floundered through the 1919 season and finally ended up sixth. The fans kept coming to Fenway nonetheless, if not to see victories, then to cheer home runs.

Babe Ruth's 11 homers of 1918 had been only a taste. In 1919, he blasted away at a record clip. First, he sailed by the American League record of 16 set by Socks Seybold in 1902. Then he surpassed the National League's record of 24 set by Gavvy Cravath in 1915. What could be next? It was noted by some antiquarian that Ned Williamson had popped 27 dingers in 1884 for Chicago during a season in which his team played at a ballpark with a 180-foot distance to the left field foul line. Playing on a real field, Ruth set a new all-time record with 29 home runs. Wise men shook their heads and predicted *that* record would live forever.

Although Ruth brought fans to Fenway Park in healthy lots, he couldn't bring enough to solve Frazee's continuous money crunch. And Ruppert's office and checkbook were so convenient. In mid-1919, right-hander Carl Mays, twice a 20-game winner, went to the Yanks for $40,000.

The backbreaker came the next winter. Desperate for cash, Frazee sold Ruth to New York. The official price was $125,000, but that was the smaller part. Ruppert lent Frazee $350,000 with Fenway Park as security. For the Yankees, *this* was the deal of the century. In his first year as a pinstriper, the Babe smashed 54 homers, making his previous record of 29 look like an off year. He raised the mark to 59 in 1921 and 60 in 1927. More important, he took the Yankees to seven pennants and four World Championships over the next 13 seasons. Of course, he had a lot of help—much of it out of Boston.

In the Big Picture, Ruth's going to New York was a good thing for baseball. It put the game's most charismatic star center stage so that he could help America forget that the Chicago White Sox had disgraced themselves and betrayed their fans by intentionally losing the 1919 World Series. To say, as some have, that he "saved" baseball is an exaggeration. Baseball wasn't quite yet on the critical list. What the Ruthian Homer did was speed the patient's recovery and take it to

new heights of health. And, of course, the response his homers received led owners to inject the baseball with rabbit in hope of spawn-
ing other Ruths, and that changed everything from a pitcher's game
to a batter's. And *that* made for a far more entertaining spectacle than
had been seen on diamonds before. So Bostonians could take solace
in the thought that their sacrifice was for the greater good.

But on the whole, they would rather have sold Frazee to New York
and kept the Babe.

When he got to New York, Ruth was installed in right field with
the Yankees. That may have been why Boston's Harry Hooper wasn't
traded to New York. The Yanks didn't need a second right fielder.
Instead, Harry was traded to Chicago. Everyone ELSE of consequence
was traded to New York.

The roll call:

Catcher Wally Schang, a three-year Red Sox regular, arrived in
New York in 1921, just in time to help them win 3 straight pennants.
A .300 hitter in Boston, he continued to be so with the Yankees.

Everett Scott had been the regular Red Sox shortstop since 1914
when he was sent to New York in 1922. A brilliant gloveman, he
cemented the defense for the 1922 and '23 champs.

Third baseman Jumpin' Joe Dugan was another more celebrated
for his glove than his bat, but he gave the Yankees solid work with
both for 6 seasons after coming over in mid-1922.

The Yankees received virtually a whole All-Star pitching staff from
the Red Sox. Waite Hoyt, Sad Sam Jones, Bullet Joe Bush, Herb
Pennock, George Pipgras, and the aforementioned Carl Mays were all
supplied by Frazee, and all—every last one of 'em—became a Yankee
20-game winner!

These were not all cash-and-carry deals. In fact, the money Frazee
got from Ruppert was seldom mentioned in print reports. Except for
the Ruth sale, New York always threw a couple of players into the
brew. And it is only fair to say that the Red Sox sometimes received
legitimate major leaguers in these transactions, though never of the
quality of the men given up. The proof of the one-sided character of
all this flesh-peddling, of course, lies in the American League standings, which saw the Yankees surge to the top while the Red Sox
plunged to the bottom and remained there through 1933.

In July of 1923, a syndicate led by longtime baseball man J.A.
Robert Quinn bought the Red Sox from Frazee and Boston cheered.
Quinn had been running the St. Louis Browns for owner Phil Ball and

doing quite well. At that time, the Browns were more successful and more popular in St. Louis than the Cardinals. But Ban Johnson and several team owners who were sick to death of the shambles the Frazee-to-Ruppert pipeline was making of the league pushed Quinn to jump in and "save" the Red Sox. Unfortunately, by the time the cavalry arrived there was precious little left unscalped.

With luck, Quinn might have been able to rebuild. He had no luck. Or, more precisely, he had no money. First the chief financial backer of the syndicate died, and then along came the Depression. At one point, Quinn had to borrow on his life insurance to pay team bills. Without the wherewithal to buy top players and with almost no one left to dangle as trade bait, Quinn spent his years in Boston in the cellar. The Sox finished last in 1922, Frazee's final year. They stayed last in 1923, leaped to seventh in 1924, and then fell back to last for six straight seasons. In 1931, the BoSox breathed sixth-place air, but the next year set a team record with 111 losses.

Managers came and went, trying to make bricks without straw. Ed Barrow left after 1920 to become the Yankees general manager (another ex–Red Soxer in New York!). Hugh Duffy, a Boston favorite who set the all-time record for batting averages back in 1894, presided in 1921 and '22 but couldn't teach anybody to hit as he had. Frank Chance, the "Peerless Leader" of four Cubs pennant-winners, escaped after one season. Lee Fohl, who'd managed for Quinn in St. Louis, lasted three years. Rough Carrigan was lured back for three seasons, but the magic was gone from his managerial wand. Then, in quick succession, it was Heinie Wagner, Shano Collins, and Marty McManus. All but McManus left in last place. Marty was seventh when he drew his final check.

As bad as the BoSox were during the Quinn years, they nevertheless put some interesting players on the field from time to time.

Outfielder Smead Jolley, for example, could hit .300 with his eyes shut but was so disastrous in the field that he couldn't stay in the majors. It was said his only defense against a fly ball was his cap. Another outfielder, Ike Boone, hit .333 and .330 in 1924 and '25 but was so painfully slow that he was sent back to the minors.

Pitcher Red Ruffing was good enough to lose 47 games in 1928 and '29. If that sounds peculiar, remember a pitcher must be doing his job when the manager keeps sending him out despite so many losses. Anyway, Ruffing proved his worth when he later won 20 games four times for the Yankees. (Another one traded away!)

First baseman Dale Alexander, so big and clumsy in the field that he may have been a harbinger of later Red Soxer Dick Stuart, could hit a ton. He came over from Detroit early in the 1932 season and became the first man ever to lead the league in batting while playing for two teams. He was also the first Red Sox batting champ.

Outfielder Earl Webb had a short major-league career, but in 1931 he went "doubles crazy" and knocked out an all-time record 67 two-base hits, more than twice as many as he ever hit before or after.

Others worth noting included pitcher Howard Ehmke, who won 20 games for the last-place 1923 Sox; catcher Charlie Berry, an ex-football star who later became an umpire; reliable outfielders Ira Flagstead and Tom Oliver; and bespectacled Danny MacFayden, who pitched heroically for the Red Sox in their worst years and then went to the downtrodden Braves just as the BoSox were improving.

In truth, even at their worst, the Sox were probably never quite as horrendous as such legendary last-placers as the 1899 Cleveland Spiders or the 1952 Pittsburgh Pirates. There was nearly always someone on the team worth coming out to cheer for. Boston fans deserve credit for supporting their losing team at a subsistence level throughout the 1920s. Alas! Bob Quinn needed much more than that to lift his club to a respectable position.

As the Depression deepened, the price of a Red Sox ticket became more of a burden than many loyal fans could bear. In 1932, attendance fell to 182,150—less than 2,400 a game—and easily the lowest figure in the team's history. The end had come for Bob Quinn.

LEFT(Y) IN THE LURCH

During the year that Frank Chance managed the Red Sox, he had in his employ a young pitcher named Frank "Lefty" O'Doul. The pitcher had a liking for nightlife and was often castigated and fined by Chance for missing curfews. If Chance had a "list," O'Doul was on it. One day the Peerless Leader stopped by the hotel barbershop where he observed Lefty enjoying a shave, haircut, manicure, shine—the works. What really raised the manager's hackles was the long, admiring look at himself Lefty took in the mirror before he left the shop.

As luck would have it, the Red Sox starting pitcher that afternoon against Cleveland was injured in the sixth inning and Chance had to call in a replacement. O'Doul was on tap and entered the game with a runner on third and two out. Unfortunately, he was both wild and hittable, a deadly combination. Instead of preventing the run from scoring, Lefty allowed that one and another and another. As hits and walks mounted, Chance was heard to mutter grimly, "I'm going to keep that looking-glass [bleep] in there, if he don't get them out all afternoon!"

By the time the inning ended, thirteen Indians had scored.

Perhaps the incident helped convince Lefty that his talent lay in hitting baseballs rather than hurling them. At any rate, he eventually found stardom as an outfielder, twice topping the National League in batting.

I'D RATHER DO IT MYSELF!

There have only been 8 unassisted triple plays in the majors during the twentieth century, and 6 of them were performed during the 1920s. Partly it may have been that the hit-and-run play was still as common as in the deadball days, while the livelier baseball made it far more dangerous. But obviously there was a certain amount of monkey-see-monkey-do. The unaided triple-killing by Cleveland second baseman Bill Wambsganss in the 1920 World Series made him famous, and, after that, every infielder was looking for a chance to gain immortality.

Certainly that was the case on September 14, 1923, when Red Sox first baseman George Burns snared a drive off the bat of Cleveland's Frank Brower and tagged runner Rube Lutzke for the second out. Burns could have easily tossed to second base to put out baserunner Riggs Stephenson, but he saw that the Clevelander was just getting himself turned around near third. Both Stephenson and Burns sprinted madly for second base and both slid in from opposite sides.

Burns, a split second quicker, made the put out and gained his headline.

QUICK THINKING

One day in September 1923, Babe Ruth lifted a towering fly against the Red Sox. Boston outfielder Dick Reichle circled under it. The Babe kept running. Reichle kept circling. Suddenly, it was obvious that

Reichle had lost sight of the ball. By the time it landed unmolested, Ruth was nearly to third base, and he had no problem reaching home plate with an inside-the-park home run.

When Reichle came to the bench at inning's end, Manager Frank Chance deadpanned, "Pretty smart, Dick! It's late in the season, and I wouldn't get hit on the head either."

Buy Me a Champion, 1933–1946

To many baseball fans in parts of the American League other than Boston, Tom Yawkey was just a rich man who tried to buy himself a pennant. It's certainly true that Yawkey spent liberally to bring star players to his Red Sox and then paid them well. But nearly every owner in his or her own way tries to "buy" a pennant for the team. Some, because of circumstance or personal preference, try to do it on the cheap. Others, again guided by circumstance or preference, are more liberal. Boston fans well remembered that Jake Ruppert bought pennants for his Yankees, because he bought them to a great extent from the Red Sox! And due to Harry Frazee's fire sales, followed by years of Bob Quinn's undercapitalized stewardship, Yawkey had little choice in his effort to rebuild the BoSox but to do it with his checkbook.

More than anything else, Tom Yawkey was a baseball *fan*. But he was not a fanatic. He wanted to see good baseball played, and naturally enough he wanted to see his own team play well. He was unstinting in his efforts to build a team that all New England could take pride in. But win or lose, he loved the Red Sox. When they won, he was the last person to take credit. When they lost, he never regarded the losses as any sort of blot upon his personal honor. It was not his way to rant and rave and precipitously fire those who did not perform up to his hopes. Every team in baseball should be blessed with an owner like Yawkey.

Yawkey came by his love of baseball honestly. His uncle and later adoptive father, Bill Yawkey, had once been half owner of the Detroit Tigers, and legend has it that Bill's willingness to spend money on the ball club just about drove his frugal partner Frank Navin crazy.

The Yawkeys had extensive lumber and ore holdings, but Tom

Yawkey's love was baseball. As soon as he could he would own his own team. He turned thirty on February 21, 1933, and came into the bulk of an eight-figure inheritance from his uncle, mother, and grandfather. Four days later, he bought the Red Sox. "I don't intend to mess with a loser," he told reporters.

Many rich men convince themselves that great wealth conveys great knowledge. The history of baseball is littered with the mistakes of egotistical owners who learned to their dismay that a big bank account is no substitute for baseball "smarts." Yawkey was too intelligent to fall into the trap of overestimating his own intelligence. His first move was to hire Eddie Collins as vice president and general manager. Collins, one of the greatest second basemen of all time, had been Yawkey's boyhood hero. But, that aside, he was one of the brightest men in the game. At the time Yawkey offered him the job, he was serving as a coach for Connie Mack in Philadelphia and was Connie's heir-apparent (succession to occur whenever Mack should choose to retire). Collins went to Mack and told him of Yawkey's offer. "If you don't take the job," Connie said, "I'll fire you."

Yawkey's instructions to Collins: "I've got the money to spend, and I intend to spend it." Shortly thereafter, Eddie secured the services of Rick Ferrell, perhaps the best catcher to wear a Red Sox uniform until Carlton Fisk. Ferrell was a consistent .300 hitter and a fine defensive backstop who was available only because the St. Louis Browns were in dire financial straits. The Yankees were fiscally sound, of course, but Collins talked them out of pitcher George Pipgras and infielder Billy Werber for about $100,000. Pipgras developed a sore arm, but Werber gave the BoSox four years of top third-basing and led the league in stolen bases in 1934–1935.

The Red Sox struggled up to seventh place in the first year of Yawkey's ownership, but better times were on the way.

So were better players.

During the remainder of the 1930s, the Red Sox imported a virtual roster of established major-league stars through the generous use of Tom Yawkey's checkbook. Some didn't work out so well, but several loom large in Red Sox history.

The first huge purchase, for $125,000 and two players, brought Lefty Grove from Philadelphia on December 12, 1933, along with second baseman Max Bishop and lefty Rube Walberg. The Depression had hit Connie Mack hard, and he began dismantling the great team that had won three straight pennants from 1929 to 1931. At the

Boston training camp in the spring of 1934, Grove was felled by a sore arm. The next thing he knew, his great fastball was gone forever. Mack immediately offered to take Grove back and return the money, but Yawkey would have none of it, knowing that all parties had dealt in good faith. As it turned out, keeping Grove was a good move. Deprived of his high hard one, Lefty relearned pitching, this time with cunning and control. He won 20 games in 1935, 17 in each of the next two years, and led the league in lowest ERA four times.

Wes Ferrell, Rick's pitcher brother, had been a four-time 20-game winner for Cleveland, but a sore arm in 1933 seemed ready to end his career. Collins got him for a fifth of what he paid for Grove on the chance there was something left. In his first Boston season, he junk-balled his way to 14 wins. In 1935, he won 25 and the year after that 20.

Between them, Grove and Ferrell led the league in temperament. Both were justly famous for their clubhouse tantrums whenever they lost a game. Woe to be the teammate whose error might have cost the victory. When manager-shortstop Joe Cronin booted a ball to make Grove a loser, he went into his office and locked the door as soon as the game ended. But the walls of his office didn't go to the ceiling. Grove stood on a bench by the partition, looked down into Cronin's office and screamed obscenities at the manager for half an hour. But no matter how towering Lefty's rage, by the next day, all was forgiven and he was friendly again.

Joe Cronin cost the Red Sox $225,000 in the fall of 1934. Only an ordinary shortstop, Cronin was one of the best hitters ever to play that position. As player-manager for the Washington Senators, he'd won the 1933 pennant. Nevertheless, it wasn't only a great player and successful manager that Washington owner Clark Griffith sold to Boston. Cronin was also his son-in-law! It was the Depression and $225,000 was a LOT of money. Cronin remained an all-star shortstop throughout the 1930s, served as Red Sox manager from 1935 through 1947, and then moved up to general manager. In 1959, he became American League president, and in 1974, A.L. chairman.

Home-run hitter Jimmie Foxx was one of the last of Connie Mack's stars to be sold off. Mack sent him to Boston in December of 1935 for $150,000 and two players. Foxx was one of the most powerful right-handed batters ever and probably the first to cut his sleeves short to intimidate pitchers with his bulging biceps. With the Athletics, Jimmie had already won two MVP Awards. He won a

third with the Red Sox in 1938 when he led the A.L. in batting and
RBI. His 175 runs driven in remains the club record. Of his 50 home
runs that season (second in the league to Hank Greenberg's 58), 35
were hit at Fenway Park. Nevertheless, teammate Doc Cramer always insisted the Fenway left-field wall hurt Foxx more than it
helped him because many of the slugger's best drives were still rising
when they hit the high wall near the top.

Other useful players obtained by Eddie Collins during the period
included outfielders Cramer, Joe Vosmik, and Ben Chapman, all of
whom had .300 seasons in Boston; pitchers Fritz Ostermueller, Bobo
Newsom, and Joe Heving; and infielders Pinky Higgins and Jim
Tabor.

Although no pennants were won—the Yankees always had too
much pitching—the BoSox returned to the respectability of the first
division and put on a good show for their fans. Attendance at Fenway
Park rose steadily.

Ironically, the greatest gate attraction—and many would say the
greatest player—ever to wear a Red Sox uniform was not one of the
already-existing stars brought in by Collins at great expense but a
player he discovered himself and got for next to nothing. In 1937, he
took a trip to San Diego to look at infielder Bobby Doerr. He liked
what he saw. Doerr joined the Sox in 1938 and went on to be the best
they ever had at second base. But what really excited Collins was the
batting swing of a skinny San Diego outfielder named Ted Williams.
The kid's stats were only fair at the time, but Collins knew he was
going to set records with that swing. In 1938, he put Williams in
Minneapolis, where he tore up Triple A. By 1939, Collins was ready
to unleash him on the majors.

Arguments over the greatest hitter of all time usually narrow down
to Ted Williams and Babe Ruth. Both were left-handed power hitters.
Ruth's cumulative totals are better in home runs, 714 to 521, and RBI,
and 2,211 to 1,839, but the Babe didn't lose five of his potentially most
productive seasons to the service. And, for much of his career, Ruth
played half his games in a ballpark that favors left-handed power
hitters. Fenway Park, Williams's home field, favors right-handers.
Williams's career batting average of .344 is only slightly better than
Ruth's .342, but Ruth played the bulk of his career during a period of
unusually high batting averages. An adjustment for time and place
would probably mean a twenty-point difference in favor of Williams.

Perhaps instead of number one and number two, Ruth and Williams should be considered one and one-A, respectively.

In 1941, Joe DiMaggio's 56-game hitting streak captured the public's imagination. As remarkable as the Yankee Clipper's achievement was, Williams was even better over the long haul of the season. He led the league in homers with 37, trailed DiMag in runs batted in by five with 120, and batted .406. He was the first hitter to go over .400 since Bill Terry of the Giants did it in 1931 and the first American Leaguer to do it since 1923. And no one has done it since!

The Red Sox had a doubleheader scheduled for the final day of the season. Williams's average was .3996, technically .400. Manager Cronin suggested he sit out the games and protect his mark, but Williams would have none of that. He played—and went six for eight.

Many felt Williams deserved the MVP Award for 1941 but the official voters opted for DiMaggio. In 1942, Ted came back to win the batting Triple Crown with 36 homers, 137 RBI, and a .356 batting average. The voters chose Yankee Joe Gordon as MVP.

The truth was that many of the sportswriters who voted for awards—including several from Boston—were not fond of Williams. Ted's greatest sin was a penchant for saying what he believed. In the "tact league" he never got past the Mendoza Line. When criticized, he tended to strike back. In short, many writers could never forgive him for acting like a young man in his twenties instead of a mature, middle-aged man. And, because of what he considered unfair criticism in his youth, Williams's loathing for some writers continued as he actually approached middle age.

Not even the most critical Boston writer could find fault with Williams's war record. While many ballplayers found sinecures playing exhibitions for the entertainment of other troops, Ted became a decorated Marine fighter pilot.

During the war years, most major-league teams marked time, filling their rosters with 4-Fs, overage veterans, and green youngsters waiting for their draft notices. In 1942, the Red Sox had finished second to the Yankees. Cronin had replaced himself with Johnny Pesky, a fine fielder who hit .331. Dom DiMaggio, Joe's brother, was an exceptional center fielder and good hitter though lacking Joe's power. Right-hander Cecil "Tex" Hughson led the A.L. with a 22–6 record. Williams and Doerr were at their best.

Then during the next three years, the team finished seventh twice while BoSox fans waited for the return of the major leaguers. In 1946, they were back and Boston ran away and hid from the rest of the league. They got off to a 32-and-9 start and coasted to the pennant by 12 games over Detroit. After all these years, Tom Yawkey finally had his flag.

Cronin had a terrific team. Doerr and Pesky were brilliant around second base. Pesky batted .335; Doerr had 18 homers and 116 RBI. Veteran slugger Rudy York was brought in to play first base and had 117 RBI. Dom DiMaggio hit .316. Hughson won 20 games, and Dave "Boo" Ferriss, a sensational wartime discovery, won 25 with only 6 losses. Maurice "Mickey" Harris won 17 and Joe Dobson 13. Williams was named MVP at last—ironically, in a year when he won no part of the Triple Crown. He was, however, second in all three categories and first in runs scored with 142.

The Red Sox were favored in the World Series—didn't they *always* win the World Series? Their opponents were the St. Louis Cardinals, who also had a habit of winning the Fall Classic whenever they appeared. The Redbirds had come to the fore in St. Louis in the mid-1920s and since had won five Series. They also had Stan Musial, Enos Slaughter, Marty Marion, and a deep pitching staff headed by 21-game-winner Howie Pollet.

Hughson outpitched Pollet in the opener, but reliever Ernie Johnson got the win when Rudy York homered in the tenth inning. The next day, Cardinals lefty Harry Brecheen shut out the Red Sox 3–0 to even things up. Two days later at Boston, Boo Ferriss returned the favor by whitewashing the Cards 4–0. It was the fiftieth shutout in Series history.

Game Four was all St. Louis, as the Cards hammered out Hughson in two innings and went on to win 12–3. Once more, the Red Sox went in front, three games to two, when Joe Dobson threw a four-hitter in Game Five. He was touched for three unearned runs, but the BoSox scored six times on his behalf. The Series returned to St. Louis with Boston hoping to wrap it up, but Harry Brecheen scattered seven hits for his second Series victory, 4–1.

Game Seven was one of the most memorable of all time. The Red Sox jumped on Murry Dickson for a run in the first inning, but after that the little Cardinal right-hander was masterful, limiting the BoSox to one hit through the next six innings. Boo Ferriss, the Red Sox starter, was not at his best. He allowed the Cardinals a run in the second and two more in the fifth when Dobson relieved him. Dickson was responsible for the two fifth-inning runs, doubling in one and scoring the other on Red Schoendienst's single.

In the top of the eighth, Dickson weakened. Glen "Rip" Russell singled as a pinch hitter and George Metkovich pinch-hit a double to put runners at second and third with no outs. Cardinal Manager Eddie Dyer signaled to his bullpen and brought in Harry Brecheen. The crafty lefty struck out Wally Moses and got Johnny Pesky to line out while the runners held. With two away, Dom DiMaggio came through for Boston, smashing a double off the right-centerfield wall to tie the game. Leon Culberson replaced DiMaggio, who'd twisted his ankle in running to second, but Brecheen ended the inning by getting a pop foul out from Williams.

Bob Klinger, the Red Sox best reliever, came on to pitch the bottom of the eighth. Enos Slaughter greeted him with a single. Klinger settled in to retire the next two Cardinals. That brought up Harry "The Hat" Walker, the Cards' most effective hitter of the Series. When he lashed a drive to right-center, Slaughter was already on his way to second. Culberson was slow in handling the hit. Had DiMaggio still been in center . . . well, who knows? Pesky took the relay and turned to see Slaughter racing through his coach's stop sign at third and on his way to the plate. He scored easily.

Boston opened the ninth with singles by York and Doerr, but then Brecheen put on the clamps. When pinch hitter Tom McBride grounded into a force play for the final out, the Red Sox had lost their first World Series.

Those more interested in assigning blame than saluting success fastened on Williams's .200 batting average on five singles (Musial hit .222), but the goat's horns were mostly assigned to Pesky, who supposedly hesitated before throwing home on Slaughter's mad dash in the seventh game. Many eyewitnesses denied that Johnny skipped a beat before making his relay, but that's the way it went out of the press box.

The Sox had dropped Tom Yawkey's first World Series, but with the crew of hitters and pitchers he and Eddie Collins had to call on, hopes were bright for many more Fall Classic appearances in the near future.

THE PERFECT DEFENSE

What kind of fear did the sight of muscular Jimmie Foxx striding to the plate engender in the hearts of pitchers? The Yankees' "Lefty" Gomez probably put it best. One day with Foxx at the plate, Gomez peered in at his catcher. And peered. And peered. Finally, shouts went up: "Throw the ball!" Quoth Lefty, "I don't want to."

No pitcher with half his marbles wanted to pitch to the man they called "The Beast." He didn't just hit homers; he demoralized pitchers with the length of his long blasts. Still, on June 16, 1938, the St. Louis Browns, not known for their pitching expertise, found a way to keep Foxx from getting the ball out of the infield!

They walked him 6 consecutive times.

A JABLONOWSKI BY ANY OTHER NAME

In 1932, Peter William Jablonowski pitched briefly for the Red Sox without much success—an 0–3 record. Soon Jablonowski was back in the minors, and while he was there he decided to change his name.

In 1936, the Washington Senators brought up a pitcher who won 14 games for them. The fellow's name was Pete Appleton. Same guy, but you couldn't tell it by the box score—or the batters.

LET THE BOSS SHOW YOU HOW IT'S DONE

By 1943, Joe Cronin was mostly a bench manager. He'd slowed in the field but he still had a good bat. In the first game of a June double-header with the Athletics, the Red Sox were down 4–1 with two men on when Joe put himself in as a pinch hitter. He homered to tie the score, and Boston eventually won.

That felt so good that Joe pinch-hit again in the nightcap. Same result. Home run.

CALLING THEM AS HE SAW THEM

Jimmie Foxx always gave his all for Joe Cronin's Red Sox, even though sometimes he didn't see eye-to-eye with his manager's decisions. Jimmie kept his own counsel until a reporter asked him, "How come Cronin isn't winning with so many of the same players that won championships for Connie Mack?"

"Well," said Jimmie in his most tactful way, "One manager knew what he was doing and the other one doesn't."

SOUND FAMILIAR?

One day in 1938, Red Sox pitchers couldn't seem to get anyone out. Manager Cronin waved pitcher after pitcher in from the bullpen until six had appeared. When the sixth departed, Joe Heving was brought in and he finished the game.

The next day the *Boston Herald* strung column-wide photos of the first six unsuccessful hurlers across the page with a double-column picture of Heving at the end. The headline: ALL THESE AND HEVING, TOO!

Frustrations and a Dream, 1947–1967

The Red Sox were favored to repeat as pennant winners in 1947, but they were bushwhacked by an incredible outbreak of aching arms. The three top starters from 1946—Tex Hughson, Dave Ferriss, and Mickey Harris—were all stricken in spring training. The hurlers who had posted a cumulative 62–28 record in 1946 slumped to 29–26. Tragically, none of them ever fully recovered.

It took a great year by Ted Williams, with ample help from Bobby Doerr, Johnny Pesky, Dom DiMaggio, and rookie Sam Mele, to bring the Sox in third behind the Yankees. Williams gained his second batting Triple Crown with a .343 batting average, 32 home runs, and 114 RBI. Yet, once more he was deprived of the Most Valuable Player Award in favor of Joe DiMaggio, whose figures were .315, 20, and 97. One Boston writer who'd had a nasty argument with Williams during the season did not list Ted among the top ten players in the league when he sent in his MVP ballot.

Joe Cronin retired as field manager after the season and moved into the front office to replace the ailing Eddie Collins. To replace himself in the dugout, he lured the fabled "Marse Joe" McCarthy out of retirement. McCarthy had won eight pennants as Yankee skipper and was considered the best manager alive, although Jimmy Dykes, the longtime White Sox manager, looked at the wealth of Yankee talent and labled him a "push-button" manager.

Cronin set out to give McCarthy all the buttons he could ask for, bringing in veteran outfielder Stan Spence from Washington and pitchers Jack Kramer and Ellis Kinder from St. Louis. The shiniest new addition was slugging shortstop Vern Stephens, another ex-Brown with terrific right-hand power. Surprisingly, McCarthy handed the shortstop job to Stephens and shifted Pesky to third although Pesky was the better man in the field. The decision had more to do with egos than skills, as did many of the choices McCarthy would be forced to make. The major question in 1948 spring training was, how would the prickly McCarthy and the temperamental Williams blend? As it turned out, that was never a problem—"Any manager who can't get along with a .400 hitter should have his head examined," McCarthy said. But, although McCarthy and Williams developed a warm friendship, other parts of the team did not jell so smoothly.

The 1948 Red Sox could hit with anyone. The team's 907 runs scored led the league as did Williams's .369 batting average. Doerr, Stephens, and Williams all drove in over 100 runs. Yet the Red Sox got out of the blocks slowly and were only 14–23 by Memorial Day.

The pitching was the weak spot. Jack Kramer led the league in winning percentage based on his 18–6 record, but his 4.35 ERA told how poorly he actually pitched. Eventually, Joe Dobson and rookie left-hander Mel Parnell came on to help Boston close with a rush. On the last day of the season, the BoSox tied Cleveland for first place. That set up a one-game playoff for all the marbles at Fenway Park the next day.

Cleveland started its sensational rookie left-hander, Gene Bearden, a 19-game winner to that point. McCarthy, unaccountably, went with thirty-six-year-old Denny Galehouse, a journeyman with eight wins on the season. Perhaps Smokey Joe Wood in his prime couldn't have stopped the "on-a-roll" Indians. Led by two homers by playing-manager Lou Boudreau, who was having the season of his career, Cleveland took the game and the pennant with an 8–3 win.

Ironically, Cleveland faced the Braves, making their last bid for Boston's fans, in the World Series. It was the closest Boston had ever come—or would come—to an "in-house" World Series.

When the Red Sox obtained Al Zarilla from St. Louis early in the 1949 season, the Red Sox had a true all-star lineup: Williams, Dom DiMaggio, and Zarilla from left to right in the outfield; .300-hitter Billy Goodman at first base completing an infield that had Doerr, Stephens, and Pesky; and peppery Birdie Tebbetts behind the plate. Yet again, Boston stumbled out of the gate and fell behind the Yankees early. On July 4, they trailed by 12 games.

The pitching staff had two aces. Mel Parnell was brilliant all year, winning 25 games, the most ever by a Red Sox lefty. Ellis Kinder, thirty-four years old and with an undistinguished career behind him, suddenly became a world-beater and won 23 games. But Joe Dobson was the only other pitcher who had appeared in at least ten games to have an ERA under 4.00. Down the stretch, as the Red Sox sought to overtake New York, McCarthy used Parnell and Kinder to start and relieve.

On the next-to-last weekend of the season, Boston swept three games from the Yankees and moved into first place by a game. They still held that lead going into the season's final weekend, which closed out with two games at Yankee Stadium. One win meant the pennant.

On Saturday, the Yankees came back from a 4–0 deficit to beat Parnell 5–4. On Sunday, New York led Kinder only 1–0 in the eighth when McCarthy pinch-hit for his starter. In the bottom of the inning, he brought in the exhausted Mel Parnell. The Yankees scored four more runs, negating a three-run rally by the Sox in the top of the ninth. Once more Boston was out a pennant by a hairsbreadth and a questionable pitching decision.

Another MVP Award for Williams was small consolation. Although Ted had won the honor in two of the last five seasons he played, his supporters could argue with some justification that it should have been five-for-five.

During the 1950 All-Star Game, Williams broke his elbow crashing into Comiskey Park's left-field wall while making a catch. The injury limited him to 89 games, and some felt that was the difference when the Red Sox finished third in a four-team race with the Yankees, Indians, and Tigers. In truth, the Sox didn't miss Ted's bat. As a team, they hit .302 and scored 1,027 runs. Sensational first baseman Walt Dropo hit .322 with 34 homers to win Rookie of the Year honors. He and Stephens tied for the league RBI crown with 144 each. Every regular hit above .300 except Stephens (.295) and Doerr (.294), and they hit 30 and 27 home runs, respectively. Billy Goodman, who played all four infield positions and filled in for Williams in the outfield, was the surprise A.L. batting champ with a .354 mark.

In short, the Sox had all the hitting they could ask for. But the pitching was another story. Parnell and Kinder slumped. No one took up the slack. The team ERA was an ugly 4.88. Before midseason, with the Sox at 32–30, McCarthy resigned. Steve O'Neill presided over the usual second-half surge.

As the 1950s wore on and the Red Sox great hitters aged, Boston slid to the middle of the pack. Dropo never repeated his rookie slugging and was traded to Detroit. Continuing back problems forced

Doerr's retirement; he was replaced at second by Billy Goodman, who finally settled down to one position. Injuries and age took Stephens, Pesky, and DiMaggio. Williams missed nearly all of two seasons when he was recalled to active duty during the Korean War.

Yet Boston's woes nearly always could be traced to pitching deficiencies. Parnell had a few more good years, Kinder became for a while one of the top relief specialists in baseball, and youngsters Tom Brewer and Frank Sullivan pitched well at times. But the Sox never had a staff or even a rotation that could compare with those in Chicago or Cleveland, much less with the Yankees, who won eight of the ten 1950's A.L. pennants.

Throughout the decade, the Sox always had a cadre of hitting talent. Right-fielder Jackie Jensen was one of the best and most consistent RBI men in the league. Goodman was always a reliable hitter. Sammy White arrived to become one of the best catchers in club history. Williams returned from shooting down Migs and hit as though he'd never been away.

One of the most exciting players on the team was center-fielder Jimmy Piersall, whose career almost ended in his rookie year of 1952. The Red Sox tried to make outfielder Piersall into a shortstop. That, together with family pressures, proved too much for him. He began exhibiting bizarre behavior on the field and eventually was sent to the minors. There, the problems continued. Eventually it was discovered that he had suffered a complete nervous breakdown. He had no memory of the preceding months or his odd conduct. Happily, he recovered, became a brilliant center fielder and sharp hitter, and was even able to write about his experience in the best-selling book *Fear Strikes Out*.

Harry Agganis's tale had a more tragic ending. "The Golden Greek" had been an All-American quarterback at Boston University and was one of the most popular athletes in New England. As a rookie first baseman with the Red Sox in 1954, he showed flashes of hitting power that led many to predict he would become one of the American League's stars. Early in 1955, he was hitting .313 when he contracted pneumonia. Complications set in and Agganis died of a pulmonary embolism at age 25.

Infielder Elijah "Pumpsie" Green was a Red Sox rookie in 1959. Never an outstanding player, his batting average for 5 major league seasons was .246. Green's significance is that he was the first black player to wear a Red Sox uniform. Such black stars as Willie Mays,

Hank Aaron, Ernie Banks, Larry Doby, Frank Robinson and Minnie Minoso had been shaping pennant races for several years, and many felt the Red Sox delay in hiring blacks—twelve seasons after Jackie Robinson arrived in Brooklyn—had a great deal to do with the poor showings of the team in the early 1960s.

Williams won his fifth and sixth batting titles in 1957–1958. His 1957 mark of .388 remains the closest approach to .400 since Ted's own 1941 season. He could have had two more batting championships in the period, but qualification was based on at-bats at the time, putting Williams, who walked so often, at a disadvantage. Because of this, the standard was changed to plate appearances.

In 1959, Ted Williams hit .254. Although a neck injury was at the root of his hitting problem, many assumed the forty-one-year-old great had finally come to the end. Tom Yawkey was one of several who hinted that it was time for Ted to hang up his bat. But Williams refused to go out on a low note.

He returned for the 1960 season determined to erase any memory of that dreadful .254. When Williams set his mind to something, it was as good as done. In his magnificent farewell, he batted .316—only four points below the league leader, Red Sox second baseman Pete Runnels—and slugged 29 home runs. His final homer came in his final at-bat against a pitcher born in 1939, Ted's rookie year. As the Fenway crowd roared its appreciation, Ted circled the bases head down and disappeared into the dugout. And into the Hall of Fame.

Williams's successor in left field arrived in 1961. Because Yastrzemski was hard to spell and harder to pronounce, most fans called him "Yaz." No one could be "another" Williams, but Yaz carved his own niche and eventually joined Ted at Cooperstown. Yaz started less spectacularly than Williams, but by his third season, he had won his first batting title. Another Red Sox batting leader was Pete Runnels, a versatile player who played both first and second base. Pete won in 1960 and 1962.

A tremendous power hitter, Dick Stuart, held down first base for the Sox in 1963–1964, hitting 75 homers and batting in 232 runs in those two years. Unfortunately, Stuart's abilities ended with his bat. His nickname, "Dr. Strangeglove," told it all. When it was determined that his defense was producing more runs for the opposition than his bat was for Boston, he was traded to the Phillies.

Tony Conigliaro, a hitter of nearly unlimited potential joined the Sox in 1964, breaking in with 24 home runs as a nineteen-year-old.

When he turned twenty, he led the league with 32. Another outstanding player through the period was Frank Malzone, perhaps the finest Red Sox third baseman since the fabled days of Jimmie Collins.

Pitching, as usual, was the Red Sox weakness. Bill Monbouquette was the best starter of the period, winning 20 games for the seventh-place 1963 Sox.

One Red Sox hurler stood out as the best in the business during the period. Six-foot-six, 240-pound Dick Radatz was baseball's most imposing reliever. He was called "The Monster," and his fastball in his prime was truly monstrous. From 1962 through 1965, Radatz won 49 games in relief and saved over 100. Perhaps he was overused. By 1966, he'd lost a foot or two off his fastball and he had no other pitches to fall back on.

Despite the excellent work of Yaz, Conigliaro, Runnels, Malzone, Radatz, Monbouquette, and a few others, the first two-thirds of the 1960s were not great times at Fenway. The Red Sox tumbled into the second division. In 1967, when new manager Dick Williams took over, Boston had finished ninth in the expanded league two years in a row.

Williams was a former journeyman outfielder but no relation to Ted by either blood or bat. He spent the spring concentrating on fundamentals and convincing the Red Sox players to believe in themselves. He hadn't taken the job to make friends, and, with his sharp tongue, he didn't make very many. Through the first half of the season, the results were not positive as other teams competed for the the A.L. lead.

Then, coming out of the All-Star break, the Red Sox ran off a ten-game winning streak. Suddenly, the pennant race was a four-team race among the Red Sox, White Sox, Twins, and Tigers. Through July, August, and September, the four teams were seldom separated by more than three games in the standings.

For Boston, the biggest differences between the ninth-place team of the year before were Yaz, always a good hitter but now blossoming as a home-run threat, and pitcher Jim Lonborg, on his way to a Cy Young season. Yaz, easily the American League MVP, won the batting Triple Crown. Others, like first baseman George Scott, shortstop Rico Petrocelli, and outfielder Reggie Smith, contributed in the clutch even though their overall statistics were only ordinary. Sox fans called their pennant quest "The Impossible Dream," but as Boston stayed in the race the "dream" began to seem plausible.

The team survived a frightening blow in August when Tony Conigliaro was seriously hurt in a terrible beaning. His eyesight was affected. He missed all of the next year. He made a partial comeback for a couple of seasons but then was forced to retire as his sight worsened.

As September neared its end, Chicago finally slipped out of the race. The Red Sox beat the Twins 6–4 on September 30, the day before the season closed, to pull into a tie with Minnesota for the lead with Detroit only a half game behind. The next day, they beat Minnesota again, 5–3, to kayo the Twins. That left Detroit with a doubleheader scheduled in California. The Tigers won the opener over the Angels and took a lead in the second game. But, with Red Sox fans on the edge of their chairs, the Angels rallied. Detroit dropped the nightcap, 8–5, and with it the tie for the pennant. "The Impossible Dream" had become a Red Sox reality.

The World Series against St. Louis proved a letdown, but only because Cardinal pitcher Bob Gibson was truly unbeatable. He won three games: 2–1, 6–0, and the finale, 7–2. Lonborg almost matched him, winning a one-hit shutout in Game Two and a three-hitter in Game Five, before weakening in Game Seven. Despite the loss, 1967 must be considered one of the most thrilling and satisfying ever for Boston fans.

BATTEN DOWN THE PITCHERS!

Oh how those Red Sox of the early 1950s could hit! In June of 1950, the St. Louis Browns arrived in Boston for a four-game series. The Brownies had one of the world's weakest pitching staffs so the Red Sox were expected to fatten their batting averages, but no one predicted the magnitude of the slaughter. In the opening game, the Red Sox scored 29 runs! The next day, they tailed off to 20. Perhaps exhausted from running the bases, Boston was content with scoring seven and then eight runs in the last two games, but that still brought the series total to 64.

However, for sheer cruelty to pitchers, look how the Sox socked Detroit in the seventh inning on June 18, 1953. Before the inning ended, Boston scored 17 runs! Outfielder Gene Stephens made three hits for a record and catcher Sammy White scored three times for another.

RISING TO THE OCCASION

Ted Williams appeared in 18 All-Star Games and hit .304 against the best pitchers the National League could offer. His final All-Star at-bat was as a pinch hitter in 1960. He singled. Ted also walked eleven times to go with his 14 All-Star hits, giving him an on-base average of .438.

No doubt his most thrilling moment—and one of the greatest in All-Star history—came in 1941 when his two-out, three-run homer in the ninth gave the American League a stunning 7–5 win. However, most fans remember his 1946 game best. Ted had four hits, including two home runs. He batted in 5 of the A.L.'s 12 runs. But the *crème de la crème* came in his last at bat. The N.L.'s Rip Sewell was famous for his *eephus* pitch, a high lob that sometimes arched as high as 40 feet before coming down through the strike zone. With absolutely nothing on it, the *eephus* was considered "home-run proof." Sewell fed Ted an *eephus* and Williams fouled it off. The game was as good as won by then, of course, and it was funny to see baseball's mightiest hitter handcuffed by what looked like a sandlot pitch. Sewell threw another *eephus*. Williams took a little hop forward and blasted the ball into the stands. He laughed all the way around the bases.

THE SECRET'S IN THE WALLET

Tommy Henrich, the Yankees' "Old Reliable," always maintained that the reason New York won pennants and the Red Sox didn't was that Tom Yawkey paid his players too well. Yawkey was known for his generous payroll. Meanwhile, the Yankee players had to deal each year with George Weiss, the New York GM who never saw a penny he couldn't pinch. According to Henrich, the Red Sox played each year for a pennant; the Yankees played to make a decent living.

The Close-Call Years, 1968–1979

Nineteen sixty-eight was the "Year of the Pitcher," as the mounds-men dominated batsmen as they hadn't done since the deadball era fifty years before. In the National League, the Cardinals' Bob Gibson posted a 1.12 ERA. In the American League, the Tigers' Denny McLain won 31 games. Both pitchers earned MVP and Cy Young Awards for their leagues, but they were hardly alone in turning batters into helpless bystanders. National League hitters in total managed a paltry .243 batting average. That, however, was heavy hitting compared to the American League's miniscule .230. Only one qualifying A.L. batter topped .300 in the batting race—Boston's Carl Yastrzem-ski, with a glorious .301.

In Boston, the phrase "Year of the Pitcher" took on a different meaning. The high hopes for the season were dashed before it began when the Red Sox 1967 Cy Young winner, Jim Lonborg, tore up his knee in a winter skiing accident. From 22–9 in 1967 he fell to 6–10 in 1968 when he was finally able to return to the mound. And, for the rest of his career, he was never able to regain the form that he'd shown in the year of "The Impossible Dream."

Tony Conigliaro's hitting was missed, too. Ken Harrelson, who'd been acquired in late 1967, helped fill the void with 35 homers and a league-leading 109 RBI, but most Sox bats went into hibernation. Although Yaz led the league in batting, his home-run total dropped from 44 to 23. First baseman George Scott stopped hitting altogether. Boston finished fourth, a half game behind Cleveland but 17 behind pennant-winning Detroit.

The American League was split into Eastern and Western Divisions in 1969. The Red Sox finished third three times in a row. By 1972, the team had changed. Eddie Kasko was in his third season as manager.

Rico Petrocelli had moved from short to third to make room for veteran Luis Aparicio. Doug Griffin held down second, and Danny Cater, acquired from the Yankees for reliever Sparky Lyle, was at first base. The outfield had swift Tommy Harper, underrated Reggie Smith, and Yastrzemski. A most valuable newcomer was catcher Carlton Fisk, who hit .293 and was named Rookie of the Year. Pitchers Marty Pattin, Sonny Siebert, and John Curtis were average, but right-hander Luis Tiant was outstanding. Tiant had once been a 20-game winner with Cleveland, but arm miseries had forced him back to the minors, where the Red Sox found him. He went 15–6 with a 1.91 ERA to earn Comeback Player of the Year laurels.

A player strike at the beginning cost thirteen days of the 1972 season, and the owners ruled that the games would not be made up. This proved crucial when the Red Sox chased the Tigers down to the wire, for the Tigers had one more game in the till than the Sox. Boston went to Detroit for the last series of the season, leading by half a game. The Tigers won the first two contests to clinch the Eastern Division title. A Red Sox victory in the third game still left them a half game behind—Detroit's "extra" game—and moaning about what might have been.

There was no catching Baltimore the next year, but in 1974 the Red Sox looked for a while like champions under new manager Darrell Johnson. The Boston farm system was one of the best in baseball. In 1974, it added outfielder Dwight Evans and shortstop Rick Burleson to the team. By late August, the Sox were in first place and pennant fever began to build in Boston. Then the Sox lost three straight in Minnesota, traveled to Baltimore to be shut out three in a row, and dropped two more to Milwaukee back at Fenway. The eight-game losing streak was more than enough to knock them out of the race.

After so much frustration, the Eastern championship in 1975 came almost easily. Boston took the division lead in late May and was never headed. Two rookies led the way. Jim Rice took over in left field as Yastrzemski moved to first base. Before he was sidelined late in the season with a broken wrist, Rice hit a robust .309 with 22 home runs and 102 RBI. In most years, he would have been Rookie of the Year in a landslide, but 1975 also saw Fred Lynn arrive in center field for the Sox. As Super Rookie, Lynn batted .331 with 21 homers and 105 RBI while simultaneously earning a reputation as the A.L.'s best outfield gloveman. After the season, he received not only the Rookie of the Year Award but also the MVP trophy. The pitching was also stronger and deeper than Red Sox fans had come to expect. Rick Wise paced the staff with 19 wins, Tiant won 18, and left-hander Bill Lee 17. Another lefty, Roger Moret, led the A.L. in winning percentage with a 14–3 mark.

Boston's opponent in the League Championship Series (LCS) was Oakland, winner of three straight pennants and favored to make short work of the Red Sox in capturing a fourth. The series opened in Boston, and Tiant thrilled the home crowd by tossing a three-hit, 7–1 victory. The next day, Reggie Cleveland was touched by the A's for three runs in five innings, but the Red Sox pulled even by scoring three of their own in the bottom of the fifth, with a two-run homer by Yaz the big blow. Moret and Dick Drago came in to hold the fort while Boston added three runs to its total to take a two-game lead. The series moved to Oakland, but the Red Sox were on a roll. They built a 5–1 lead before Rick Wise weakened for two runs in the eighth. However, Drago, the Sox's top reliever all season, was once more equal to the task, shutting down Oakland and making Boston an upset pennant winner.

One of the keys to the victory was Oakland's sloppy outfield play. Meanwhile, the Red Sox shone in that department, particularly Yastrzemski, who'd moved back to left because of Rice's injury.

If the Red Sox had faced a great team in the LCS, they found themselves up against an even greater one in the World Series. Cincinnati's "Big Red Machine" of Pete Rose, Johnny Bench, Tony Perez, Joe Morgan, George Foster, and Dave Concepcion bore comparison with such legendary clubs as the 1927 Yankees. Once more the Sox were decided underdogs.

But again Tiant got Boston away and winging, as he shut out the Reds 5–0 on five hits in Game One. The next day, Lee also held the Reds in check through eight innings. He left in the ninth with a 2–1 lead and a runner on. Drago came in and got two out, but two hits and two Cincinnati runs followed before he got the third.

In Game Three, Cincinnati jumped off to a 5–1 lead before the Red Sox rallied. They tied it at 5–5 on Evans's two-run homer in the ninth. After Cincinnati's Cesar Geronimo opened the bottom of the tenth with a single, pinch hitter Ed Armbruster tried to sacrifice him to second. The ball landed just in front of the plate and Fisk leaped for it, colliding with Armbruster. When Fisk got to the ball, he threw wildly to second, allowing Geronimo to go to third and Armbruster to reach second. The Red Sox claimed interference but umpire Larry Barnett didn't see it that way. When the arguing ceased, Moret relieved Jim Willoughby, who'd been outstanding but unlucky. Rose was walked to load the bases. Moret struck out pinch hitter Merv Rettenmund for what would have been the second out had Arbruster been retired. As things stood, however, there was only one away and the Sox still had to keep their outfield drawn in. Morgan lifted a fly over Lynn's head for what might have been the third out, but instead the ball dropped for a hit while Geronimo trotted in from third with the winning run.

Undaunted, Boston sent Tiant out to even the Series in Game Four. It wasn't vintage El Tiante, but his 9-hit complete game was enough for a 5–4 win. The next day, however, Cincinnati forged back into the lead with a 6–3 victory as Tony Perez blasted a pair of homers.

That set the stage for the historic sixth game. After a day off for travel, Game Six was postponed another 72 hours by rain. That looked like a break for Boston because it meant Tiant was ready to pitch again. Lynn staked him to a lead with a 3-run homer in the bottom of the first inning. That lasted until the top of the fifth when the Reds solved Tiant for three runs of their own. In the seventh inning, Cincinnati added two more runs. Then Geronimo opened the eighth with a homer and Tiant was lifted.

Trailing 6–3, the Red Sox started the bottom of the eighth with a single by Lynn and a walk to Petrocelli. Rawley Eastwick relieved for the Reds and struck out Evans. Burleson lined to short for the second out. That left it up to pinch hitter Bernie Carbo, who'd homered as a pinch hitter in Game Three. This time he pounded one into the center-field bleachers to tie the game. Only one other man—Chuck Essegian of the Dodgers in 1959—had ever hit a pair of pinch-hit homers in a World Series.

The Red Sox loaded the bases with no outs in the bottom of the ninth, only to be retired without scoring. The Reds also threatened to win. In the eleventh inning, Morgan lined one for the right-field seats that had home run written all over it, but Evans made a great leaping catch and then threw in time to double up a runner off first. In the top of the twelfth, Cincinnati had two on and one out before Rick Wise, working in relief, retired Concepcion and Geronimo.

Pat Darcy, the Reds' eighth reliever of the game, had pitched two faultless innings when he opened the 12th against Carlton Fisk. The Red Sox catcher greeted him with a blast down the left-field line that was surely gone—but fair or foul? As he moved down the first-base line, Fisk waved his arms urging the ball fair. When his drive bounced off the foul pole, the Series was tied again.

After the thrills of Game Six, the seventh game was necessarily anticlimactic. In almost any other Series, it would have been memorable. Boston got off to a three-run lead behind Bill Lee, but the Reds got two back on Perez's homer in the sixth and tied the score in the the seventh. In the ninth, Ken Griffey walked for the Reds and reached third with two outs. Joe Morgan's looping single gave Cincinnati a 4–3 lead. Boston went down in order in their half of the ninth. As expected, "The Big Red Machine" reigned as World Champions, but the Red Sox had come oh-so-close in what many regarded as the greatest World Series ever.

After the thrills of '75, 1976 was one of the saddest years in Red Sox history. Holdouts by Fisk, Lynn, and Burleson got the team off to a grumpy start, and it puttered through an undistinguished season before finally edging Cleveland for third place. Johnson was let go after 85 games and replaced as manager by Don Zimmer.

In July, the Red Sox suffered a loss far greater than any they had ever encountered on the field. Tom Yawkey died. In his more than forty years of ownership he'd never seen his team win a World Series and had only enjoyed three pennants. But, if ultimate victory always escaped him, his years with the Sox were still a triumph. He'd brought them back from near extinction during the Depression, made them contenders, and kept them so in most seasons. A "fans' " owner, he always saw that the folks who bought the seats got their money's worth at Fenway Park.

But, with Yawkey gone, the uncertainty at the top—ownership was split three ways—contributed to the frustrations of the next couple of years.

In one way, the 1977 Red Sox were like the Sox of 30 years before: lots of hit, not much pitch. Boston batters slugged 213 home runs, led by 39 by Jim Rice. No fewer than eight Red Sox hit at least 14 dingers. However, the starting pitching was lackluster at best. Zimmer called in reliever Bill Campbell, acquired over the winter from Minnesota, a total of 69 times, often for several innings at a stretch. Campbell was marvelous, saving 31 games and leading the team in wins with 13, but his overuse probably contributed to his rapid decline in succeeding seasons. The Sox took over first place for a while in August but eventually lost out to the Yankees by 2½ games.

The pitching staff was revamped for 1978. Dennis Eckersley was acquired from Cleveland and went 20–8. Mike Torrez from the Yankees won 16. Campbell was struck down with a bad arm, but rookie Bob Stanley saved ten games and was a terrific 15–2. The hitting fell off a little, but no one could blame Jim Rice, who led the A.L. with 46 homers and 139 RBI on his way to an MVP season.

The Sox rolled to a ten-game lead in mid-July and were being compared with the greatest aggregations of Boston's past. A division title seemed assured, probably a pennant, and possibly the long-sought World Series win. Then the Sox began to lose and the Yankees, who'd been slumbering in fourth place, began to win. By September 7, when New York arrived at Fenway for a 4-game set, the lead was down to four games. In a new version of the Boston Massacre, the Yankees slaughtered the Red Sox 15–3, 13–2, 7–0, and 7–4. By the following weekend when Boston invaded Yankee Stadium, New York was a game and a half in front. When the home team took the first two games of the series, the Red Sox looked dead in the water.

Boston won the third game to get back within hailing distance. Then in the final two weeks of the season, they rallied. On the last day, they tied the Yanks. Thirty years after losing the 1948 pennant in a one-game playoff, the Red Sox had a chance for revenge. The scene was even the same—Fenway Park.

Alas, it was not to be. The Red Sox staked Mike Torrez to a 2–0 lead through six innings. In the seventh, New York got two on with two out and light-hitting Bucky Dent at the plate. Dent lifted a routine fly into left field which Yaz appeared to have a play on. But suddenly the ball was in the screen and the Yankees led 3–2. New York added two more runs for an apparently safe lead going into the ninth. The Sox rallied for a pair and had the tying run at third before Yankee reliever Goose Gossage retired Yaz for Boston's final out of the season. Ninety-nine victories were only good for second place!

The Red Sox closed the decade with a generic year—91 wins, third place. Lynn won the batting title. He and Rice each hit 39 homers and drove in 122 and 130 runs, respectively. Despite the glory of 1975, the 1970s would be remembered in Boston more for pennants lost than for the one pennant gained.

SUCCESS STORY

Haywood Sullivan is a throwback to an earlier era when ballplayers occasionally rose to become club owners. Two of the best-known examples were Charles Comiskey, who started as an 1880s' first baseman and ended up owning the Chicago White Sox, and Clark

Griffith, a star pitcher of the 1890s who went on to own the Washington Senators.

Sullivan was a baseball and football star at the University of Florida. He could have had a pro football career as a quarterback but chose instead to sign with the Red Sox as a catcher. A back injury limited him to 60 games with the Sox over four seasons before he was dealt to Kansas City in 1961. He managed in the minors for two years and then took over as skipper of the A's in 1965. The next year, at age thirty-five, he became Red Sox vice-president in charge of player personnel. In 1978, when the club was purchased from the Yawkey estate, he became a partner, completing his rise from foot soldier to general.

IT'S ALL RELATIVE

Carl Yastrzemski's .301 batting average in 1968 led the American League, but it looked rather pallid when compared to some of the great marks of the past—say with Ted Williams's .406 in 1941. In fact, it was exactly 100 points lower than the .401 Bill Terry hit for the New York Giants in 1930, the last .400 hitter before Williams and the last in the National League.

But there's another way to look at it. When Terry had his big year, hitting was at its all-time high because of a number of factors that had nothing to do with Terry's batting eye. For one thing, the 1930 baseball was livelier than a caffeine cocktail. The whole National League averaged .303. In 1968, the pendulum had swung all the way in the other direction. The pitchers were in charge, and the American League averaged only .230 that year.

By comparison, Terry outhit his league by 98 points, .401 to .303; Yaz outhit his by 71, .301 to .230. In other words, if Yaz had been hitting in 1930 circumstances, he probably would have hit .374. That would have only put him sixth in the 1930 N.L., but it may be a better gauge of Yaz's 1968 hitting.

Oh, by the way, Williams outhit the American League by 140 points in 1941.

Battles in the East, 1980–1992

Near the end of the 1980 season, Don Zimmer was fired. In the three seasons he'd managed the Red Sox from start to finish, they'd won 97, 99, and 91 games and come close to two division titles. But "close," as everyone knows, only counts in horeshoes and hand grenades. The frustration of being almost on top was getting to Boston fans and management, some of whom believed that another manager might have won the couple extra games each season necessary for the brass ring. With five games left in 1980, the Sox stood 82–73 and were out of the race and Zim was out of a job.

His successor was Ralph Houk, the man who'd won three pennants with the 1961–1963 Yankees. But the team Houk inherited was less talented than those Yankee teams and less talented than the team Zimmer had managed. Carlton Fisk became a free agent over the winter and signed with the White Sox. Fred Lynn and Rick Burleson were traded away before they, too, could become free agents. Butch Hobson was also traded and Carney Lansford replaced him at third base.

The 1981 season was like no other in that a player strike in the middle caused it to be split into first and second stanzas, with the winners of each segment playing off for the division crown. The Red Sox were unaffected, having won neither end of the season, but they did complete a winning year under Houk, going 59–49 overall in the bisected schedule. Lansford won the batting title with a .336 mark, and Dwight Evans tied for the home-run leadership with 22.

Houk's Red Sox made some noise early in 1982, but they didn't have the starting pitching to stay the course. Third place was the best they could do.

The most significant Red Sox happening in 1982 was the arrival of

Wade Boggs. He didn't get into the starting lineup until late July when an injury sidelined Carney Lansford. From then to the end of the season, he batted .361. Although Boggs didn't bat enough times to be eligible for the batting title, his overall mark of .349 was 17 points better than the actual winner, Kansas City's Willie Wilson. His hitting enabled the Sox to trade Lansford to Oakland for slugging outfielder Tony Armas.

Yastrzemski retired after the 1983 season. He'd worn a Red Sox uniform for 23 seasons. Inevitably, Yaz's career would be compared with that of Ted Williams, the left fielder he'd replaced as a rookie in 1961. It was a comparison neither he nor more than a handful of players in history could stand up to. Although he'd won three batting titles, his .285 career batting average of was far below Williams's .344. Williams also topped Yaz in homers, 521 to 452, despite playing in over a thousand fewer games. Yastrzemski's longevity gave him the club career lead in games, at bats, hits, runs, doubles, runs batted in, and total bases. Yaz's fans could argue that he played through a period of unusually low batting averages and that he was far superior to Williams in the field. If he ultimately fell short of Williams's accomplishments, Yastrzemski was nevertheless a certainty for the Hall of Fame in his first year of eligibility.

Boston fans had little to cheer about for three seasons except individual accomplishments. The Red Sox were essentially a .500 ballclub—a little under in 1983, a little over in '84, and right on the mark with an 81–81 when John McNamara became the manager in 1985. Boggs won his first batting title in 1983 with a .361 mark and repeated in '85 at .368. His 240 base hits were the most in the American League since 1928. Rice led the league in homers with 39 and tied for the runs-batted-in title with 126 in 1983. The next year, Tony Armas led the A.L. in both departments with 43 and 123; Rice was second in RBI with 122.

Going in, the 1986 season looked to be more of the same. The most noticeable change in the regular lineup was the addition of Don Baylor as the designated hitter. He'd come to the Red Sox for Mike Easler in a trade of designated hitters of (DHs). Both were considered near the end of their careers. The pitching had potential. Bob Ojeda had been swapped to the New York Mets for a couple of relievers. Bruce Hurst, Dennis "Oil Can" Boyd, and Bob Nipper were okay, and Bob Stanley was still available for the bullpen. Roger Clemens, the hard-throwing right-hander, had begun well in 1984 and '85 only to have both seasons curtailed by injury. After arm surgery the previous August, he was a big question mark.

It took a while for Boston fans to get their hopes up. Even when Clemens proved he was all the way back with his major-league-record 20-strikeout game against Seattle in April, fans were not ready to jump on a BoSox bandwagon. In mid-May, Boston took a tenuous lead in the East. Nipper and Hurst were sidelined at times, but Manager McNamara juggled his staff and the Sox stayed in front.

When it became obvious that the Red Sox really might pull it off, GM Lou Gorman went out and got some help, adding Spike Owen to take over shortstop, Dave Henderson to platoon with slowing Tony Armas in center field, and veteran pitcher Tom Seaver to bolster the pitching. In the meantime, Baylor was enjoying a wonderful year that would see him end with 31 homers and 94 RBI. Jim Rice, in his last big season, knocked in 120, and first baseman Bill Buckner had 102. Wade Boggs won another batting title with his .357 mark.

The man of the hour, day, and season, however, was Clemens, whose 24-4 mark and league-leading 2.48 ERA made him irreplaceable. Fittingly, he was voted both the Most Valuable Player and the Cy Young Award. He even found time to be named MVP of the All-Star Game.

The League Championship Series pitted the Red Sox against the California Angels, seeking their first-ever pennant. In a stunning reversal of form, Clemens was pounded into submission, 8-1, in the opener at Fenway. Bruce Hurst evened the series with a 9-2 win in Game Two. The scene then shifted to California, where the Angels jumped on Boyd late for a 5-3 win. Clemens came back in Game Four and pitched shutout ball into the ninth, only to see the Angels rally for three runs to tie. The game went into extra innings, with California winning in the 11th.

Had the LCS been in its original 3-out-of-5 format, the Sox would have been eliminated, but a best-of-7 format had gone into effect in 1985. That seemed academic the next day. The Angels held a 5-4 lead with two outs in the top of the ninth and a 2-2 count on Boston's Dave Henderson. A Red Sox runner was on base, but the Angels had their ace reliever, Donnie Moore, on the mound. As Moore delivered, 64,000 Angels fans were on their feet and the Angels bench stood poised to erupt from the dugout. But Henderson deposited the pitch into the left-field seats to turn the game around.

California managed to tie the score in the bottom of the ninth, but they were only delaying the inevitable. Henderson's sacrifice fly in the eleventh inning brought home the winning run for Boston. The stunned Angels and jubilant Red Sox returned to Boston where McNamara's band completed its comeback by winning Game Six 10–6 and Game Seven 8–1. A combination of veteran hitters, young pitchers, and a bit of luck had put the Red Sox back in the World Series for the first time since 1975.

The opponents were the New York Mets, who'd won 108 regular-season games. As usual, Boston was the underdog. Bruce Hurst opened for the Red Sox at Shea Stadium against Ron Darling. Hurst held the Mets to four hits in eight innings, but Darling was even stingier, allowing three singles in seven frames. The Red Sox, however, pushed over a run in the seventh, and, when Calvin Schiraldi blanked New York in the ninth, Boston was up a game. The next day was billed as the pitching matchup of the year—Clemens vs. the Mets' Doc Gooden. Neither lasted past the fifth inning, but the Red Sox bats prevailed, 9–3.

The Red Sox brought a 2–0 lead back to Boston but lost the next two games. So much for home-field advantage! In Game Five, Hurst was back on the mound for the Sox. He wasn't as sharp as in the opener. He allowed ten hits but only three runs in going the route. In the meantime, the Sox scored four times in the first four innings against Gooden and held on for the win.

Game Six had been the memorable one in the Sox's last Series appearance, and it was to be the one everybody remembered from this one. Clemens went the first seven innings for Boston and was in line for a 3–2 win. But Calvin Schiraldi gave up a tying run in the eighth. In the top of the tenth, Dave Henderson crashed a homer off Rick Aguilera and Boston added a second run before they were retired.

Leading 5–3, only three outs separated Boston from its first Series win since 1918. Schiraldi retired the first two Mets of the inning. Then Gary Carter singled and Kevin Mitchell followed with another hit. Schiraldi zipped two strikes past Ray Knight—one strike away from victory—but the New Yorker looped a single into center. Carter scored to make the score 5–4 and Mitchell raced to third.

Bob Stanley was brought in to face Mookie Wilson. He worked the count to 2–2, but then Wilson fouled off two in a row as the tension built. On his seventh delivery, Stanley wild pitched. Mitchell scored and Knight went to second. The game was tied. Wilson fouled two more of Stanley's offerings. On the tenth pitch of his at bat, Mookie slapped an easy bounding ball to hobbled first baseman Bill Buckner. Somehow it went unhindered through Buckner's aching legs; Knight raced home with the winning run.

It was a crushing defeat. A rain postponement gave Boston an extra day before Game Seven, but whether that would help them recover or just magnify the Game Six defeat was impossible to say. Bruce Hurst went to the mound for the Red Sox in search of his third Series win. The Sox scored three in the second inning on back-to-back homers by Dwight Evans and Rich Gedman and Boggs's RBI single. Hurst pitched five shutout innings, but then was rocked for three runs in the sixth. Schiraldi came in to pitch the seventh. Knight greeted him with a homer for the go-ahead run. Before the inning ended, the Mets added two more runs to go up 6–3. Boston closed to 6–5 in the eighth, but New York matched them with two runs in the bottom of the inning. When the Sox went down one-two-three in the ninth, Boston had lost its fourth World Series since Babe Ruth had been traded to the Yankees.

Whether the "Curse of the Bambino" hovered over Fenway Park made little difference in 1987 as the Sox slumped to fifth place in the East. Boggs won another batting title with his .363 average and Clemens's 20–9 was good for his second consecutive Cy Young Award. Dwight Evans cracked 30 homers and drove in 123. Mike Greenwell hit .328, but the Sox had too many holes in the lineup as Baylor, Rice, Buckner, and catcher Rich Gedman all slumped.

Nothing very exciting happened during the first half of 1988. At the All-Star Game break, with the team record at 43–42, McNamara was replaced as manager by coach Joe Morgan. When the Sox won twelve straight coming out of the break, they found themselves in the thick of the division race. Evans and Greenwell supplied RBI power and Boggs, who won his fifth batting title at .366, led the league in runs scored with 123. Ellis Burks hit a solid .293 in center field. Clemens and Hurst had matching 18-win seasons, and big Lee Smith was a force out of the bullpen with 29 saves. By the end of the season, the Sox were slumping, losing seven of their last ten, but by then everyone else in the East was out of the race.

Some ex–Red Sox helped Oakland win the opening game of the LCS. Dave Henderson drove in Carney Lansford for the go-ahead run off Bruce Hurst in the eighth inning, and then Dennis Eckersley came in to nail down the save. The next day, the Athletics edged Clemens, 4–3. The series moved to Oakland, and the Red Sox jumped off to a five-run lead in Game Three only to lose, 10–6. The A's wrapped up the pennant with a 4–1 win the next day.

Injuries waylaid the Red Sox in 1989. The lineup varied from game to game. Rice, Burks, and second baseman Marty Barrett missed extended periods and most of the other regulars were out from time to time. A muscle tear limited Clemens to 17 wins. Only a spurt at the end allowed the team to climb to a winning 83–79 record.

Ellis Burks led the Red Sox in homers in 1990 with only 21, the lowest total by a Sox leader since 1974. His modest 89 RBI also topped the club. Wade Boggs batted a career-low .302. But overall the team had a solid lineup that led the A.L. with a .272 average. Tony Pena came over from St. Louis to give the Sox quality catching. His influence was credited for the surprisingly strong showing of the pitching staff. By early September, Boston held a 6½ game lead, but then a shoulder injury sidelined Clemens.

As if to show how irreplaceable the Rocket Man was, the Sox promptly went into a slump to give the lead to Toronto. However, the Blue Jays returned the favor, losing six of their last eight to practically force Boston into the Eastern title.

The Oakland A's were widely regarded as unstoppable, and their performance in the LCS did nothing to change that opinion. They took the Red Sox in four straight again. The most memorable moment of the Series came in Game Four with Clemens on the mound. In the second inning, he was unceremoniously ejected from the game for allegedly directing vulgar language toward the delicate ears of the home-plate umpire. With him went any slight hopes the Red Sox may have harbored for a miracle comeback.

Boston was apparently out of the A.L. East race by August in 1991. Sox fans held a mock funeral to inter their hopes. But the team came back from the dead to make it close in September before finally finishing seven games behind Toronto. Clemens led the league in strikeouts with 241 and he pitched better all season than his 18–10 record would suggest, a fact recognized when he received his third Cy Young Award after the season. The news Joe Morgan got was less welcome; he was replaced as manager by Butch Hobson, the one-time Sox third baseman.

Perhaps Morgan was the luckier of the two, since he didn't have to endure the 1992 season—one of the darkest in Red Sox history. Promising first baseman Carlos Quintana missed the entire season due to injuries suffered in an auto accident. Ellis Burks and Mike Greenwell played only 115 games between them. As if losing three of their best hitters was not crippling enough, Wade Boggs suffered through a season-long slump that saw his batting average end at an un-Boggsian .259, and Slugger Jack Clark was not even a ghost of his former self. The punchless Red Sox scored a mere 599 runs while finishing last in the A.L. East.

Wasted was the great pitching of Roger Clemens, who nearly won another Cy Young, and some good work by lefthander Frank Viola. They and a few others gave Boston the league's second-best ERA.

On the bright side, the rash of injuries and disappointments allowed Hobson to work many of the young Red Sox prospects into the lineup. And, while none of them excelled, that year of experience should pay dividends in 1993. So should the free agent addition of veteran National League slugger Andre Dawson, who is expected to add punch to the lineup and a steadying influence in the clubhouse. If the pitching continues strong, the Red Sox should move up this season.

Fenway Park

A few years ago, a National League pitcher remarked that he could stand on a mound in any one of the "cookie-cutter" stadiums and not know if he was in Philadelphia, Pittsburgh, or Cincinnati. A visit to one of those, all-purpose stadiums with ersatz grass, analogous foul lines, and antiseptic ambience will leave any Red Sox fan homesick for Fenway Park. Fenway is unmistakably of baseball, by baseball, and, most definitely, for baseball.

For their first eleven seasons in the American League, the Red Sox played at the Huntington Avenue Grounds. But in 1912, Fenway was built. Sox owner John I. Taylor named it without any great show of originality: "It's in the Fenway section [of Boston], isn't it? Then call it Fenway Park."

It was a good time for building legendary ballparks. Pittsburgh's late lamented Forbes Field went up in 1909, the same year as Philadelphia's long-departed Shibe Park; the original Comiskey Park opened in 1910; Detroit's Navin Field (now Tiger Stadium), Cincinnati's Crosley Field, and Fenway Park all saw their first baseball in the same year; Brooklyn's hallowed Ebbets Field became home to "Dem Bums" in 1913; and Chicago's Weeghman Park (now Wrigley Field) was built in 1914, although the Cubs didn't move into it until two years later. Boston even saw a second baseball stadium built—Braves Field (remember the Braves?) was opened in August of 1915.

Fenway was scheduled to open with the Red Sox against New York on April 18, 1912, but two days of rain pushed the initial game back two days. Those who worried about ill omens were mollified by Boston's 11-inning, 7–6 win against the team then known as the "Highlanders." Tris Speaker drove in the winning run against New York to send 27,000 Red Sox fans home happy. The event would have been front-page news in Boston had it not been bumped by the story of the sinking of the Titanic.

The Red Sox were able to initiate their new park into the World Series in that first year, as Boston beat the Giants in a classic. Two years later, Fenway hosted another World Series, but this one didn't involve the Red Sox. The 1914 Braves put on a "miracle" drive at the end of the season to win one of their two twentieth-century National League pennants. And, because Braves Field was still only a construction site, they played—and astonishingly beat—Connie Mack's Philadelphia Athletics for the World Championship. The Red Sox won pennants in 1915 and '16, but by then Braves Field, with its larger capacity, was open and the Boston games of both Series were played there.

That wasn't the last time the Red Sox deserted their home for Braves Field. Sunday baseball was approved in 1929, but for the first couple of years the Sox played their Sunday games at Braves Field because Fenway Park was near a church. Finally, on July 3, 1932, Fenway saw its first Sunday game—a 13–2 loss to the Yankees.

On May 8, 1926, a fire destroyed the bleachers along the left-field foul line. Team owner Bob Quinn was barely able to meet his payroll and had nothing left over for new seats. For the rest of the time he owned the Sox, infielders could dash behind the third-base grandstand to catch foul balls.

As soon as Tom Yawkey took over, he launched a rebuilding program. Another fire in left was a setback, but by 1934, Fenway was as good as new. Better!

That year, a crowd of 46,766 showed up on August 12 to say good-bye to Babe Ruth, then in his last season with the Yankees. A week later, that record was broken by the 46,995 who came out for a doubleheader with the pennant-bound Tigers. The all-time Fenway Park record was set on September 22, 1935—47,627 for a Yankee doubleheader. The park will never see such crowds again unless there's a major reconstruction because fire laws passed during World War II prohibited such overcrowding.

Fenway Park's most famous feature—the left-field wall—deserves mention. Originally, it was just a humdrum, ten-foot-high wood fence, but a ten-foot-high incline, which acted much as today's warning tracks do, extended all the way across left field at the fence. Duffy Lewis quickly became the master of playing the incline, and it became known as "Duffy's Cliff." Visiting outfielders unfamiliar with this particular piece of real estate had fits playing balls off the wall. The wall itself was raised to its present 37.17 feet in 1917. The lower part was concrete; the upper part was tin-covered wood. Since 1976, it has all been a hard plastic.

When Yawkey revamped Fenway in 1934, he had "Duffy's Cliff" flattened. The 23-foot screen was placed on top in 1936, not to save baseballs, but to save windows on Lansdowne Street. Until 1947, fans could read ads about Gem Blades, Lifebouy Soap, and Vimms on the wall, but that year it was covered with a coat of paint and became the "Green Monster."

That same year, 1947, saw lights for night games placed in Fenway. By then, thirteen of the existing major-league clubs were playing at night, so it looked as if it might be more than a fad. The Red Sox first home night game was June 13, 1947. They beat the White Sox 5–3.

To recount the many magnificent plays that have made Fenway Park more than a patch of steel, concrete and grass (real grass!) would take more space than is available here, but one history note must be mentioned. The first two (and so far only) American League Playoff games were played at Fenway Park. We forget who won.

2
PUZZLES

1. The Monster who pitched in front of The Green Monster
5. Leonard, Ruth, Grove, Parnell, Hurst all threw——
10. A "bender" that is sometimes the chief
11. 1,451 RBI
12. Won 25 in 1949
13. Triple Crown in 1967
16. Three-time RBI champ of the 1950s
17. Batting champ of 1950
20. 23-game winner in 1949
21. All-time doubles champion
22. Jimmie, Shano, or Eddie
24. Rocket
26. 34–5 in 1912
29. Rookie of the Year in 1950
31. One Joe hurt us in 1975; another led in '88
33. Everett or Boomer
34. This one was splendid
35. Vern Stephens

1. Batting champ in 1960 and '62
2. Won three Series games in 1903 (variant spelling)
3. Three times better than a single
4. Sox first home-run champ
6. "The Beast"
7. "The Hawk"
8. No. 1 at second base
9. Lewis or Hugh
10. Managed 1915–1916 champions
12a. Rookie of the Year and MVP in 1975
14. Holder of Red Sox record for rookie hits
15. Play or header
18. Won number 300 in 1941
19. Author of *Fear Strikes Out*
21. Ted or Dick (or Dib in 1935)
22. Clark Griffith's son-in-law
23. You'll find it at home (but don't try to eat off it)
25. In French, *wrong-zone;* but he was right at third
27. "The Little Professor"
28. Wade or cranberry
30. Waved it fair in Game 6
32. Lewis, Speaker, and——

RED SOX HEROES

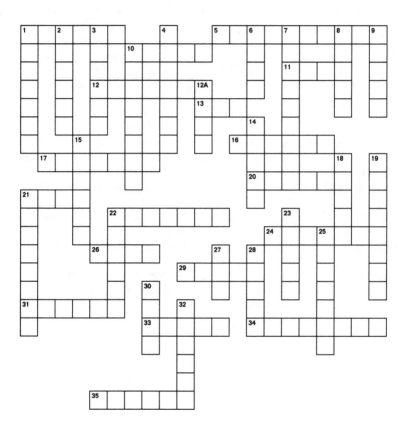

ACROSS

1. Double play or a win over Minnesota
4. Foe in 1903
7. Where you'll find the manager and subs
8. The best place to be when on gameday
11. He scored from first in 1946
13. A half game better in 1972
14. Better to be on it than be it
15. Nee Orioles
18. The Yankee Clipper batted this way
19. Not really enough; it takes one more
21. Had us down three games to one in 1986
23. Park I and II
26. Walter Johnson pitched for them
30. One-ninth of a game
31. Every runner wants to get there
32. The Junior Circuit
34. Maryland's favorite birds
35. New York or Damn
36. What Armbruster tried to do in 1975

DOWN

1. The 1991 World Champions
2. Won the playoff in 1948
3. Perfect color for a Monster
5. What to do between the top and bottom of the seventh
6. Sox not at Fenway
9. Robin Yount's team
10. Clemens struck out 20 in one game
12. Outs, strikes, or bases
14. How certain northern birds are after a loss
16. Outfield limit
17. A hose of a different color
20. From Philly to K.C. to Oakland
22. Yankee shortstop who ruined Sox in 1978
24. He makes up the lineup
25. Brett's team
27. Once were the Senators
28. Outside the lines
29. 1986 Series opponents
33. Innings or on a side

RED SOX VILLAINS

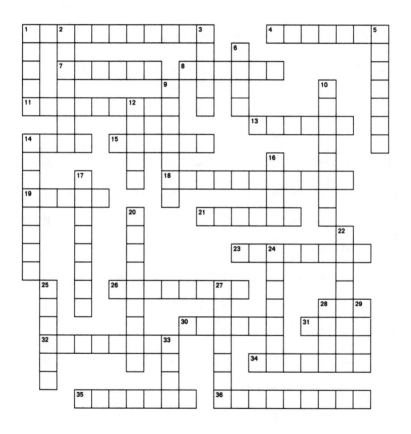

WHO'S IN CHARGE HERE?

Namesearch: Managers

In the NAMESEARCH maze below are the last names of 20 men who have managed the Red Sox at one time or another. All you have to do is circle them. Of course, to make it sporting, we spelled some backward, some diagonally, some down, some up, and only a few across. The first names or nicknames of the managers included are:

Joe	Darrell	Marse Joe	Ralph
Billy	Ed	Joe (again)	Don
Jimmy	Jake	Eddie	Butch
Lee	Lou	Pinky	John
Johnny	Hugh	Frank	Rough

M	C	C	A	R	T	H	Y	R	H	T	Y	G	Z	B	N
O	A	R	N	S	E	C	D	G	W	B	R	U	I	A	O
R	K	W	U	H	L	O	S	T	A	H	L	Z	G	R	M
G	E	S	N	O	O	T	D	U	R	U	T	I	K	R	E
A	W	N	A	U	A	B	T	J	A	F	R	T	E	O	N
N	J	I	B	K	R	V	S	H	M	R	C	B	O	W	T
R	F	G	G	E	K	H	R	O	A	R	N	W	D	U	P
D	R	G	F	J	O	O	L	C	N	A	G	J	L	P	E
U	Z	I	M	M	E	R	V	O	C	O	L	L	I	N	S
H	C	H	A	N	C	E	D	R	M	K	H	A	Y	A	K
R	H	R	B	S	W	N	O	S	N	H	O	J	F	O	Y
T	E	A	L	H	T	N	N	C	D	P	F	I	F	M	O
P	F	G	O	E	I	R	K	U	A	E	R	D	U	O	B
A	L	C	R	N	A	M	R	E	H	U	A	S	D	E	S

64

Red Sox Heroes Answers

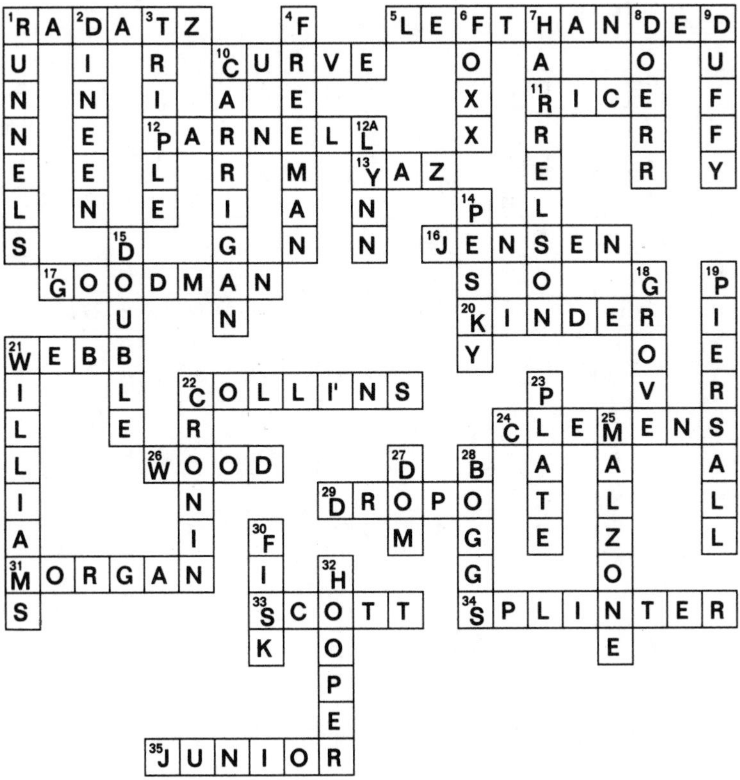

Red Sox Villains Answers

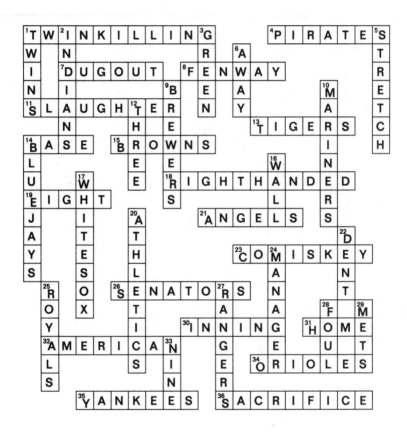

```
M  C  C  A  R  T  H  Y  R  H  T  Y  G  Z  B  N
O  A  R  N  S  E  C  D  G  W  B  R  U  I  A  O
R  K  W  U  H  L  O  S  T  A  H  L  Z  G  R  M
G  E  S  N  O  O  T  D  U  R  U  T  I  K  R  E
A  W  N  A  U  A  B  T  J  A  F  R  T  E  O  N
N  J  I  B  K  R  V  S  H  M  R  C  B  O  W  T
R  F  G  G  E  K  H  R  O  A  R  N  W  D  U  P
D  R  G  F  J  O  O  L  C  N  A  G  J  L  P  E
U  Z  I  M  M  E  R  V  O  C  O  L  L  I  N  S
H  C  H  A  N  C  E  D  R  M  K  H  A  Y  A  K
R  H  R  B  S  W  N  O  S  N  H  O  J  F  O  Y
T  E  A  L  H  T  N  N  C  D  P  F  I  F  M  O
P  F  G  O  E  I  R  K  U  A  E  R  D  U  O  B
A  L  C  R  N  A  M  R  E  H  U  A  S  D  E  S
```

3
TRIVIA QUESTIONS AND ANSWERS

PILGRIMS' PROGRESS, 1901–1909

1. Before they were the Red Sox, the team was called the
   a. Beaneaters ✓
   b. Celtics
   c. Red Caps
   d. Pilgrims

2. The team's first manager was
   a. Eddie Collins
   b. Jimmy Collins ✓
   c. Tom Collins
   d. Phil Collins

3. The original owner of the Boston A.L. team was
   a. Tom Yawkey
   b. Arthur Soden ✓
   c. Ban Johnson
   d. Charles Somers

4. Boston's A.L. team played its first home games at
   a. Huntington Avenue ✓
      Grounds
   b. Braves Field
   c. Fenway Park
   d. South End Grounds

5. In their first season, the Bostons finished second to
   a. Philadelphia Athletics
   b. Chicago White ✓
      Stockings
   c. Cleveland Indians
   d. St. Louis Browns

6. The first Boston player to lead the American League in home runs
   was
   a. Babe Ruth
   b. Jimmy Collins
   c. Buck Freeman
   d. Tris Speaker ✓

7. The Pittsburgh pitcher who beat Boston three times in the first
   modern World Series was
   a. Deacon Phillippe
   b. Preacher Roe
   c. Parson Weems
   d. Pop Haines ✓

8. Boston's pitching hero with three wins in the 1903 World Series
   was
   a. Cy Young
   b. Bill Dinneen
   c. Long Tom Hughes ✓
   d. Jesse Tannehill

9. The song the Royal Rooters incessantly sang during the 1903 World Series was
   a. "Auld Lang Syne"
   b. "Slide, Kelly, Slide" ✓
   c. "Sweetheart of Sigma Chi"
   d. "Tessie"

10. Whose wild pitch against Boston in 1904 cost New York the pennant?
    a. Sad Sam Jones
    b. Fat Freddy Fitzsimmons
    c. Happy Jack Chesbro
    d. Iron Man Joe ✓ McGinnity

11. Which team won the 1904 World Series?
    a. Boston
    b. New York Giants
    c. Chicago Cubs ✓
    d. No one

12. The first pitcher to throw a perfect game in the twentieth century was
    a. Don Larsen
    b. Nolan Ryan
    c. Cy Young
    d. Rube Waddell ✓

13. The team was named the Red Sox by
    a. Owner John I. Taylor
    b. Sportswriter Tim Murnane
    c. Mayor John F. Fitzgerald
    d. A.L. President Ban ✓ Johnson

14. What famous Philadelphia Athletics pitcher defeated Cy Young in a 20-inning game?
    a. Eddie Plank
    b. Rube Waddell
    c. Chief Bender
    d. Jack Coombs ✓

15. The Red Sox manager who died—an apparent suicide—during spring training in 1907 was
    a. Jake Stahl
    b. Chick Stahl
    c. George Stallings ✓
    d. Chic Sales

THE BEST OF TIMES, 1910–1918

1. The only brothers to manage the same major-league team were the
   a. Alous
   b. Sewells
   c. Stahls
   d. Ferrells

2. The strong-armed Red Sox right fielder for this decade was
   a. Duffy Lewis
   b. Harry Hooper
   c. Tris Speaker
   d. Larry Gardner

3. The second Red Sox player to lead the American League in home runs was
   a. Babe Ruth
   b. Tris Speaker
   c. Braggo Roth
   d. Chick Stahl

4. How many consecutive games did Smokey Joe Wood win in 1912 to tie the record?
   a. 10
   b. 16
   c. 19
   d. 24

5. Who made an infamous muff of a fly ball in the 1912 World Series?
   a. Josh Devore
   b. Tris Speaker
   c. Fred Merkle
   d. Fred Snodgrass

6. The Red Sox hurler with the most wins in a season to date is
   a. Cy Young
   b. Dutch Leonard
   c. Smokey Joe Wood
   d. Ray Collins

7. What was Manager Rough Carrigan's position in the field?
   a. Catcher
   b. First base
   c. Third base
   d. Outfield

8. Who was the only pitcher to defeat the Red Sox in the 1915 World Series?
   a. Christy Mathewson
   b. Grover Alexander
   c. Herb Pennock
   d. Walter Johnson

9. What was the Red Sox home field in the 1915 and 1916 World Series?
   a. Fenway Park
   b. Braves Field
   c. Huntington Avenue Grounds
   d. Harvard Stadium

10. Where did Tris Speaker go when he was traded before the 1916 season?
    a. Detroit Tigers
    b. Boston Braves
    c. New York Yankees
    d. Cleveland Indians

11. Who was the winning pitcher in the 14-inning, 2–1 second game of the 1916 World Series?
    a. Babe Ruth
    b. Grover Alexander
    c. Christy Mathewson
    d. Sherry Smith

12. Who relieved Babe Ruth and went on to retire 26 batters in a row?
    a. Hugh Bedient
    b. Ernie Shore
    c. Carl Mays
    d. Rube Foster

13. What effect did the goverment's "work or fight" order have on the 1918 baseball season?
    a. None
    b. It was cancelled
    c. It ended on September 1
    d. Players held two jobs

14. The Red Sox's opponents in the 1918 World Series were the
    a. Brooklyn Dodgers
    b. Chicago Cubs
    c. New York Giants
    d. Philadelphia Phillies

15. Who made the decision to turn Babe Ruth into an outfielder?
    a. Rough Carrigan
    b. Harry Frazee
    c. Ed Barrow
    d. Jack Barry

THE WORST OF TIMES, 1919–1932

1. What was Harry Frazee's big Broadway hit?
   a. *No, No, Nanette*
   b. *Good News*
   c. *The Jazz Singer*
   d. *Where's Charley?*

2. Which of the following pitchers was *not* sent to the Yankees by the Red Sox?
   a. Herb Pennock
   b. Waite Hoyt
   c. Howard Ehmke
   d. Carl Mays

3. What was the security for the loan that was part of the deal that sent Babe Ruth to New York?
   a. Harry Frazee's estate
   b. Fenway Park
   c. Frazee's life insurance
   d. Rights to Frazee's next show

4. Whose all-time home-run record did Babe Ruth break in 1919?
   a. Frank Baker
   b. Ned Williamson
   c. King Kelly
   d. Roger Connor

5. The Red Sox longtime shortstop who became a Yankee in 1922 was
   a. Everett Scott
   b. Jack Barry
   c. Roger Peckinpaugh
   d. Stuffy McInnis

6. After he left the Red Sox, what team did Ed Barrow go to work for?
   a. Tigers
   b. Indians
   c. Yankees
   d. White Sox

7. Before managing the Red Sox, Frank Chance was the first baseman in an infield with what doubleplay combination?
   a. Honus Wagner and Dots Miller
   b. Fred Parent and Hobe Ferris
   c. Joe Tinker and Johnny Evers
   d. Jack Barry and Eddie Collins

8. What Red Sox pitcher won 20 games for a last-place team in 1923?
   a. Jack Quinn
   b. Howard Ehmke
   c. Herb Pennock
   d. Bullet Joe Bush

9. Before buying the Red Sox, Bob Quinn was a successful executive with the
   a. Chicago White Sox
   b. Philadelphia Phillies
   c. St. Louis Browns
   d. St. Louis Cardinals

10. The only Red Sox player ever to get an unassisted triple play was
    a. Ira Flagstead   c. Rabbit Warstler
    b. George Burns   d. Johnny Neun

11. Perhaps the worst fielder ever to play the outfield for the Red Sox was
    a. Tom Oliver   c. Harry Hooper
    b. Babe Ruth   d. Smead Jolley

12. What former Red Sox pennant-winning manager came back to try (unsuccessfully) again in 1927?
    a. Rough Carrigan   c. Jake Stahl
    b. Jimmy Collins   d. Ed Barrow

13. What future Hall of Fame pitcher lost 47 games for the Red Sox in 1928–1929?
    a. Danny MacFayden   c. Waite Hoyt
    b. Red Ruffing   d. Ed Morris

14. The Red Sox player who set the all-time record for doubles in a season was
    a. Phil Todt   c. Earl Webb
    b. Moon Harris   d. Buddy Myer

15. The first Red Sox player to lead the American League in hitting was
    a. Ted Williams   c. Tris Speaker
    b. Dale Alexander   d. Cedric Durst

BUY ME A CHAMPION, 1933–1946

1. What team had Tom Yawkey's uncle owned?
   a. St. Louis Browns   c. Philadelphia Phillies
   b. Boston Braves   d. Detroit Tigers

2. Who did Yawkey hire as his vice president and general manager?
   a. Eddie Collins   c. Tris Speaker
   b. Rough Carrigan   d. Ed Barrow

3. In one of the GM's first moves, what Hall of Fame catcher came from St. Louis?
   a. Wes Ferrell
   b. Rick Ferrell
   c. Charlie Farrell
   d. Duke Farrell

4. What Red Sox player led the A.L. in stolen bases in 1934–1935?
   a. Tom Oliver
   b. Billy Werber
   c. Doc Cramer
   d. Max Bishop

5. Because of the Depression, what club owner sent two future Hall of Famers to the Red Sox in the 1930s?
   a. Clark Griffith
   b. Jake Ruppert
   c. Connie Mack
   d. Phil Ball

6. What Sox lefty led the A.L. in ERA four times in the late 1930s?
   a. Lefty Liefield
   b. Lefty O'Doul
   c. Lefty Grove
   d. Lefty Gomez

7. Joe Cronin was whose son-in-law?
   a. Tom Yawkey
   b. Connie Mack
   c. Eddie Collins
   d. Clark Griffith

8. The American League's MVP in 1938 with 175 RBI was
   a. Jimmie Foxx
   b. Joe Cronin
   c. Ted Williams
   d. Dale Alexander

9. Eddie Collins discovered Ted Williams on a trip to look at
   a. Johnny Pesky
   b. Bobby Doerr
   c. Pinky Higgins
   d. Dom DiMaggio

10. What was Ted Williams's batting average with one day left in the 1941 season?
    a. .406
    b. .399
    c. .3996
    d. .4001

11. Who was chosen over Williams as 1942 MVP?
    a. Joe DiMaggio
    b. Joe Gordon
    c. Joe Cronin
    d. Joe Kuhel

12. The leading A.L. pitcher in 1942, with a 22–6 mark, was
   a. Tex Hughson
   b. Tex Carleton
   c. Tex Ritter
   d. Tex Schramm

13. What Cardinal pitcher won 3 games in the 1946 World Series?
   a. Howie Pollett
   b. Harry Brecheen
   c. Murry Dickson
   d. Max Lanier

14. Whose tenth-inning homer won Game One of the 1946 Series?
   a. Ted Williams
   b. George Metkovich
   c. Bobby Doerr
   d. Rudy York

15. Whose hit drove home Enos Slaughter with the winning run in Game Seven?
   a. Harry Walker
   b. Stan Musial
   c. Whitey Kurowski
   d. Marty Marion

FRUSTRATIONS AND A DREAM, 1947–1967

1. Which of the following Red Sox pitchers did NOT come down with a sore arm in 1947?
   a. Tex Hughson
   b. Joe Dobson
   c. Boo Ferriss
   d. Mickey Harris

2. Vern Stephens was acquired by the Red Sox in a deal with the
   a. Cleveland Indians
   b. Detroit Tigers
   c. St. Louis Browns
   d. Washington Senators

3. Who was the starting pitcher for Boston in the 1948 playoff?
   a. Joe Dobson
   b. Denny Galehouse
   c. Jack Kramer
   d. Mel Parnell

4. What did Ted Williams do in the 1950 All-Star Game?
   a. Struck out 4 times
   b. Broke his elbow
   c. Hit 2 home runs
   d. Sprained his ankle

5. Who won the 1950 American League batting title?
   a. Ted Williams
   b. Johnny Pesky
   c. Al Zarilla
   d. Billy Goodman

6. What Red Sox outfielder suffered a widely publicized mental breakdown in 1952?
   a. Al Zarilla
   b. Jimmy Piersall
   c. Ted Williams
   d. Jackie Jensen

7. What Red Sox first baseman (and former All-American football star) died early in the 1955 season?
   a. Walt Dropo
   b. Jackie Jensen
   c. Harry Agganis
   d. Norm Zauchin

8. The first black player to wear a Red Sox uniform was
   a. Pumpsie Green
   b. Willie Tasby
   c. Billy Harrell
   d. Felix Mantilla

9. Since Ted Williams hit .406 in 1941, what major-league player has come the closest to hitting .400?
   a. Wade Boggs
   b. Ted Williams
   c. George Brett
   d. Rod Carew

10. In his final at bat, Ted Williams
    a. homered
    b. was intentionally walked
    c. struck out
    d. was hit by a pitch

11. Former Red Sox first baseman Dick Stuart was called
    a. The Boston Strangler
    b. Old Ironglove
    c. E-three
    d. Dr. Strangeglove

12. How old was Tony Conigliaro when he led the American League in home runs?
    a. 19
    b. 20
    c. 36
    d. 41

13. Reliever Dick Radatz was called
    a. Radical
    b. The Ogre
    c. The Green Monster
    d. The Monster

14. What Cardinals pitcher won three games in the 1967 World Series?
    a. Nelson Briles
    b. Bob Gibson
    c. Steve Carlton
    d. Ray Washburn

15. Name Boston's Cy Young Award winner of 1967.
    - a. Jim Lonborg
    - b. Gary Bell
    - c. Jose Santiago
    - d. John Wyatt

THE CLOSE-CALL YEARS, 1968–1979

1. What kind of accident derailed Jim Lonborg after his Cy Young season?
   - a. Train
   - b. Skiing
   - c. Auto
   - d. Mountain climbing

2. What was 1968 "The Year of"?
   - a. "Narrow Defeats"
   - b. "Chaos"
   - c. "The Pitcher"
   - d. "Managers"

3. The surprise A.L. RBI leader in 1968 was
   - a. Ken Harrelson
   - b. George Scott
   - c. Carl Yastrzemski
   - d. Reggie Smith

4. In which year did the American League split into East and West Divisions?
   - a. 1968
   - b. 1969
   - c. 1970
   - d. 1971

5. What Red Sox player won Rookie of the Year honors in 1972?
   - a. Carlton Fisk
   - b. Doug Griffin
   - c. Dwight Evans
   - d. Rick Burleson

6. Who was the Red Sox first full-time designated hitter?
   - a. Tommy Harper
   - b. Orlando Cepeda
   - c. Carl Yastrzemski
   - d. Dwight Evans

7. What Red Sox pitcher won Comeback Player of the Year in 1972?
   - a. Bill Lee
   - b. Marty Pattin
   - c. Sonny Siebert
   - d. Luis Tiant

8. When he won Rookie of the Year and MVP honors in 1975, Fred Lynn led the American League in
   - a. hits
   - b. runs
   - c. RBI
   - d. batting

9. The nickname for the Cincinnati Reds in the mid-1970s was the
   - a. "Big Red Bonecrushers"
   - b. "Big Red Raiders"
   - c. "Big Red Machine"
   - d. "Big Red Steam Roller"

10. The Red Sox pitching hero of the 1975 World Series, with two victories, was
    - a. Luis Tiant
    - b. Roger Moret
    - c. Rick Wise
    - d. Jim Willoughby

11. What Red Soxer became only the second player ever to hit two pinch-hit homers in a World Series?
    - a. Rick Miller
    - b. Jim Rice
    - c. Bernie Carbo
    - d. Cecil Cooper

12. Whose great catch of a Joe Morgan drive kept Red Sox hopes alive in Game Six of the 1975 World Series?
    - a. Carl Yastrzemski
    - b. Rick Miller
    - c. Fred Lynn
    - d. Dwight Evans

13. What Reds pitcher gave up Carlton Fisk's winning homer in Game Six?
    - a. Pat Darcy
    - b. Pedro Borbon
    - c. Will McEnaney
    - d. Rawley Eastwick

14. Who led Red Sox pitchers in 1977 with 13 wins?
    - a. Luis Tiant
    - b. Rick Wise
    - c. Bill Campbell
    - d. Reggie Cleveland

15. What Red Sox pitcher gave up Bucky Dent's playoff-game homer in 1978?
    - a. Mike Torrez
    - b. Bob Stanley
    - c. Dennis Eckersley
    - d. Luis Tiant

BATTLES IN THE EAST, 1980-1992

1. Who was the Red Sox third baseman Carney Lansford replaced in 1981?
   - a. Frank Malzone
   - b. Joe Morgan
   - c. Butch Hobson
   - d. Rico Petrocelli

2. What was unusual about the 1981 pennant race?
   - a. Ended in a tie
   - b. Split into 2 parts
   - c. East winner had losing record
   - d. Cleveland won

3. Who won the 1981 A.L. batting title?
   - a. Dwight Evans
   - b. Carl Yastrzemski
   - c. Jim Rice
   - d. Carney Lansford

4. How many batting titles did Yaz win in his career?
   - a. 3
   - b. 4
   - c. 5
   - d. 7

5. The Red Soxer who won both the home-run and RBI crowns in 1984 was
   - a. Jim Rice
   - b. Dwight Evans
   - c. Bill Buckner
   - d. Tony Armas

6. Roger Clemens's 20 strikeouts in a game in 1986 were against the
   - a. New York Yankees
   - b. Cleveland Indians
   - c. Texas Rangers
   - d. Seattle Mariners

7. With the Sox trailing 3 games to 1 in the 1986 LCS and trailing with two out in the ninth, whose homer kept them alive?
   - a. Tony Armas
   - b. Spike Owen
   - c. Dave Henderson
   - d. Bill Buckner

8. Name the Red Sox hurler with two wins in the 1986 World Series.
   - a. Oil Can Boyd
   - b. Bruce Hurst
   - c. Roger Clemens
   - d. Bob Stanley

9. Who hit the ball that trickled between Buckner's legs in Game Six?
   a. Ray Knight
   b. Mookie Wilson
   c. Gary Carter
   d. Keith Henderson

10. As of 1991, how many batting titles had Wade Boggs won?
    a. 3
    b. 4
    c. 5
    d. 7

11. In 1988, the Sox caught fire when who was named manager?
    a. John McNamara
    b. Joe Morgan
    c. Ralph Houk
    d. Dick Williams

12. The 1988 Sox lost the LCS to what team?
    a. Minnesota Twins
    b. California Angels
    c. Oakland Athletics
    d. Kansas City Royals

13. How many LCS games did the Red Sox win from 1988 through 1991?
    a. None
    b. Seven
    c. Two
    d. Four

14. What happened to Roger Clemens in the second inning of Game Four of the 1990 LCS?
    a. He was ejected
    b. He gave up four homers
    c. He was injured
    d. He was hit by a batted ball

15. What did Boston fans hold to show how they felt about the Red Sox chances in August 1991?
    a. Coronation Ball
    b. Pool for clinching date
    c. Mock funeral
    d. Manager hanged in effigy

MATCH THE PLAYER TO THE NUMBER

1. ____Wade Boggs	25	
2. ____Roger Clemens	.406	
3. ____Jimmie Foxx	67	
4. ____Mel Parnell	.301	
5. ____Jeff Rearden	34	
6. ____Earl Webb	20	
7. ____Ted Williams	40	
8. ____Smokey Joe Wood	511	
9. ____Carl Yastrzemski	175	
10. ____Cy Young	240	

"WHAT HAPPENS WHEN OUR THIRD BASEMAN IS REALLY TIRED?"

Answer: "Wade boggs down."

Here's a little just-for-fun quiz in which the logical answers incorporate great Red Sox names. If you hate puns and think ESPN's Chris Berman and his fanciful player-nicknames are a yawn, skip this. If you have a slightly bent sense of the ridiculous, read on.

1. "How do you open a great second baseman?"
2. "What does a slugging left fielder eat for breakfast?"
3. "What should you call a brilliant center fielder in the U.S. House of Representatives?"
4. "Where did a premier reliever of the 1950s start to school?"
5. "Speaking of schools, whose parent-teacher meetings does the 1973 A.L. base-stealing champ attend?"
6. "How should you measure radioactivity on a speedy center fielder of the early 1960s?"

7. "What cowboy song does a pre–World War I infielder and manager sing?"
8. "Meanwhile, what is that blues a good-hitting second sacker and utility man of the 1950s is singing?"
9. "What does a 25-game winner from 1946 go around on?"
10. "Do you think that 1975's 19-game winner is a smart aleck?"

Answers to Pilgrims' Progress, 1901–1909

1. d. Pilgrims
2. b. Jimmy Collins
3. d. Charles Somers
4. a. Huntington Avenue Grounds
5. b. Chicago White Stockings
6. c. Buck Freeman
7. a. Deacon Phillippe
8. b. Bill Dinneen
9. d. "Tessie"
10. c. Happy Jack Chesbro
11. d. No one
12. c. Cy Young
13. a. Owner John I. Taylor
14. b. Rube Waddell
15. b. Chick Stahl

Answers to the Best of Times, 1910–1918

1. c. Stahls
2. b. Harry Hooper
3. d. Chick Stahl
4. b. 16
5. d. Fred Snodgrass
6. c. Smokey Joe Wood
7. a. Catcher
8. b. Grover Alexander
9. b. Braves Field
10. d. Cleveland Indians
11. a. Babe Ruth

12. b. Ernie Shore
13. c. It ended on September 1
14. b. Chicago Cubs
15. c. Ed Barrow

Answers to the Worst of Times, 1919–1932

1.   a. *No, No, Nanette*
2.   c. Howard Ehmke
3.   b. Fenway Park
4.   b. Ned Williamson
5.   a. Everett Scott
6.   c. Yankees
7.   c. Joe Tinker and Johnny Evers
8.   b. Howard Ehmke
9.   c. St. Louis Browns
10. b. George Burns
11. d. Smead Jolley
12. a. Rough Carrigan
13. b. Red Ruffing
14. c. Earl Webb
15. b. Dale Alexander

Buy Me a Champion, 1933–1946

1.   d. Detroit Tigers
2.   a. Eddie Collins
3.   b. Rick Ferrell
4.   b. Billy Werber
5.   c. Connie Mack
6.   c. Lefty Grove
7.   d. Clark Griffith
8.   a. Jimmie Foxx
9.   b. Bobby Doerr
10. c. .3996
11. b. Joe Gordon
12. a. Tex Hughson
13. b. Harry Brecheen

14. d. Rudy York
15. a. Harry Walker

Answers to Frustrations and a Dream, 1947-1967

1. b. Joe Dobson
2. c. St. Louis Browns
3. b. Denny Galehouse
4. b. Broke his elbow
5. d. Billy Goodman
6. b. Jimmy Piersall
7. c. Harry Agganis
8. a. Pumpsie Green
9. b. George Brett
10. a. homered
11. d. "Dr. Strangeglove"
12. b. 20
13. d. The Monster
14. b. Bob Gibson
15. a. Jim Lonborg

Answers to the Close-Call Years, 1968-1979

1. b. Skiing
2. c. "The Pitcher"
3. a. Ken Harrelson
4. b. 1969
5. a. Carlton Fisk
6. b. Orlando Cepeda
7. d. Luis Tiant
8. b. runs
9. c. Big Red Machine
10. a. Luis Tiant
11. c. Bernie Carbo
12. d. Dwight Evans
13. a. Pat Darcy
14. c. Bill Campbell
15. a. Mike Torrez

Answers to Battles in the East, 1980–1992

1. c. Butch Hobson
2. b. Split into two parts
3. d. Carney Lansford
4. a. 3
5. d. Tony Armas
6. d. Seattle Mariners
7. c. Dave Henderson
8. b. Bruce Hurst
9. b. Mookie Wilson
10. c. 5
11. b. Joe Morgan
12. c. Oakland Athletics
13. a. None
14. a. He was ejected
15. c. Mock funeral

Answers to Match the Player to the Number

1. 240, Wade Boggs's hits in 1985 (club record)
2. 20, Roger Clemens's strikeouts in one 1986 game (major-league record)
3. 175, Jimmie Foxx's RBI in 1938 (club record)
4. 25, Mel Parnell's wins in 1949 (club record for a lefty)
5. 40, Jeff Reardon's saves in 1991 (club record)
6. 67, Earl Webb's doubles in 1931 (major league record)
7. .406, Ted Williams's 1941 batting average (last .400 season)
8. 34, Smokey Joe Wood's wins in 1912 (club record)
9. .301, Carl Yastrzemski's batting average in 1968 (the lowest to ever lead a major league)
10. 511, Cy Young's career victories (193 with the Red Sox)

"What Happens When Our Third Baseman is Really Tired?" Answers

1. "With a Bobby Doerr–key."
2. "Jim Rice Krispies."

3. "Tris Speaker of the House."
4. "Ellis Kindergarten."
5. "The Tommy Harper Valley P.T.A."
6. "With a Gary Geiger counter."
7. "Jack Barry Me Not on the Lone Prairie."
8. "A Billy Goodman Is Hard to Find."
9. "A Dave Ferriss wheel."
10. "He's a real Rick Wise-acre."

4
RED SOX STATISTICAL LEADERS, RECORD HOLDERS, AWARD WINNERS, AND HALL-OF-FAMERS

RED SOX WITH 600 OR MORE AT BATS IN A SEASON

AB	PLAYER	YEAR	AB	PLAYER	YEAR
677	Jim Rice	1978	621	Joe Vosmik	1938
673	Bill Buckner	1985	621	Johnny Pesky	1946
663	Rick Burleson	1977	621	Wade Boggs	1989
661	Doc Cramer	1940	620	Johnny Pesky	1942
658	Doc Cramer	1938	619	Frank Malzone	1962
657	Jim Rice	1984	619	Jim Rice	1979
653	Wade Boggs	1985	619	Wade Boggs	1990
648	Dom DiMaggio	1948	618	Reggie Smith	1971
646	Tom Oliver	1930	618	Jim Rice	1986
646	Chuck Shilling	1961	618	Jody Reed	1991
646	Carl Yastrzemski	1962	617	Dwight Evans	1985
644	Jim Rice	1977	612	Dick Stuart	1963
644	Rick Burleson	1980	612	Marty Barrett	1988
643	Doc Cramer	1936	610	Vern Stephens	1949
639	Dom DiMaggio	1951	610	Mike Greenwell	1990
639	Tony Armas	1984	609	Jimmy Piersall	1957
638	Johnny Pesky	1947	609	Dwight Evans	1982
636	Jerry Remy	1982	608	Tony Lupien	1943
635	Vern Stephens	1948	607	Del Pratt	1922
634	Frank Malzone	1957	607	Mel Almada	1935
633	Jimmy Collins	1904	605	Dom DiMaggio	1949
630	Dwight Evans	1984	604	Bobby Doerr	1943
629	Bill Buckner	1986	604	Johnny Pesky	1949
628	Vern Stephens	1950	604	Frank Malzone	1959
627	Frank Malzone	1958	603	Dick Stuart	1964
627	Rick Burleson	1979	603	Carl Yastrzemski	1969
626	Rick Burleson	1978	602	Fred Parent	1905
626	Jim Rice	1983	601	Jimmy Piersall	1956
625	Wade Boggs	1984	601	George Scott	1966
625	Marty Barrett	1986	601	Mike Easler	1984
623	Bill Werber	1934	600	Fred Parent	1906
622	Dom DiMaggio	1948			

RED SOX WITH 175 OR MORE HITS IN A SEASON

HITS	PLAYER	YEAR	HITS	PLAYER	YEAR
240	Wade Boggs	1985	187	Wade Boggs	1990
222	Tris Speaker	1912	186	Ted Williams	1942
214	Wade Boggs	1988	186	Dom DiMaggio	1949
213	Jim Rice	1978	186	Carl Yastrzemski	1970
210	Wade Boggs	1983	186	Dwight Evans	1984
208	Johnny Pesky	1946	185	Jimmy Collins	1901
207	Johnny Pesky	1947	185	Ted Williams	1939
207	Wade Boggs	1986	185	Ted Williams	1941
206	Jim Rice	1977	185	Dom DiMaggio	1948
205	Johnny Pesky	1942	185	Johnny Pesky	1949
205	Wade Boggs	1989	185	Vern Stephens	1950
203	Wade Boggs	1984	185	Frank Malzone	1957
201	Joe Vosmik	1938	185	Frank Malzone	1958
201	Jim Rice	1979	184	Jim Rice	1984
201	Bill Buckner	1985	183	Tris Speaker	1910
200	Bill Werber	1934	183	Del Pratt	1922
200	Doc Cramer	1940	183	Doc Cramer	1939
200	Jim Rice	1986	183	Pete Runnels	1958
200	Wade Boggs	1987	183	Pete Runnels	1962
198	Jimmie Foxx	1936	183	Carl Yastrzemski	1963
198	Doc Cramer	1938	182	Jackie Jensen	1956
197	Jimmie Foxx	1938	181	George Burns	1923
196	Earl Webb	1931	181	Ted Williams	1947
195	Patsy Dougherty	1903	181	Mike Greenwell	1990
194	Ted Williams	1949	181	Wade Boggs	1991
194	Rick Burleson	1977	180	Walt Dropo	1950
193	Tris Speaker	1914	179	Stuffy McInnis	1921
193	Ted Williams	1940	179	Rick Burleson	1980
193	Dom DiMaggio	1950	179	Marty Barrett	1986
192	Mike Greenwell	1988	178	Dom DiMaggio	1942
191	Carl Yastrzemski	1962	178	Dwight Evans	1982
191	Jim Rice	1983	178	Jerry Remy	1982
190	Tris Speaker	1913	178	Mike Greenwell	1989
189	Tom Oliver	1930	177	Buck Freeman	1902
189	Dom DiMaggio	1951	177	Vern Stephens	1949
189	Carl Yastrzemski	1967	177	Fred Lynn	1979
188	Doc Cramer	1936	177	Jim Rice	1982
188	Ted Williams	1948	176	Tris Speaker	1915
188	Mike Easler	1984	176	Mel Almada	1935

HITS	PLAYER	YEAR	HITS	PLAYER	YEAR
176	Ted Williams	1946	175	Joe Cronin	1937
176	Billy Goodman	1955	175	Reggie Smith	1971
176	Jimmy Piersall	1956	175	Fred Lynn	1975
176	Pete Runnels	1959	175	Jody Reed	1991
176	Reggie Smith	1970			

RED SOX WITH 25 OR MORE HOME RUNS IN A SEASON

HR	PLAYER	YEAR	HR	PLAYER	YEAR
50	Jimmie Foxx	1938	30	Ted Williams	1951
46	Jim Rice	1978	30	Felix Mantila	1964
44	Carl Yastrzemski	1967	30	Reggie Smith	1971
43	Ted Williams	1949	30	Butch Hobson	1977
43	Tony Armas	1984	30	Nick Esasky	1989
42	Dick Stuart	1963	29	Babe Ruth	1919
41	Jimmie Foxx	1936	29	Vern Stephens	1948
40	Carl Yastrzemski	1969	29	Ted Williams	1954
40	Rico Petrocelli	1969	29	Ted Williams	1960
40	Carl Yastrzemski	1970	29	Rico Petrocelli	1970
39	Vern Stephens	1949	29	Dwight Evans	1985
39	Jim Rice	1977	28	Ted Williams	1950
39	Fred Lynn	1979	28	Ted Williams	1955
39	Jim Rice	1979	28	Jackie Jensen	1959
39	Jim Rice	1983	28	Tony Conigliaro	1966
38	Ted Williams	1946	28	Rico Petrocelli	1971
38	Ted Williams	1957	28	Carl Yastrzemski	1977
37	Ted Williams	1941	28	Butch Hobson	1979
36	Jimmie Foxx	1937	28	Jim Rice	1984
36	Jimmie Foxx	1940	28	Jack Clark	1991
36	Ted Williams	1942	27	Bobby Doerr	1948
36	Tony Conigliaro	1970	27	Bobby Doerr	1950
36	Tony Armas	1983	27	Norm Zauchin	1955
35	Jimmie Foxx	1939	27	George Scott	1966
35	Jackie Jensen	1958	27	Mike Easler	1984
35	Ken Harrelson	1968	27	Jim Rice	1985
34	Walt Dropo	1950	26	Jackie Jensen	1955
34	Dwight Evans	1987	26	Ted Williams	1958
33	Dick Stuart	1964	26	Carlton Fisk	1973
33	George Scott	1977	26	Carlton Fisk	1977
32	Ted Williams	1947	26	Dwight Evans	1986
32	Tony Conigliaro	1965	25	Ted Williams	1948
32	Dwight Evans	1982	25	Jackie Jensen	1954
32	Dwight Evans	1984	25	Reggie Smith	1969
31	Ted Williams	1939	25	Jim Rice	1976
31	Don Baylor	1986	25	Tony Perez	1980
30	Vern Stephens	1950			

RED SOX WITH 100 OR MORE RBI IN A SEASON

RBI	PLAYER	YEAR	RBI	PLAYER	YEAR
175	Jimmie Foxx	1938	114	Jim Rice	1977
159	Vern Stephens	1949	113	Ted Williams	1940
159	Ted Williams	1949	112	Jackie Jensen	1959
145	Ted Williams	1939	112	Butch Hobson	1977
144	Walt Dropo	1950	111	Joe Cronin	1940
144	Vern Stephens	1950	111	Bobby Doerr	1948
143	Jimmie Foxx	1936	111	Carl Yastrzemski	1969
139	Jim Rice	1978	111	Dwight Evans	1988
137	Ted Williams	1942	110	Joe Cronin	1937
137	Vern Stephens	1948	110	Bill Buckner	1985
130	Jim Rice	1979	110	Jim Rice	1986
127	Jimmie Foxx	1937	109	Duffy Lewis	1912
127	Ted Williams	1948	109	Bobby Doerr	1949
126	Ted Williams	1951	109	Ken Harrelson	1968
126	Jim Rice	1983	108	Nick Esasky	1989
123	Ted Williams	1946	107	Joe Cronin	1939
123	Tony Armas	1984	107	Tony Armas	1983
123	Dwight Evans	1987	106	Pinky Higgins	1937
122	Jackie Jensen	1958	106	Pinky Higgins	1938
122	Fred Lynn	1979	106	Bob Johnson	1944
122	Jim Rice	1984	105	Jimmie Foxx	1939
121	Buck Freeman	1902	105	Bobby Doerr	1940
121	Carl Yastrzemski	1967	105	Jimmie Foxx	1941
120	Ted Williams	1941	105	Fred Lynn	1975
120	Bobby Doerr	1950	105	Tony Perez	1980
119	Roy Johnson	1934	104	Buck Freeman	1903
119	Jimmie Foxx	1940	104	Dwight Evans	1984
119	Rudy York	1946	103	Earl Webb	1931
119	Mike Greenwell	1988	103	Jackie Jensen	1957
118	Dick Stuart	1963	103	Frank Malzone	1957
117	Jackie Jensen	1954	103	Vic Wertz	1960
116	Bobby Doerr	1946	103	Rico Petrocelli	1970
116	Jackie Jensen	1955	103	Jim Rice	1985
116	Tony Conigliaro	1970	102	Bobby Doerr	1942
114	Buck Freeman	1901	102	Carl Yastrzemski	1970
114	Babe Ruth	1919	102	Jim Rice	1975
114	Ted Williams	1947	102	Carl Yastrzemski	1976
114	Dick Stuart	1964	102	Carlton Fisk	1977

RBI	PLAYER	YEAR	RBI	PLAYER	YEAR
102	Carl Yastrzemski	1977	100	Del Pratt	1921
102	Bill Buckner	1986	100	Dwight Evans	1989
101	Jim Tabor	1941			

RED SOX WITH 90 OR MORE BASES ON BALLS IN A SEASON

BB	PLAYER	YEAR	BB	PLAYER	YEAR
162	Ted Williams	1947	101	Vern Stephens	1949
162	Ted Williams	1949	101	Carl Yastrzemski	1969
156	Ted Williams	1946	100	Johnny Pesky	1949
145	Ted Williams	1941	99	Jimmie Foxx	1937
145	Ted Williams	1942	99	Johnny Pesky	1948
144	Ted Williams	1951	99	Bily Goodman	1955
136	Ted Williams	1954	99	Jackie Jensen	1958
128	Carl Yastrzemski	1970	99	Dwight Evans	1989
126	Ted Williams	1948	98	Ted Williams	1958
125	Wade Boggs	1988	98	Rico Petrocelli	1969
119	Jimmie Foxx	1938	97	Dwight Evans	1986
119	Ted Williams	1957	96	Ted Williams	1940
119	Carl Yastrzemski	1968	96	Bob Johnson	1944
114	Dwight Evans	1985	96	Dom DiMaggio	1949
112	Dwight Evans	1982	96	Carl Yastrzemski	1961
107	Ted Williams	1939	96	Dwight Evans	1984
107	Wade Boggs	1989	96	Wade Boggs	1985
106	Topper Rigney	1926	96	Jack Clark	1991
106	Eddie Lake	1945	95	Pete Runnels	1959
106	Carl Yastrzemski	1971	95	Carl Yastrzemski	1963
106	Dwight Evans	1987	93	Jimmie Foxx	1941
105	Jimmie Foxx	1936	92	Don Buddin	1959
105	Carl Yastrzemski	1973	92	Wade Boggs	1983
105	Wade Boggs	1986	91	Joe Cronin	1938
105	Wade Boggs	1987	91	Ted Williams	1955
104	Johnny Pesky	1950	91	Gary Geiger	1961
104	Carl Yastrzemski	1974	91	Joe Foy	1966
102	Ted Williams	1956	91	Carl Yastrzemski	1967
101	Babe Ruth	1919	91	Rico Petrocelli	1971
101	Jimmie Foxx	1940	90	Dom DiMaggio	1941
101	Dom DiMaggio	1948	90	Billy Klaus	1956

RED SOX BATTERS WITH 90 OR MORE STRIKEOUTS IN A SEASON

SO	PLAYER	YEAR	SO	PLAYER	YEAR
162	Butch Hobson	1977	102	Jim Rice	1983
156	Tony Armas	1984	102	Jim Rice	1984
152	George Scott	1966	99	Don Buddin	1949
144	Dick Stuart	1963	99	Ed Bressoud	1964
134	Mike Easler	1984	99	Rico Petrocelli	1966
133	Jack Clark	1991	99	Carlton Fisk	1973
131	Tony Armas	1983	99	Dwight Evans	1988
130	Dick Stuart	1964	98	Dwight Evans	1980
129	Mike Easler	1985	98	Jim Rice	1982
126	Jim Rice	1978	98	Ellis Burks	1987
123	Jim Rice	1976	98	Dwight Evans	1987
122	Jim Rice	1975	97	Jim Rice	1979
122	Butch Hobson	1978	97	Dwight Evans	1983
119	Jimmie Foxx	1936	96	Jimmie Foxx	1937
119	Dwight Evans	1978	96	Tom Brunansky	1992
119	George Scott	1978	95	Reggie Smith	1967
118	Ed Bressoud	1962	95	George Scott	1970
118	Lu Clinton	1963	93	Rudy York	1946
117	Dwight Evans	1986	93	Ed Bressoud	1963
117	Nick Esasky	1988	93	Rico Petrocelli	1967
116	Tony Conigliaro	1965	93	Tony Conigliaro	1970
115	Dwight Evans	1984	93	Tommy Harper	1973
112	Tony Conigliaro	1966	93	Tony Perez	1980
112	George Scott	1977	92	Dwight Evans	1976
111	Tony Conigliaro	1969	91	Joe Foy	1968
111	Don Baylor	1986	91	Carl Yastrzemski	1969
108	Rico Petrocelli	1971	91	Rico Petrocelli	1972
106	Don Buddin	1958	90	Carl Yastrzemski	1964
105	Norm Zauchin	1955	90	Ken Harrelson	1968
105	Dwight Evans	1985	90	Carl Yastrzemski	1968
105	Tom Brunansky	1990	90	Bernie Carbo	1974
104	Tommy Harper	1972	90	Fred Lynn	1975
103	Jimmie Foxx	1941	90	Tony Armas	1985
102	George Scott	1971			

RED SOX WITH 20 OR MORE STOLEN BASES IN A SEASON

SB	PLAYER	YEAR	SB	PLAYER	YEAR
54	Tommy Harper	1973	25	Fred Parent	1905
52	Tris Speaker	1912	25	Tris Speaker	1911
46	Tris Speaker	1913	25	Larry Gardner	1912
42	Tris Speaker	1914	25	Tommy Harper	1972
40	Harry Hooper	1910	25	Ellis Burks	1988
40	Bill Werber	1934	24	Fred Parent	1903
38	Harry Hooper	1911	24	Clyde Engle	1911
36	Harry Lord	1909	24	Harry Hooper	1918
35	Patsy Dougherty	1903	23	Harry Lord	1908
35	Tris Speaker	1909	23	Harry Hooper	1919
35	Tris Speaker	1910	23	Mike Menosky	1920
33	Tommy Dowd	1901	23	Jack Rothrock	1929
31	Amby McConnell	1908	23	Bill Werber	1936
30	Buddy Myer	1928	23	Carl Yastrzemski	1970
30	Jerry Remy	1978	22	Jimmy Collins	1903
29	Chick Stahl	1901	22	Jake Stahl	1910
29	Harry Hooper	1912	22	Duffy Lewis	1914
29	Hal Janvrin	1914	22	Harry Hooper	1915
29	Tris Speaker	1915	22	Pete Fox	1943
29	Bill Werber	1935	22	Jackie Jensen	1954
28	Clyde Engle	1913	22	Reggie Smith	1968
28	Tommy Harper	1974	21	Heinie Wagner	1912
27	Harry Niles	1909	21	Harry Hooper	1917
27	Larry Gardner	1911	21	Ellis Burks	1989
27	Harry Hooper	1916	20	Patsy Dougherty	1902
27	Ben Chapman	1937	20	Fred Parent	1904
27	Ellis Burks	1987	20	Heinie Wagner	1907
26	Amby McConnell	1909	20	Heinie Wagner	1908
26	Heinie Wagner	1910	20	Amos Strunk	1918
26	Harry Hooper	1913	20	Mel Almada	1935
26	Joe Foy	1968			

RED SOX WITH BATTING AVERAGES OF .315 OR BETTER FOR A SEASON

BA	PLAYER	YEAR	BA	PLAYER	YEAR
.406	Ted Williams	1941	.329	Jimmy Collins	1901
.388	Ted Williams	1957	.329	Carl Yastrzemski	1970
.383	Tris Speaker	1912	.328	George Burns	1923
.369	Ted Williams	1948	.328	Dom DiMaggio	1950
.368	Wade Boggs	1985	.328	Ted Williams	1958
.366	Wade Boggs	1988	.328	Mike Greenwell	1987
.363	Tris Speaker	1913	.327	Ted Williams	1939
.363	Wade Boggs	1988	.326	Pete Runnels	1962
.361	Wade Boggs	1983	.326	Carl Yastrzemski	1967
.360	Jimmie Foxx	1939	.325	Jimmy Collins	1902
.357	Wade Boggs	1986	.325	Joe Cronin	1938
.356	Ted Williams	1942	.325	Bobby Doerr	1944
.354	Billy Goodman	1950	.325	Al Zarilla	1950
.349	Jimmie Foxx	1938	.325	Jim Rice	1979
.346	Buck Freeman	1901	.325	Wade Boggs	1984
.345	Ted Williams	1954	.325	Mike Greenwell	1988
.345	Ted Williams	1956	.324	Del Pratt	1921
.344	Ted Williams	1940	.324	Joe Vosmik	1928
.343	Ted Williams	1947	.324	Bob Johnson	1944
.343	Ted Williams	1949	.324	Johnny Pesky	1947
.342	Patsy Dougherty	1902	.324	Jim Rice	1986
.342	Ted Williams	1946	.323	Earl Webb	1930
.340	Tris Speaker	1910	.322	Tris Speaker	1915
.340	Ben Chapman	1938	.322	Babe Ruth	1919
.338	Tris Speaker	1914	.322	Walt Dropo	1950
.338	Jimmie Foxx	1936	.322	Pete Runnels	1958
.336	Carney Lansford	1981	.321	Bill Werber	1934
.335	Joe Harris	1923	.321	Carl Yastrzemski	1963
.334	Tris Speaker	1911	.321	Dave Stapleton	1980
.333	Ike Boone	1924	.320	Roy Johnson	1934
.333	Earl Webb	1931	.320	Lou Finney	1940
.333	Fred Lynn	1979	.320	Pete Runnels	1960
.332	Wade Boggs	1991	.320	Jim Rice	1977
.331	Patsy Dougherty	1903	.318	Chick Stahl	1902
.331	Johnny Pesky	1942	.318	Bobby Doerr	1939
.331	Fred Lynn	1975	.318	Ted Williams	1951
.330	Ike Boone	1925	.316	Joe Harris	1922
.330	Wade Boggs	1989	.316	Dom DiMaggio	1946

BA	PLAYER	YEAR	BA	PLAYER	YEAR
.315	Larry Gardner	1912	.315	Jackie Jensen	1956
.315	Roy Johnson	1935	.315	Carlton Fisk	1977
.315	Pete Fox	1944	.315	Jim Rice	1978

RED SOX WITH .520 OR BETTER SLUGGING AVERAGE

SLG	PLAYER	YEAR	SLG	PLAYER	YEAR
.735	Ted Williams	1941	.569	Dwight Evans	1987
.731	Ted Williams	1957	.567	Tris Speaker	1912
.704	Jimmie Foxx	1938	.566	Fred Lynn	1975
.694	Jimmie Foxx	1939	.556	Ted Williams	1951
.667	Ted Williams	1946	.555	Babe Ruth	1918
.657	Babe Ruth	1919	.550	Jim Rice	1983
.648	Ted Williams	1942	.539	Vern Stephens	1949
.637	Fred Lynn	1979	.538	Jimmie Foxx	1937
.635	Ted Williams	1954	.538	Carlton Fisk	1972
.634	Ted Williams	1947	.536	Joe Cronin	1938
.631	Jimmie Foxx	1936	.536	Carl Yastrzemski	1965
.622	Carl Yastrzemski	1967	.535	Jackie Jensen	1958
.615	Ted Williams	1948	.534	Dwight Evans	1982
.609	Ted Williams	1939	.532	Dwight Evans	1984
.605	Ted Williams	1956	.531	Tony Armas	1984
.600	Jim Rice	1978	.531	Mike Greenwell	1987
.596	Jim Rice	1979	.530	Tony Conigliaro	1964
.594	Ted Williams	1940	.528	Earl Webb	1931
.593	Jim Rice	1977	.528	Bobby Doerr	1944
.592	Carl Yastrzemski	1970	.528	Bob Johnson	1944
.589	Rico Petrocelli	1969	.527	Reggie Smith	1969
.588	Wade Boggs	1987	.523	Earl Webb	1930
.584	Ted Williams	1958	.522	Dwight Evans	1981
.583	Walt Dropo	1950	.521	Dick Stuart	1963
.581	Jimmie Foxx	1940	.521	Buck Freeman	1901
.570	Mike Greenwell	1987	.520	Joe Harris	1923

RED SOX WITH 48 OR MORE GAMES PITCHED IN A SEASON

GP	PITCHER	YEAR	GP	PITCHER	YEAR
79	Dick Radatz	1964	53	Wilcy Moore	1931
74	Rob Murphy	1989	53	Arnie Earley	1963
71	Sparky Lyle	1969	53	Dick Drago	1979
70	Mike Fornieles	1960	53	Joe Sambito	1986
70	Greg Harris	1992	53	Greg Harris	1991
69	Ellis Kinder	1953	52	Murray Wall	1958
69	Bill Campbell	1977	52	Vicente Romo	1969
68	Rob Murphy	1990	52	Bob Bolin	1971
66	Dick Radatz	1963	52	Bob Stanley	1978
66	Bob Stanley	1986	52	Bob Stanley	1980
65	Jack Lamabe	1963	51	Jack Wilson	1937
64	Bob Stanley	1983	51	Dennis Lamp	1991
64	Lee Smith	1988	51	Danny Darwin	1992
64	Lee Smith	1989	50	Jose Santiago	1967
64	Tony Fossas	1991	50	Lee Stange	1968
63	Ellis Kinder	1951	50	Sparky Lyle	1971
63	Dick Radatz	1965	50	Jeff Gray	1991
63	Sparky Lyle	1970	49	Mace Brown	1943
62	Dick Radatz	1962	49	Ike Delock	1957
62	Tom Burgmeier	1980	49	Don McMahon	1966
62	Calvin Schiraldi	1987	49	Sparky Lyle	1968
60	John Wyatt	1967	49	Wes Gardner	1987
60	Tony Fossas	1992	48	Dutch Leonard	1916
58	Diego Segui	1974	48	Emerson Dickman	1939
57	Mike Fornieles	1961	48	Ellis Kinder	1950
57	Arnie Earley	1965	48	Ellis Kinder	1954
57	Bob Stanley	1984	48	Ike Delock	1956
57	Bob Stanley	1988	48	Vicente Romo	1970
57	Jeff Rearden	1991	48	Bob Stanley	1982
55	Bob Heffner	1964	48	Mark Clear	1983
55	Mark Clear	1982	48	Bob Stanley	1985
54	Joe Willoughby	1976			

RED SOX PITCHERS WITH 34 OR MORE STARTS IN A SEASON

GS	PITCHER	YEAR	GS	PITCHER	YEAR
43	Cy Young	1902	35	Bill Monbouquette	1962
42	Bill Dinneen	1902	35	Bill Monbouquette	1964
41	Cy Young	1901	35	Bill Monbouquette	1965
41	Cy Young	1904	35	Marty Pattin	1972
40	Babe Ruth	1916	35	Luis Tiant	1973
39	Howard Ehmke	1923	35	Rick Wise	1975
39	Jim Lonborg	1967	35	Luis Tiant	1975
38	Smokey Joe Wood	1912	35	Dennis Eckersley	1978
38	Babe Ruth	1917	35	Oil Can Boyd	1985
38	Sad Sam Jones	1921	35	Roger Clemens	1988
38	Wes Ferrell	1935	35	Roger Clemens	1989
38	Wes Ferrell	1936	35	Roger Clemens	1991
38	Luis Tiant	1974	35	Frank Viola	1992
38	Luis Tiant	1976	34	Ted Lewis	1901
37	Bill Dinneen	1904	34	Cy Young	1905
37	Cy Young	1907	34	Cy Young	1906
37	Bill Lee	1974	34	Buck O'Brien	1912
36	Dutch Leonard	1917	34	Dutch Leonard	1916
36	Howard Ehmke	1924	34	Red Ruffing	1928
36	Bill Monbouquette	1963	34	Milt Gaston	1930
36	Earl Wilson	1967	34	Mel Parnell	1953
36	Mike Torrez	1978	34	Earl Wilson	1963
36	Mike Torrez	1979	34	Gary Peters	1970
36	Roger Clemens	1987	34	Bill Lee	1975
35	Cy Young	1903	34	Rick Wise	1976
35	Bill Dinneen	1903	34	John Tudor	1983
35	Boo Ferriss	1946	34	Mike Boddicker	1989
35	Tex Hughson	1946	34	Mike Boddicker	1990
35	Frank Sullivan	1955			

RED SOX PITCHERS WITH 20 OR MORE COMPLETE GAMES IN A SEASON

CG	PITCHER	YEAR	CG	PITCHER	YEAR
41	Cy Young	1902	25	Tom Hughes	1903
40	Cy Young	1904	25	Smokey Joe Wood	1911
39	Bill Dinneen	1902	25	Sad Sam Jones	1921
38	Cy Young	1901	25	Red Ruffing	1928
37	Bill Dinneen	1904	25	Luis Tiant	1974
35	Smokey Joe Wood	1912	24	George Winter	1905
35	Babe Ruth	1917	23	Bill Dinneen	1905
34	Cy Young	1903	23	Babe Ruth	1916
33	Cy Young	1907	23	Luis Tiant	1973
32	Bill Dinneen	1902	22	Bill Dinneen	1906
32	Cy Young	1905	22	Rube Foster	1915
31	Ted Lewis	1901	22	Howard Ehmke	1922
31	Wes Ferrell	1935	22	Lefty Grove	1936
30	Jesse Tannehill	1904	22	Tex Hughson	1942
30	Carl Mays	1918	22	Jim Lonborg	1968
29	Norwood Gibson	1904	21	George Winter	1907
28	Cy Young	1906	21	Sad Sam Jones	1919
28	Howard Ehmke	1923	21	Lefty Grove	1937
28	Wes Ferrell	1936	21	Tex Hughson	1946
27	Jesse Tannehill	1905	21	Mel Parnell	1950
27	Carl Mays	1917	20	Joe Harris	1906
27	Mel Parnell	1949	20	Eddie Cicotte	1910
26	George Winter	1901	20	Sad Sam Jones	1920
26	Buck O'Brien	1912	20	Bullet Joe Bush	1921
26	Dutch Leonard	1917	20	Ed Morris	1928
26	Babe Ruth	1918	20	Milt Gaston	1929
26	Howard Ehmke	1924	20	Milt Gaston	1930
26	Boo Ferriss	1945	20	Tex Hughson	1943
26	Boo Ferriss	1946			

RED SOX PITCHERS WITH 18 OR MORE WINS IN A SEASON

GW	PITCHER	YEAR	GW	PITCHER	YEAR
34	Smokey Joe Wood	1912	20	Ray Collins	1914
33	Cy Young	1901	20	Howard Ehmke	1923
32	Cy Young	1902	20	Lefty Grove	1935
28	Cy Young	1903	20	Wes Ferrell	1936
26	Cy Young	1904	20	Tex Hughson	1946
25	Wes Ferrell	1935	20	Bill Monbouquette	1963
25	Boo Ferriss	1946	20	Luis Tiant	1973
25	Mel Parnell	1949	20	Dennis Eckersley	1978
24	Babe Ruth	1917	20	Roger Clemens	1987
24	Roger Clemens	1986	19	Ray Collins	1913
23	Bill Dinneen	1904	19	Dutch Leonard	1914
23	Smokey Joe Wood	1911	19	Ernie Shove	1915
23	Babe Ruth	1916	19	Howard Ehmke	1924
23	Sam Jones	1921	19	Ed Morris	1928
23	Ellis Kinder	1949	19	Dick Newsome	1941
22	Jesse Tannehill	1905	19	Tom Brewer	1956
22	Cy Young	1907	19	Rick Wise	1975
22	Carl Mays	1917	18	Cy Young	1905
22	Tex Hughson	1942	18	Babe Ruth	1915
22	Jim Lonborg	1967	18	Dutch Leonard	1916
22	Luis Tiant	1974	18	Carl Mays	1916
21	Bill Dinneen	1902	18	Tex Hughson	1944
21	Bill Dinneen	1903	18	Joe Dobson	1947
21	Jesse Tannehill	1904	18	Jack Kramer	1948
21	Cy Young	1908	18	Mel Parnell	1950
21	Carl Mays	1918	18	Mel Parnell	1951
21	Bob Ferriss	1945	18	Mickey McDermott	1953
21	Mel Parnell	1953	18	Frank Sullivan	1955
21	Luis Tiant	1976	18	Luis Tiant	1975
21	Roger Clemens	1990	18	Roger Clemens	1988
20	Tom Hughes	1903	18	Bruce Hurst	1988
20	Hugh Bedient	1912	18	Roger Clemens	1991
20	Buck O'Brien	1912	18	Roger Clemens	1992

RED SOX PITCHERS WITH 15 OR MORE LOSSES IN A SEASON

GL	PITCHER	YEAR	GL	PITCHER	YEAR
25	Red Ruffing	1928	16	Cy Young	1904
22	Red Ruffing	1929	16	George Winter	1905
21	Bill Dinneen	1902	16	George Winter	1907
21	Joe Harris	1906	16	Dutch Leonard	1913
21	Cy Young	1906	16	Sad Sam Jones	1920
21	Slim Harris	1927	16	Sad Sam Jones	1921
20	Sad Sam Jones	1919	16	Alex Ferguson	1922
20	Howard Ehmke	1925	16	Jack Quinn	1922
20	Milt Gaston	1930	16	Ted Wingfield	1926
20	Jack Russell	1930	16	Bob Weiland	1932
19	Cy Young	1905	16	Fritz Ostermueller	1936
19	Bill Dinneen	1906	16	Jim Bagby	1940
19	Ted Wingfield	1925	16	Frank Sullivan	1960
19	Milt Gaston	1929	16	Earl Wilson	1963
18	George Winter	1906	16	Ray Culp	1971
18	Red Ruffing	1925	16	Mike Torrez	1980
18	Paul Zahniser	1926	15	Cy Young	1907
18	Hal Wiltse	1927	15	Eddie Cicotte	1911
18	Danny MacFayden	1929	15	Bullet Joe Bush	1918
18	Jack Russell	1929	15	Bullet Joe Bush	1920
18	Jack Russell	1931	15	Curt Fullerton	1923
18	Bill Monbouquette	1965	15	Hal Wiltse	1926
18	Dave Morehead	1965	15	Red Ruffing	1926
17	Smokey Joe Wood	1911	15	Ed Morris	1928
17	Dutch Leonard	1917	15	Danny MacFayden	1928
17	Herb Pennock	1922	15	Ed Durham	1930
17	Howard Ehmke	1923	15	Gordon Rhodes	1933
17	Jack Quinn	1923	15	Johnny Welch	1934
17	Bill Piercy	1923	15	Wes Ferrell	1936
17	Alex Ferguson	1924	15	Jack Wilson	1938
17	Howard Ehmke	1924	15	Tex Hughson	1943
17	Hod Lisenbee	1930	15	Tom Brewer	1960
17	Jim Lonborg	1965	15	Don Schwall	1962
17	Marty Pattin	1973	15	Dave Morehead	1964
17	Bill Lee	1974	15	Bob Stanley	1987
16	Ted Lewis	1901			

RED SOX PITCHERS WITH A WINNING PERCENTAGE OF .667 OR BETTER IN A SEASON (MINIMUM OF 15 DECISIONS)

PCT.	PITCHER	W–L	YEAR
.882	Bob Stanley	15–2	1978
.872	Smokey Joe Wood	34–5	1912
.867	Roger Moret	13–2	1973
.857	Roger Clemens	24–4	1986
.824	Roger Moret	14–3	1975
.806	Boo Ferriss	25–6	1946
.793	Ellis Kinder	23–6	1949
.792	Dutch Leonard	19–5	1914
.789	Lefty Grove	15–4	1939
.786	Tex Hughson	22–6	1942
.783	Tex Hughson	18–5	1944
.783	Jack Kramer	18–5	1948
.781	Mel Parnell	25–7	1949
.778	Lefty Grove	15–4	1938
.778	Roger Clemens	21–6	1990
.767	Cy Young	33–10	1901
.762	Sad Sam Jones	16–5	1918
.757	Cy Young	29–9	1903
.750	Babe Ruth	18–6	1915
.750	Jose Santiago	12–4	1967
.750	Bruce Hurst	18–6	1988
.750	Joe Hesketh	12–4	1991
.744	Cy Young	32–11	1902
.741	Tom Hughes	20–7	1903
.737	Smokey Joe Wood	14–5	1915
.737	Wes Ferrell	14–5	1934
.727	Ray Culp	16–6	1968
.724	Mel Parnell	21–8	1953
.722	Eddie Cicotte	13–5	1909
.722	Fritz Ostermueller	13–5	1938
.714	Rube Foster	20–8	1915
.714	Dick Radatz	15–6	1963
.714	Luis Tiant	15–6	1972
.714	Dennis Eckersley	20–8	1978
.710	Carl Mays	22–9	1917
.710	Jim Lonborg	22–9	1967
.706	Joe Dobson	12–5	1941

PCT.	PITCHER	W–L	YEAR
.704	Ray Collins	19–8	1913
.704	Ernie Shore	19–8	1915
.696	Dick Ellsworth	16–7	1968
.692	Joe Dobson	18–8	1947
.690	Hugh Bedient	20–9	1912
.690	Roger Clemens	20–9	1987
.688	Jesse Tannehill	22–10	1905
.688	Smokey Joe Wood	11–5	1913
.688	Rick Wise	11–5	1977
.682	Don Schwall	15–7	1961
.680	Ray Culp	17–8	1969
.680	Mike Boddicker	17–8	1990
.679	Tom Brewer	19–9	1956
.677	Boo Ferris	21–10	1945
.667	Bill Monbouquette	20–10	1963
.667	Herb Pennock	16–8	1919
.667	Dutch Leonard	14–7	1915
.667	Frank Sullivan	14–7	1956
.667	Charley Smith	12–6	1910
.667	Jack Wilson	12–6	1940
.667	Mike Fornieles	10–5	1960
.667	Mike Paxton	10–5	1977
.667	Tom Bolton	10–5	1990

RED SOX WITH 250 OR MORE INNINGS PITCHED IN A SEASON

IP	PLAYER	YEAR	IP	PLAYER	YEAR
385	Cy Young	1902	274	Sad Sam Jones	1920
380	Cy Young	1904	274	Boo Ferriss	1946
371	Cy Young	1901	273	Norwood Gibson	1904
371	Bill Dinneen	1902	273	Bullet Joe Bush	1918
344	Smokey Joe Wood	1912	273	Milt Gaston	1930
343	Cy Young	1907	273	Lefty Grove	1935
342	Cy Young	1903	273	Jim Lonborg	1967
336	Bill Dinneen	1904	272	Jesse Tannehill	1905
326	Babe Ruth	1917	272	Ray Collins	1914
324	Babe Ruth	1916	272	Luis Tiant	1973
322	Wes Ferrell	1935	271	Roger Clemens	1991
321	Cy Young	1905	269	Danny MacFayden	1930
317	Howard Ehmke	1923	268	Dennis Eckersley	1978
316	Ted Lewis	1901	267	Bill Monbouquette	1963
315	Howard Ehmke	1924	266	Tex Hughson	1943
311	Luis Tiant	1974	265	Boo Ferriss	1945
301	Wes Ferrell	1936	264	George Winter	1905
299	Bill Dinneen	1903	264	Roger Clemens	1988
299	Cy Young	1908	262	Lefty Grove	1937
299	Sad Sam Jones	1921	261	Howard Ehmke	1925
295	Mel Parnell	1949	260	Frank Sullivan	1955
294	Dutch Leonard	1917	260	Luis Tiant	1975
293	Carl Mays	1918	260	Bill Lee	1975
289	Carl Mays	1917	259	Hugh Bedient	1913
289	Red Ruffing	1928	259	Dutch Leonard	1913
288	Cy Young	1906	258	Ed Morris	1928
285	Bill Lee	1973	257	George Winter	1907
282	Jesse Tannehill	1904	256	Jack Quinn	1922
282	Bill Lee	1974	255	Rube Foster	1915
282	Roger Clemens	1987	255	Rick Wise	1975
281	Tex Hughson	1942	254	Bullet Joe Bush	1921
279	Luis Tiant	1976	254	Ted Wingfield	1925
278	Tex Hughson	1946	254	Roger Clemens	1986
277	Smokey Joe Wood	1911	253	Lefty Grove	1936
276	Buck O'Brien	1912	253	Marty Pattin	1972
274	Dutch Leonard	1916	253	Roger Clemens	1989

IP	PLAYER	YEAR	IP	PLAYER	YEAR
252	Ellis Kinder	1949	250	Eddie Cicotte	1910
252	Mike Torrez	1979	250	Mike Torrez	1978
251	Ray Culp	1970			

RED SOX PITCHERS WITH 140 OR MORE STRIKEOUTS IN A SEASON

SO	PITCHER	YEAR	SO	PITCHER	YEAR
291	Roger Clemens	1988	163	Dave Morehead	1965
258	Smokey Joe Wood	1912	162	Dick Radatz	1963
256	Roger Clemens	1987	162	Dennis Eckersley	1978
246	Jim Lonborg	1967	161	Bill Monbouquette	1961
241	Roger Clemens	1991	160	Cy Young	1902
238	Roger Clemens	1986	158	Cy Young	1901
231	Smokey Joe Wood	1911	155	Ken Brett	1970
230	Roger Clemens	1989	155	Gary Peters	1970
210	Cy Young	1905	154	Oil Can Boyd	1985
209	Roger Clemens	1990	153	Bill Dinneen	1904
208	Roger Clemens	1992	153	Lefty Grove	1937
206	Luis Tiant	1973	153	Bill Monbouquette	1962
200	Cy Young	1904	151	Ray Culp	1971
197	Ray Culp	1970	150	Cy Young	1908
190	Ray Culp	1968	150	Dennis Eckersley	1979
190	Bruce Hurst	1987	148	Bill Dinneen	1903
189	Bruce Hurst	1985	147	Cy Young	1907
181	Dick Radatz	1964	146	John Tudor	1982
176	Cy Young	1903	145	Mike Boddicker	1988
176	Luis Tiant	1974	144	Dutch Leonard	1913
175	Dutch Leonard	1914	144	Dutch Leonard	1916
174	Bill Monbouquette	1963	144	Dutch Leonard	1917
172	Tex Hughson	1946	144	Dick Radatz	1962
172	Ray Culp	1969	143	Mike Boddicker	1990
170	Babe Ruth	1916	142	Sonny Siebert	1970
168	Marty Pattin	1972	142	Luis Tiant	1975
167	Bruce Hurst	1986	142	Ferguson Jenkins	1976
166	Earl Wilson	1964	141	Rick Wise	1975
166	Bruce Hurst	1988	140	Cy Young	1906
164	Earl Wilson	1965			

RED SOX PITCHERS WITH 90 OR MORE BASES ON BALLS IN A SEASON

BB	PITCHER	YEAR	BB	PITCHER	YEAR
134	Mel Parnell	1949	98	Milt Gaston	1930
121	Don Schwall	1962	98	Gordon Rhodes	1934
121	Mike Torrez	1979	97	Bob Weiland	1932
119	Howard Ehmke	1923	97	Joe Dobson	1949
119	Wes Ferrell	1936	96	Red Ruffing	1928
119	Bobo Newsom	1937	96	Tracy Stallard	1961
119	Jack Wilson	1937	96	Bob Ojeda	1984
118	Babe Ruth	1916	95	Sad Sam Jones	1919
118	Red Ruffing	1929	95	Ed Morris	1929
117	Emmett O'Neill	1945	95	Charlie Wagner	1942
116	Mel Parnell	1953	95	Tom Brewer	1954
113	Dave Morehead	1965	94	Dutch Leonard	1913
112	Tom Brewer	1956	94	Bullet Joe Bush	1920
112	Dave Morehead	1964	93	Bullet Joe Bush	1921
111	Earl Wilson	1962	93	Danny MacFayden	1930
110	Don Schwall	1961	93	Gordon Rhodes	1933
109	Mickey McDermott	1953	93	Tom Brewer	1957
108	Babe Ruth	1917	93	Tom Brewer	1958
108	Alex Ferguson	1924	93	Roger Clemens	1989
108	Wes Ferrell	1935	92	Ted Wingfield	1925
106	Mel Parnell	1950	92	Boo Ferriss	1947
106	Mike Nagy	1969	92	Joe Dobson	1948
105	Earl Wilson	1963	92	Mickey McDermott	1951
103	Rip Collins	1922	92	Mickey McDermott	1952
100	Bob Weiland	1933	91	Ted Lewis	1901
100	Frank Sullivan	1955	91	Bullet Joe Bush	1918
100	Bill Monbouquette	1961	91	Jack Wilson	1938
99	Bill Dinneen	1902	91	Ray Culp	1970
99	Hal Wiltse	1926	90	Cy Morgan	1908
99	Fritz Ostermueller	1934	90	Jim Bagby	1938
99	Ellis Kinder	1944	90	Oscar Judd	1942
99	Dave Morehead	1963	90	Mel Parnell	1948
99	Mike Torrez	1978			

RED SOX PITCHERS WITH 4 OR MORE SHUTOUTS IN A SEASON

SH	PITCHER	YEAR	SH	PITCHER	YEAR
10	Cy Young	1904	5	Joe Dobson	1948
10	Smokey Joe Wood	1912	5	Mel Parnell	1953
9	Babe Ruth	1916	5	Bill Monbouquette	1964
8	Carl Mays	1918	5	Luis Tiant	1978
8	Roger Clemens	1988	5	Bob Ojeda	1984
7	Cy Young	1903	5	Roger Clemens	1992
7	Ray Collins	1914	4	Jesse Tannehill	1904
7	Dutch Leonard	1914	4	George Winter	1907
7	Bullet Joe Bush	1918	4	Smokey Joe Wood	1909
7	Luis Tiant	1974	4	Ray Collins	1910
7	Roger Clemens	1987	4	Ray Collins	1912
6	Bill Dinneen	1903	4	Ernie Shore	1915
6	Jesse Tannehill	1905	4	Dutch Leonard	1917
6	Cy Young	1907	4	Herb Pennock	1920
6	Rube Foster	1914	4	Jack Quinn	1922
6	Dutch Leonard	1914	4	Howard Ehmke	1924
6	Babe Ruth	1917	4	Danny MacFayden	1929
6	Lefty Grove	1936	4	Tex Hughson	1942
6	Boo Ferriss	1946	4	Tex Hughson	1943
6	Tex Hughson	1946	4	Mel Parnell	1949
6	Ellis Kinder	1949	4	Mickey McDermott	1953
6	Ray Culp	1968	4	Tom Brewer	1956
6	Luis Tiant	1972	4	Bill Monbouquette	1962
5	Cy Young	1901	4	Gary Peters	1970
5	Tom Hughes	1903	4	Sonny Siebert	1971
5	Bill Dinneen	1904	4	Marty Pattin	1972
5	Cy Young	1905	4	John Curtis	1973
5	Smokey Joe Wood	1911	4	Bill Lee	1975
5	Rube Foster	1915	4	Rick Wise	1976
5	Sad Sam Jones	1918	4	Bob Stanley	1979
5	Herb Pennock	1919	4	Bruce Hurst	1986
5	Sad Sam Jones	1919	4	Roger Clemens	1990
5	Sad Sam Jones	1921	4	Roger Clemens	1991
5	Boo Ferriss	1945			

RED SOX PITCHERS WITH ERAS OF 2.70 OR LESS IN A SEASON

YEAR	PITCHER	ERA	YEAR	PITCHER	ERA
1914	Dutch Leonard	1.00	1907	Ralph Glaze	2.32
1908	Cy Young	1.26	1915	Dutch Leonard	2.36
1915	Smokey Joe Wood	1.49	1916	Dutch Leonard	2.36
1910	Ray Collins	1.62	1911	Ray Collins	2.39
1901	Cy Young	1.63	1913	Dutch Leonard	2.39
1915	Ernie Shore	1.64	1916	Carl Mays	2.39
1914	Rube Foster	1.65	1992	Roger Clemens	2.41
1910	Smokey Joe Wood	1.68	1908	Eddie Cicotte	2.43
1917	Carl Mays	1.74	1915	Babe Ruth	2.44
1916	Babe Ruth	1.75	1908	Cy Morgan	2.46
1905	Cy Young	1.82	1911	Larry Pape	2.46
1910	Charley Hall	1.91	1914	Ray Collins	2.48
1912	Smokey Joe Wood	1.91	1905	Jesse Tannehill	2.48
1972	Luis Tiant	1.91	1919	Carl Mays	2.48
1990	Roger Clemens	1.93	1986	Roger Clemens	2.48
1904	Cy Young	1.97	1912	Ray Collins	2.54
1909	Eddie Cicotte	1.97	1939	Lefty Grove	2.54
1907	Cy Young	1.99	1903	Tom Hughes	2.57
1911	Smokey Joe Wood	2.02	1912	Buck O'Brien	2.57
1917	Babe Ruth	2.02	1942	Tex Hughson	2.59
1904	Jesse Tannehill	2.04	1913	Ray Collins	2.63
1907	George Winter	2.07	1916	Ernie Shore	2.63
1903	Cy Young	2.08	1943	Tex Hughson	2.64
1918	Bullet Joe Bush	2.11	1935	Lefty Grove	2.70
1915	Rube Foster	2.12			
1902	Cy Young	2.15			
1917	Dutch Leonard	2.17			
1909	Frank Arellanes	2.18			
1904	Bill Dinneen	2.20			
1904	Norwood Gibson	2.21			
1909	Smokey Joe Wood	2.21			
1918	Carl Mays	2.21			
1917	Ernie Shore	2.22			
1918	Babe Ruth	2.22			
1903	Bill Dinneen	2.23			
1918	Sad Sam Jones	2.25			
1944	Tex Hughson	2.26			
1910	Charlie Smith	2.30			

RED SOX PITCHERS WITH 9 OR MORE SAVES IN A SEASON

SV	PITCHER	YEAR	SV	PITCHER	YEAR
40	Jeff Reardon	1991	13	Dick Drago	1979
33	Bob Stanley	1983	12	Leo Kiely	1958
31	Bill Campbell	1977	12	Lee Stange	1968
29	Dick Radatz	1964	12	Steve Crawford	1985
29	Lee Smith	1988	12	Joe Sambito	1986
27	Ellis Kinder	1953	11	Ike Delock	1957
27	Jeff Reardon	1992	11	Mike Fornieles	1959
25	Dick Radatz	1963	11	Sparky Lyle	1968
25	Lee Smith	1989	11	Vicente Romo	1969
24	Dick Radatz	1962	11	Bob Veale	1973
24	Tom Burgmeier	1980	10	Wilcy Moore	1931
22	Dick Radatz	1965	10	Murray Wall	1958
22	Bob Stanley	1984	10	Diego Segui	1974
21	Jeff Reardon	1990	10	Jim Willoughby	1976
20	John Wyatt	1967	10	Bob Stanley	1978
20	Sparky Lyle	1970	10	Bob Stanley	1985
18	Ellis Kinder	1955	10	Wes Gardner	1987
17	Sparky Lyle	1969	9	Mace Brown	1943
16	Sparky Lyle	1971	9	Bob Klinger	1946
16	Bob Stanley	1986	9	Ellis Kinder	1950
15	Ellis Kinder	1954	9	Ike Delock	1956
15	Mike Fornieles	1961	9	Don McMahon	1966
15	Bob Bolin	1973	9	Ken Tatum	1971
15	Dick Drago	1975	9	Bill Campbell	1979
14	Ellis Kinder	1951	9	Mark Clear	1981
14	Mike Fornieles	1960	9	Calvin Schiraldi	1986
14	Bob Stanley	1980	9	Rob Murphy	1989
14	Mark Clear	1982	9	Jeff Gray	1990
14	Bob Stanley	1982			

RED SOX ALL-STAR SELECTIONS

1933	Rick Ferrell, C		Bobby Doerr, 2B
1934	Rick Ferrell, C		Boo Ferriss, P
1935	Joe Cronin, SS		Mickey Harris, P
	Rick Ferrell, C		Johnny Pesky, SS
	Lefty Grove, P		Hal Wagner, C
1936	Joe Cronin, SS		Ted Williams, OF
	Rick Ferrell, C		Rudy York, 1B
	Jimmie Foxx, 1B	1947	Bobby Doerr, 2B
	Lefty Grove, P		Ted Williams, OF
1937	Doc Cramer, OF	1948	Joe Dobson, P
	Joe Cronin, SS		Bobby Doerr, 2B
	Jimmie Foxx, 1B		Vern Stephens, SS
	Lefty Grove, P		Birdie Tebbetts, C
1938	Doc Cramer, OF		Ted Williams, OF
	Joe Cronin, SS	1949	Dom DiMaggio, OF
	Jimmie Foxx, 1B		Billy Goodman, 1B
	Lefty Grove, P		Mel Parnell, P
1939	Doc Cramer, OF		Vern Stephens, SS
	Joe Cronin, SS		Birdie Tebbetts, C
	Jimmie Foxx, 1B		Ted Williams, OF
	Lefty Grove, P	1950	Dom DiMaggio, OF
1940	Doc Cramer, OF		Bobby Doerr, 2B
	Lou Finney, OF		Walt Dropo, 1B
	Jimmie Foxx, 1B		Vern Stephens, SS
	Ted Williams, OF		Ted Williams, OF
1941	Joe Cronin, SS	1951	Dom DiMaggio, OF
	Dom DiMaggio, OF		Bobby Doerr, 2B
	Bobby Doerr, 2B		Mel Parnell, P
	Jimmie Foxx, 1B		Vern Stephens, SS
	Ted Williams, OF		Ted Williams, OF
1942	Dom DiMaggio, OF	1952	Dom DiMaggio, OF
	Bobby Doerr, 2B		George Kell, 3B
	Tex Hughson, P	1953	Billy Goodman, 2B
	Ted Williams, OF		George Kell, 3B
1943	Bobby Doerr, 2B		Sammy White, C
	Tex Hughson, P	1954	Jimmy Piersall, OF
	Oscar Judd, P		Ted Williams, OF
1944	Bobby Doerr, 2B	1955	Jackie Jensen, OF
	Pete Fox, OF		Frank Sullivan, P
	Tex Hughson, P		Ted Williams, OF
	Bob Johnson, OF	1956	Tom Brewer, P
1945	No game		Jimmy Piersall, OF
1946	Dom DiMaggio, OF		Frank Sullivan, P

	Mickey Vernon, 1B	1971	Luis Aparicio, SS
	Ted Williams, OF		Bill Siebert, P
1957	Frank Malzone, 3B		Carl Yastrzemski, OF
	Ted Williams, OF	1972	Luis Aparicio, SS
1958	Jackie Jensen, OF		Carlton Fisk, C
	Frank Malzone, 3B		Reggie Smith, OF
	Ted Williams, OF		Carl Yastrzemski, OF
1959	Frank Malzone, 3B	1973	Carlton Fisk, C
	Pete Runnels, 1B		Bill Lee, P
	Ted Williams, OF		Carl Yastrzemski, OF
1960	Frank Malzone, 3B	1974	Carlton Fisk, C
	Bill Monbouquette, P		Luis Tiant, P
	Pete Runnels, 2B		Carl Yastrzemski, OF
	Ted Williams, OF	1975	Fred Lynn, OF
1961	Mike Fornieles, P		Carl Yastrzemski, OF
	Don Schwall, P	1976	Carlton Fisk, C
1962	Bill Monbouquette, P		Fred Lynn, OF
	Pete Runnels, 2B		Luis Tiant, P
1963	Frank Malzone, 3B		Carl Yastrzemski, OF
	Bill Monbouquette, P	1977	Rick Burleson, SS
	Dick Radatz, P		Bill Campbell, P
	Carl Yastrzemski, OF		Carlton Fisk, C
1964	Eddie Bressoud, SS		Fred Lynn, OF
	Frank Malzone, 3B		Jim Rice, OF
	Dick Radatz, P		George Scott, 1B
1965	Felix Mantilla, 2B		Carl Yastrzemski, OF
	Carl Yastrzemski, OF	1978	Rick Burleson, SS
1966	George Scott, 1B		Dwight Evans, OF
	Carl Yastrzemski, OF		Carlton Fisk, C
1967	Tony Conigliaro, OF		Fred Lynn, OF
	Jim Lonborg, P		Gerry Remy, 2B
	Rico Petrocelli, SS		Jim Rice, OF
	Carl Yastrzemski, OF		Carl Yastrzemski, OF
1968	Ken Harrelson, OF	1979	Rick Burleson, SS
	Jose Santiago, P		Fred Lynn, OF
	Gary Bell, P		Jim Rice, OF
	Carl Yastrzemski, OF		Bob Stanley, P
1969	Mike Andrews, 2B		Carl Yastrzemski, 1B
	Ray Culp, P	1980	Tom Burgmeier, P
	Rico Petrocelli, SS		Carlton Fisk, C
	Reggie Smith, OF		Fred Lynn, OF
	Carl Yastrzemski, OF		Jim Rice, OF
1970	Jerry Moses, C	1981	Dwight Evans, OF
	Carl Yastrzemski, OF	1982	Mark Clear, P

	Dennis Eckersley, P		Dwight Evans, OF
	Carl Yastrzemski, 1B		Bruce Hurst, P
1983	Jim Rice, OF	1988	Wade Boggs, 3B
	Bob Stanley, P		Roger Clemens, P
	Carl Yastrzemski, 1B		Mike Greenwell, OF
1984	Tony Armas, OF	1989	Wade Boggs, 3B
	Jim Rice, OF	1990	Wade Boggs, 3B
1985	Wade Boggs, 3B		Ellis Burks, OF
	Rich Gedman, C		Roger Clemens, P
	Jim Rice, OF	1991	Wade Boggs, 3B
1986	Wade Boggs, 3B		Roger Clemens, P
	Roger Clemens, P		Jeff Reardon, P
	Rich Gedman, C	1992	Wade Boggs, 3B
	Jim Rice, OF		Roger Clemens, P
1987	Wade Boggs, 3B		

RED SOX HALL-OF-FAMERS

PLAYER	ACTIVE YEARS	ENSHRINEMENT YEAR
Luis Aparicio	1971–1973	1984
Ed Barrow	m1918–1920	1953
Lou Boudreau	1951–1952	1970
	m1952–1954	
Jesse Burkett	1905	1946
Frank Chance	m1923	1946
Jack Chesbro	1909	1946
Eddie Collins	e1933–1951	1939
Jimmy Collins	1901–1907	1945
	m1901–1906	
Joe Cronin	1935–1945	1956
	m1935–1947	
Bobby Doerr	1937–1951	1986
Hugh Duffy	m1921–1922	1945
Rick Ferrell	1933–1937	1984
Jimmie Foxx	1936–1942	1951
Lefty Grove	1934–41	1947
Bucky Harris	m1934	1975
Billy Herman	m1964–1966	1975
Harry Hooper	1909–1920	1971
Waite Hoyt	1919–1920	1969
Ferguson Jenkins	1976–1977	1990
George Kell	1952–1954	1983
Heinie Manush	1936	1964
Juan Marichal	1974	1983
Joe McCarthy	m1948–1950	1957
Herb Pennock	1915–1922	1948
Red Ruffing	1924–1930	1967
Babe Ruth	1914–1919	1936
Tom Seaver	1986	1992
Al Simmons	1943	1953
Tris Speaker	1907–1915	1937
Ted Williams	1939–1960	1966
Carl Yastrzemski	1961–1983	1989

PLAYER	ACTIVE YEARS	ENSHRINEMENT YEAR
Tom Yawkey	e1933–1976	1980
Cy Young	1901–1908	1937
	m1907	

m = Red Sox manager
e = Red Sox executive

RED SOX ALL-TIME TEAMS VOTED BY THE FANS

1969

C	Birdie Tebbetts
1B	Jimmie Foxx
2B	Bobby Doerr
3B	Frank Malzone
SS	Joe Cronin
OF	Ted Williams
OF	Carl Yastremski
OF	Tris Speaker
RHP	Cy Young
LHP	Lefty Grove

Ted Williams—Greatest player

1982

	FIRST TEAM		SECOND TEAM
C	Carlton Fisk	C	Birdie Tebbetts
1B	Jimmie Foxx	1B	George Scott
2B	Bobby Doerr	2B	Jerry Remy
3B	Rico Petrocelli	3B	Frank Malzone
SS	Rick Burleson	SS	Johnny Pesky
OF	Ted Williams	OF	Jim Rice
OF	Carl Yastrzemski	OF	Dom DiMaggio
OF	Dwight Evans	OF	Fred Lynn
RHP	Cy Young	RHP	Luis Tiant
LHP	Babe Ruth	LHP	Lefty Grove
REL P	Dick Radatz	REL P	Sparky Lyle
MGR	Dick Williams	MGR	Joe Cronin

Ted Williams—Greatest player

RED SOX RAWLINGS GOLD GLOVE AWARD WINNERS

1957	Frank Malzone, 3B	1976	Dwight Evans, OF
1958	Frank Malzone, 3B (2)	1977	Carl Yastrzemski, OF (7)
	Jim Piersall, CF	1978	Dwight Evans, OF (2)
1959	Frank Malzone, 3B (3)		Fred Lynn, OF (2)
	Jackie Jensen, RF	1979	Rick Burleson, SS
1963	Carl Yastrzemski, OF		Dwight Evans, OF (3)
1965	Carl Yastrzemski, OF (2)		Fred Lynn, OF (3)
1967	George Scott, 1B	1980	Fred Lynn, OF (4)
	Carl Yastrzemski, OF (3)	1981	Dwight Evans, OF (4)
1968	George Scott, 1B (2)	1982	Dwight Evans, OF (5)
	Reggie Smith, OF	1983	Dwight Evans, OF (6)
	Carl Yastrzemski, OF (4)	1984	Dwight Evans, OF (7)
1969	Carl Yastrzemski, OF (5)	1985	Dwight Evans, OF (8)
1971	Carl Yastrzemski, OF (6)	1990	Mike Boddicker, P
1972	Carlton Fisk, C		Ellis Burks, OF
	Doug Griffin, 2B	1991	Wade Boggs, 3B
1975	Fred Lynn, OF		

RED SOX RETIRED NUMBERS

9—Ted Williams—Number formally retired May 29, 1984

4—Joe Cronin—Number formally retired May 29, 1984

1—Bobby Doerr—Number formally retired May 19, 1988

8—Carl Yastrzemski—Number formally retired August 6, 1989

BOSTON WRITERS MVP AWARD (THOMAS A. YAWKEY AWARD)

From 1937 through 1952, the Boston chapter of the Baseball Writers Association of America (the BBWAA) voted the award to either a Red Sox player or a Boston Braves player. The Braves moved to Milwaukee after the 1952 season. After club-owner Tom Yawkey's death in 1976, the writers renamed the award in his honor.

Year	Player	Year	Player
1937	Jim Turner*	1966	Tony Conigliaro
1938	Jimmie Foxx	1967	Carl Yastrzemski
1939	Joe Cronin	1968	Ken Harrelson
1940	Johnny Cooney*	1969	Rico Petrocelli
1941	Ted Williams	1970	Carl Yastrzemski
1942–1944	No award	1971	Reggie Smith
1945	Tommy Holmes*	1972	Carlton Fisk
1946	Ted Williams	1973	Tommy Harper
1947	Bob Elliott*	1974	Carl Yastrzemski
1948	Johnny Sain*	1975	Fred Lynn
1949	Ted Williams	1976	Carl Yastrzemski
1950	Billy Goodman	1977	Carlton Fisk
1951	Ellis Kinder	1978	Jim Rice
1952	Walker Cooper*	1979	Rick Burleson
1953	Ellis Kinder	1980	Rick Burleson
1954	Jackie Jensen	1981	Dwight Evans
1955	Ted Williams	1982	Dwight Evans
1956	Jim Piersall	1983	Jim Rice
1957	Frank Malzone	1984	Dwight Evans and
1958	Jackie Jensen		Tony Armas
1959	Frank Malzone	1985	Wade Boggs
1960	Vic Wertz	1986	Roger Clemens
1961	Chuck Schilling	1987	Dwight Evans
1962	Eddie Bressoud	1988	Mike Greenwell
1963	Carl Yastrzemski	1989	Nick Esasky
1964	Dick Radatz	1990	Roger Clemens
1965	Carl Yastrzemski	1991	Roger Clemens

*Boston Brave

RED SOX AMERICAN LEAGUE MVP AWARDS (VOTED BY BBWAA)

YEAR	PLAYER	BA	HR	RBI
1938	Jimmie Foxx, 1B	*.349	50	*175
1946	Ted Williams, LF	.342	38	123
1949	Ted Williams, LF	.343	*43	*159
1958	Jackie Jensen, RF	.286	35	*122
1967	Carl Yastrzemski, LF	*.326	*44	*121
1975	Fred Lynn, CF	.331	21	105
1978	Jim Rice, LF	.315	*46	*139

		W–L	ERA	SO
1986	Roger Clemens, P	*24–4	*2.48	238

*Led league

RED SOX CY YOUNG AWARD WINNERS (VOTED BY BBWAA)

YEAR	PLAYER	W–L	ERA	SO
1967	Jim Lonborg	*22–9	3.16	*246
1986	Roger Clemens	*24–4	*2.48	238
1987	Roger Clemens	*20–9	2.56	256
1991	Roger Clemens	18–10	*2.62	*241

*Led league

ANNUAL MAN OF THE YEAR AWARD
(CHOSEN BY THE BOSOX CLUB OF BOSTON)

The annual Man of the Year is selected for his contributions to the success of the Red Sox and for his cooperation in community endeavors.

1967	Rico Petrocelli, SS	1980	Steve Renko, P
1968	Mike Andrews, 2B	1981	Jerry Remy, 2B
1969	Lee Stange, P	1982	Bob Stanley, P
1970	Jerry Moses, C	1983	Carl Yastrzemski, DH
1971	John Kennedy, INF	1984	Mike Easler, DH
1972	Bob Montgomery, C	1985	Wade Boggs, 3B
1973	Tommy Harper, LF	1986	Marty Barrett, 2B
1974	Rick Miller, CF	1987	Bruce Hurst, P
1975	Denny Doyle, 2B	1988	Bill Fischer, Coach
1976	Reggie Cleveland, P	1989	Dennis Lamp, P
1977	Butch Hobson, 3B	1990	Tony Pena, C
1978	Bill Campbell, P	1991	Tony Fossas, P
1979	Tom Burgmeier, P		

TV38 10TH PLAYER AWARD

Each year, Channel 38, the Red Sox flagship station, honors a player who is voted by fans as having performed above and beyond the normal expectations during the season.

1975	Fred Lynn, CF	1984	Marty Barrett, 2B
1976	Carl Yastrzemski, 1B	1985	Steve Lyons, CF
1977	Butch Hobson, 3B	1986	Roger Clemens, P
1978	Carlton Fisk, C	1987	Dwight Evans, 1B-RF
1979	Bob Watson, 1B	1988	Dwight Evans, RF-1B
1980	Dave Stapleton, 2B	1989	Nick Esasky, 1B
1981	Dwight Evans, RF	1990	Jody Reed, 2B
1982	Wade Boggs, 3B	1991	Joe Hesketh, P
1983	Wade Boggs, 3B	1992	Bob Zupcic, OF

RED SOX NO-HITTERS

May 5, 1904	Cy Young (H)	vs. Philadelphia 3–0*
Aug 17, 1904	Jesse Tannehill (A)	vs. Chicago 6–0
Sep 27, 1905 (G1)	Bill Dinneen (H)	vs. Chicago 2–0
Jun 30, 1908	Cy Young (A)	vs. New York 8–0
Jul 29, 1911 (G1)	Smokey Joe Wood (H)	vs. St. Louis 5–0
Jun 21, 1916	Rube Foster (H)	vs. New York 2–0
Aug 30, 1916	Dutch Leonard (H)	vs. St. Louis 4–0
Jun 23, 1917 (G1)	Ernie Shore (H)	vs. Washington 4–0*

(Shore didn't start the game. Babe Ruth walked the first batter and was ejected for arguing with the umpire. Shore relieved. The base runner was out attempting to steal. Shore was given credit for a perfect game in facing only 26 batters.)

Jun 3, 1918	Dutch Leonard (A)	vs. Detroit 5–0
Sep 7, 1923	Howard Ehmke (A)	vs. Philadelphia 4–0
Jul 14, 1956	Mel Parnell (H)	vs. Chicago 4–0
Jun 26, 1962	Earl Wilson (H)	vs. Los Angeles 2–0
Aug 1, 1962	Bill Monbouquette (A)	vs. Chicago 1–0
Sep 16, 1965	Dave Morehead (H)	vs. Cleveland 2–0

H = Home
A = Away
 * = Perfect game

NO-HITTERS PITCHED AGAINST THE SOX

Sep 18, 1908	Dusty Rhoads, Cleveland (A) 2–1
Aug 17, 1911	Ed Walsh, Chicago (A) 5–0
Apr 24, 1917	George Mogridge, New York (H) 2–1
Jul 1, 1920	Walter Johnson, Washington (H) 1–0
Aug 21, 1926	Ted Lyons, Chicago (H) 6–0
Aug 8, 1931	Bob Burke, Washington (A) 5–0
Sep 18, 1934	Bobo Newsom, St. Louis (A) 1–2
	(Lost in 10th but pitched 9 hitless innings)
Sep 28, 1951 (G1)	Allie Reynolds, New York (A) 8–0
Jul 20, 1958 (G1)	Jim Bunning, Detroit (H) 3–0
Aug 6, 1967	Dean Chance, Minnesota (5 innings) (A) 2–0
Apr 27, 1968	Tom Phoebou, Baltimore (A) 6–0
Jul 4, 1983	Dave Righetti, New York (A) 4–0

H = Home
A = Away

RED SOX TRIPLE CROWN WINNERS

1942	Ted Williams	36 home runs 137 runs batted in .356 batting average
1947	Ted Williams	32 home runs 114 runs batted in .343 batting average
1967	Carl Yastrzemski	44 home runs 121 runs batted in .326 batting average

Almost—2 of 3

1903	Buck Freeman	13 home runs 104 runs batted in (.287 batting average)
1919	Babe Ruth	19 home runs 114 runs batted in (.322 batting average)
1938	Jimmie Foxx	(50 home runs) 175 runs batted in .349 batting average
1941	Ted Williams	37 home runs (120 runs batted in) .406 batting average
1949	Ted Williams	43 home runs 159 runs batted in (.343 batting average)
1978	Jim Rice	46 home runs 139 runs batted in (.315 batting average)
1984	Tony Armas	43 home runs 123 runs batted in (.268 batting average)

RED SOX GRAND SLAMS

In 91 seasons, the Red Sox have hit 248 grand slams; 139 have come at Fenway Park and 4 at the old Huntington Avenue Grounds. Not surprisingly, Ted Williams holds the BoSox career grand-slam record with 17. The season record was set by Babe Ruth in 1919 when he blasted 4 slams, all on the road. Those were the only grand slams the Bambino hit in a Red Sox uniform. Jim Tabor (July 4, 1939) and Rudy York (July 22, 1946) each hit two in a single game, and Jimmie Foxx (May 20–21, 1940) hit slams in consecutive games.

CAREER	NO.
Ted Williams	17
Rico Petrocelli	9
Bobby Doerr	8
Jim Rice	8
Jimmie Foxx	7
Jackie Jensen	7
Carl Yastrzemski	7
Jim Tabor	6
Ellis Burks	5
Tony Conigliaro	5
Dom DiMaggio	5
Dwight Evans	5
Joe Foy	5
Vern Stephens	5
Vic Wertz	5

SEASON	NO.	YEAR
Babe Ruth	4	1919
Jimmie Foxx	3	1938
Jimmie Foxx	3	1940
Ted Williams	3	1955
Vic Wertz	3	1960
Dick Stuart	3	1964
Carl Yastrzemski	3	1969

CLUB, SEASON	
9	1941, 1950, 1987
8	1952, 1964
7	1938, 1940, 1955, 1986

RED SOX WORST BATTERS (AMONG REGULARS WITH 400 OR MORE AT BATS)

YEAR	PLAYER	POSITION	GAMES	AT BAT	HR	RBI	BA
1901	Hobe Ferris	(2B)	138	523	2		.250
	Tommy Dowd	(OF)	138	594		52	
1902	Patsy Dougherty	(OF)	108	438	0	34	
	Hobe Ferris	(2B)	134	499			.244
1903	Candy LaChance	(1B)	141	522	1	53	
	Hobe Ferris	(2B)	141	525			.251
1904	Candy LaChance	(1B)	157	573	1	47	
	Hobe Ferris	(2B)	156	563			.213
1905	Fred Parent	(SS)	153	602	0	33	
	Chick Stahl	(OF)	134	500	0		
	Hobe Ferris	(2B)	141	523			.220
1906	Moose Grimshaw	(1B)	110	428	0		
	Hobe Ferris	(2B)	130	495		44	
	Fred Parent	(SS)	149	600			.235
1907	Bob Unglaub	(1B)	139	544	1		
	Denny Sullivan	(OF)	144	551	1	26	
	Hobe Ferris	(2B)	150	561			.241
1908	Heinie Wagner	(SS)	153	526	1		.247
	Jack Thoney	(OF)	109	416		30	
1909	Harry Lord	(3B)	136	534	0	31	
	Amby McConnell	(2B)	121	453	0		.238
1910	Heinie Wagner	(SS)	142	491	1		
	Harry Hooper	(OF)	155	584		27	.267
1911	Steve Yerkes	(SS)	142	502	1		
	Larry Gardner	(3B)	142	492		44	
	Clyde Engle	(1B)	146	514			.270
1912	Steve Yerkes	(2B)	131	523	0	42	
	Harry Hooper	(OF)	147	590			.242
1913	Duffy Lewis	(OF)	149	551	0		
	Steve Yerkes	(2B)	136	483	0		.267
	Harry Hooper	(OF)	148	586		40	
1914	Harry Hooper	(OF)	141	530	1		
	Hal Janvrin	(IF)	143	492	1		
	Everett Scott	(SS)	144	539		37	.239
1915	Tris Speaker	(OF)	150	547	0		
	Harry Hooper	(OF)	149	566		51	.235

YEAR	PLAYER	POSITION	GAMES	AT BAT	HR	RBI	BA
1916	Dick Hoblitzell	(1B)	130	417	0		.259
	Harry Hooper	(OF)	151	575		37	
1917	Everett Scott	(SS)	157	528	0		.241
	Harry Hooper	(OF)	151	559		45	
1918	Everett Scott	(SS)	126	443	0		.221
	Dave Shean	(2B)	115	425	0	34	
	Stuffy McInnis	(1B)	117	423	0		
	Amos Strunk	(OF)	114	413	0		
1919	Everett Scott	(SS)	138	507	0	38	
	Oscar Vitt	(3B)	133	469	0		.243
1920	Stuffy McInnis	(1B)	148	559	2		.200
	Harry Hooper	(OF)	139	536		53	
	Everett Scott	(SS)	154	569			.269
1921	Stuffy McInnis	(1B)	152	584	0		
	Nemo Leibold	(OF)	123	467	0	30	
	Eddie Foster	(3B)	120	412	0	30	
	Everett Scott	(SS)	154	576			.262
1922	Shano Collins	(OF)	135	472	1		.271
	Mike Menosky	(OF)	126	406		32	
1923	Norm McMillan	(IF)	131	459	0	42	.253
1924	Bill Wambsganss	(2B)	156	636	0		.274
	Ira Flagstead	(OF)	189	560		43	
1925	Doc Prothro	(3B)	119	415	0	51	
	Phil Todt	(1B)	141	544			.278
1926	Fred Haney	(3B)	138	462	0		.221
	Ira Flagstead	(OF)	98	415		31	
1927	Jack Rothrock	(IF)	117	428	1	36	
	Phil Todt	(1B)	140	516			.236
1928	Buddy Myer	(3B)	147	536	1		
	Ira Flagstead	(OF)	140	510	1	39	
	Phil Todt	(1B)	144	539			.252
1929	Russ Scarritt	(OF)	151	540	1		
	Bobby Reeves	(3B)	140	460		28	.248
1930	Tom Oliver	(OF)	154	646	0	46	
	Bill Regan	(2B)	134	507			.266
1931	Tom Oliver	(OF)	148	586	0		
	Hal Rhyne	(SS)	147	565	0		.273
	Jack Rothrock	(OF)	133	475		42	

YEAR	PLAYER	POSITION	GAMES	AT BAT	HR	RBI	BA
1932	Tom Oliver	(OF)	122	455	0		
	Marv Olson	(2B)	115	403	0	25	.248
1933	Billy Werber	(SS-3B)	108	425		39	.259
1934	Rick Ferrell	(C)	132	437	1		
	Bill Cissell	(2B)	102	416		44	
	Lyn Lary	(SS)	129	419			.241
1935	Mel Almada	(OF)	151	607		59	
	Billy Werber	(3B)	124	462			.255
1936	Doc Cramer	(OF)	154	643	0	41	
	Billy Werber	(3B)	145	535			.275
1937	Doc Cramer	(OF)	133	560	0	51	
	Jimmie Foxx	(1B)	150	569			.285
1938	Doc Cramer	(OF)	148	658	0	71	
	Bobby Doerr	(2B)	145	509			.289
1939	Doc Cramer	(OF)	137	589	0	56	
	Joe Vosmik	(OF)	145	554			.276
1940	Doc Cramer	(OF)	150	661	1		
	Dom DiMaggio	(OF)	108	418		46	
1941	Lou Finney	(OF)	127	497		53	
	Jim Tabor	(3B)	126	498			.279
1942	Johnny Pesky	(SS)	147	620	2		
	Dom DiMaggio	(OF)	151	622		48	
	Jim Tabor	(3B)	139	508			.252
1943	Skeeter Newsome	(SS)	114	449	1	22	
	Jim Tabor	(3B)	137	537			.242
1944	Skeeter Newsome	(SS)	136	472	0	41	.242
1945	Skeeter Newsome	(2B)	125	438	1	48	
	George Metkovich	(1B)	138	539			.260
1946	Johnny Pesky	(SS)	153	621	2	55	
	Bobby Doerr	(2B)	151	583			.271
1947	Johnny Pesky	(SS)	155	638	0	39	
	Jake Jones	(1B)	109	404			.235
1948	Billy Goodman	(1B)	127	445	1		
	Johnny Pesky	(3B)	143	565		55	
	Birdie Tebbetts	(C)	128	446			.280
1949	Billy Goodman	(1B)	122	443	0		
	Birdie Tebbetts	(C)	122	403		48	.270

YEAR	PLAYER	POSITION	GAMES	AT BAT	HR	RBI	BA
1950	Johnny Pesky	(3B)	127	490	1	49	
	Bobby Doerr	(2B)	149	586			.294
1951	Billy Goodman	(1B)	141	546	0		
	Johnny Pesky	(SS)	131	480		41	
	Dom DiMaggio	(OF)	146	630			.296
1952	Billy Goodman	(2B)	103	513	4		
	Dom DiMaggio	(OF)	122	486		33	
	Hoot Evers	(OF)	106	401			.262
1953	Billy Goodman	(2B)	128	514	2	41	
	Dick Gernert	(1B)	139	494			.253
1954	Billy Goodman	(2B)	127	489	1	36	
	Harry Agannis	(1B)	132	434			.251
1955	Billy Goodman	(2B)	149	599	0	52	
	Norm Zauchin	(1B)	130	477			.239
1956	Billy Klaus	(3B)	135	520	7	59	.271
1957	Billy Klaus	(SS)	127	477	10	42	.252
1958	Pete Runnels	(2B)	147	568	8		
	Jimmy Piersall	(OF)	130	417	8		
	Don Buddin	(SS)	136	497		43	
	Dick Gernert	(1B)	122	431			.237
1959	Pete Runnels	(2B)	147	560	6		
	Don Buddin	(SS)	151	485		53	.241
1960	Pete Runnels	(2B)	143	528	2	35	
	Don Buddin	(SS)	124	428			.245
1961	Chuck Schilling	(2B)	158	646	5	62	
	Gary Geiger	(OF)	140	499			.232
1962	Chuck Schilling	(2B)	119	413	7	35	.230
1963	Chuck Schilling	(2B)	146	576	8	33	
	Lou Clinton	(OF)	148	560			.232
1964	Lee Thomas	(OF)	107	401	13	42	.257
1965	Felix Mantilla	(2B)	150	534	18		
	Carl Yastrzemski	(OF)	133	494		72	
	Tony Conigliaro	(OF)	138	521			.269
1966	George Smith	(2B)	128	403	8	37	.213
1967	Mike Andrews	(2B)	142	494	8	40	
	Reggie Smith	(OF)	158	565			.246
1968	Mike Andrews	(2B)	147	536	9	45	
	Rico Petrocelli	(SS)	123	406			.234

YEAR	PLAYER	POSITION	GAMES	AT BAT	HR	RBI	BA
1969	Mike Andrews	(2B)	121	464			
	George Scott	(3B)	152	549		52	.253
1970	George Scott	(3B)	127	480	16	63	
	Mike Andrews	(2B)	144	589			.253
1971	Doug Griffin	(2B)	125	483	3	27	
	Luis Aparicio	(SS)	125	491			.232
1972	Doug Griffin	(2B)	125	470	2	35	
	Rico Petrocelli	(3B)	147	521			.240
1973	Luis Aparicio	(SS)	132	499	0		
	Rick Miller	(OF)	143	441		43	
	Carlton Fisk	(C)	135	508			.246
1974	Tommy Harper	(OF-DH)	118	443	5	24	.237
1975	Rick Burleson	(SS)	158	580	4	36	
	Rico Petrocelli	(3B)	115	402			.239
1976	Denny Doyle	(2B)	117	432	0	26	
	Dwight Evans	(OF)	146	501			.242
1977	Denny Doyle	(2B)	137	455	2	49	.240
1978	Jerry Remy	(2B)	148	583	2	44	
	George Scott	(1B)	120	412			.233
1979	Rick Burleson	(SS)	153	627	5		
	Dwight Evans	(OF)	152	489		58	
	Butch Hobson	(3B)	146	528			.261
1980	Dave Stapleton	(2B)	106	449	7	45	
	Dwight Evans	(OF)	148	463			.266
1981	*Jerry Remy	(2B)	88	358	0	31	
	Carl Yastrzemski	(DH)	91	338			.246
1982	Jerry Remy	(2B)	155	636	0		
	Rick Miller	(OF)	135	409		38	.254
1983	Jerry Remy	(2B)	146	592	0		
	Glenn Hoffman	(SS)	142	473		41	
	Tony Armas	(OF)	145	574			.218
1984	Jackie Gutierrez	(SS)	151	449	2	29	.263
1985	Marty Barrett	(2B)	156	534	5	56	
	Dwight Evans	(OF)	159	617			.263
1986	Marty Barrett	(2B)	158	625	4		

*1981: strike year, 300 at-bats

	Player	Pos					
	Tony Armas	(OF)	121	425		58	
	Don Baylor	(DH)	160	585			.238
1987	Spike Owen	(SS)	132	437	2		.289
	Marty Barrett	(2B)	137	559		43	
1988	Marty Barrett	(2B)	150	612	1		
	Wade Boggs	(3B)	155	584		58	
	Todd Benzinger	(1B)	120	406			.254
1989	Wade Boggs	(3B)	156	621	3		
	Jody Reed	(SS-2B)	146	524	3	40	
	Nick Esasky	(1B)	154	564			.277
1990	Jody Reed	(2B)	155	598	5	51	
	Dwight Evans	(DH)	123	445			.249
1991	Jody Reed	(2B)	153	618	5		
	Luis Rivera	(SS)	129	414		40	
	Tom Brunansky	(OF)	142	459			.229
1992	Tony Pena	(C)	133	410	1	38	.241

RED SOX INDIVIDUAL SEASON RECORDS

BATTING

GAMES, most ....163, Jim Rice, 1978
AT-BATS: Left-handed, most .... 673, Bill Buckner, 1985
  Right-handed, most ....677, Jim Rice, 1978
PLATE APPEARANCES, most .... 758*, Wade Boggs, 1985
HITS, most.. 240, Wade Boggs, 1985
GAMES HIT SAFELY IN, most .... 135***, Wade Boggs, 1985
MULTIPLE-HIT GAMES, most .... 72, Wade Boggs, 1985
HITTING STREAKS, longest .... 34, Dom DiMaggio, 1949
  Longest start of season .... 20, Eddie Bressoud, 1964
BATTING AVERAGE
  Left-handed, highest ....406, Ted Williams, 1941
  Right-handed, highest ....360, Jimmie Foxx, 1939

SINGLES, most .... 187*, Wade Boggs, 1985
DOUBLES, most ....67**, Earl Webb, 1931
TRIPLES, most............................ 22, Tris Speaker, 1913; Chick Stahl, 1904
HOME RUNS, most ....50, Jimmie Foxx, 1938
  At home ....35, Jimmie Foxx, 1938
  At home by left-handed hitter .... 28, Fred Lynn, 1979
  On road .... 26, Ted Williams, 1957
    By right-handed hitter ....23, Jim Rice, 1983
  One month .... 14, Jackie Jensen, June, 1958
  By position, 1B ....50, Jimmie Foxx, 1938
    2B... 27, Bobby Doerr, 1948 and 1950
    SS.. 40*, Rico Petrocelli, 1969
    3B... 30, Butch Hobson, 1977
    LF .... 44, Carl Yastrzemski, 1967
    CF....................................38#, Fred Lynn, 1979; ##, Tony Armas, 1984
    RF .... 36, Tony Conigliaro, 1970
    C.. 26, Carlton Fisk, 1973 and 1977
    DH ....31, Jim Rice, 1977
    P... 7, Wes Ferrell, 1935
  Two consecutive games .... 5****, Carl Yastrzemski, May 19–20, 1976
  First 2 major-league games .... 2**, Sam Horn, 1987
  Grand slams .... 4, Babe Ruth, 1919
LONG HITS, most ....92, Jimmie Foxx, 1938
EXTRA BASES ON LONG HITS ....201, Jimmie Foxx, 1938
TOTAL BASES, most...406, Jim Rice, 1978

SLUGGING PERCENTAGE,
Left-handed, highest .... .735, Ted Williams, 1941
Right-handed, highest .... .704, Jimmie Foxx, 1938

RUNS, most .... 150, Ted Williams, 1949
RUNS BATTED IN, most .... 175, Jimmie Foxx, 1938
Game-winning, most.. 23, Mike Greenwell, 1988
STOLEN BASES, most .... 54, Tommy Harper, 1973
Most caught stealing .... 19, Mike Menosky, 1920

BASES ON BALLS, most .... 162, Ted Williams, 1947 and 1949
Intentional .... 33*, Ted Williams, 1957
STRIKEOUTS, Left-handed, most .... 134, Mike Easler, 1984
Right-handed, most .... 162, Butch Hobson, 1977
Fewest .... 9, Stuffy McInnis (584 AB), 1921
GROUNDED INTO DOUBLEPLAYS,
Left-handed, most .... 30***, Carl Yastrzemski, 1964
Right-handed, most ....36***, Jim Rice, 1984
Fewest .... 1, Ellis Burks (558 AB), 1987
HIT BY PITCHER, most .... 35*, Don Baylor, 1986
SACRIFICES, most, including flies .... 54, Jack Barry, 1917
Most, no flies .... 35, Fred Parent, 1905
Most, flies .... 12, Jackie Jensen, 1955 and 1959; Jim Piersall, 1956

MANAGING, most games won at the start .... 12, Joe Morgan, 1988

#Plus 1 HR as DH
##Plus 5 HR as DH

PITCHING

GAMES, most .... 79, Dick Radatz, 1964
  Most by left-hander ....74, Rob Murphy, 1989
  Started, most ....43, Cy Young, 1902
  Complete, most ....41, Cy Young, 1902 and 1904
  Finished, most .... 67, Dick Radatz, 1964

WINS, most .... 34, Smokey Joe Wood, 1912
  Wins, left-hander ....25, Mel Parnell, 1949
  Won consecutively .... 16**, Smokey Joe Wood, 1912
  Won consecutively, at home ..13, Tex Hughson, 1944; Boo Ferriss, 1946
  Won consecutively, start of season .... 14, Roger Clemens, 1986
  Won, most at home ....19, Cy Young, 1901
  Won, most at Fenway Park .... 18, Smokey Joe Wood, 1912
  Won, most on road .... 16, Smokey Joe Wood, 1912
  Won, most in relief .... 16, Dick Radatz, 1964
LOSSES, most... 25, Red Ruffing, 1928
  Lost, consecutively.. 14, Joe Harris, 1906
WINNING PERCENTAGE, highest .... .882, Bob Stanley (15–2), 1978

INNINGS, most ....385, Cy Young, 1902
  Relief, most ....168.1*, Bob Stanley, 1982
  Consecutive hitless, most .... 25.1, Cy Young, 1904
  Batters, most retired without a hit ....76, Cy Young, 1904
  Consecutive scoreless, most .... 45.2, Cy Young, 1904

HITS, most...350, Cy Young, 1902
RUNS, most .... 162, Red Ruffing, 1929; Jack Russell, 1930
EARNED RUNS, most .... 139, Jack Russell, 1930
EARNED RUN AVERAGE, lowest .... 1.00****, Dutch Leonard (223 innings), 1914

STRIKEOUTS, most... 291, Roger Clemens, 1988
  Left-hander, most .... 190, Bruce Hurst, 1987
  Consecutive games, most, 10 or more ....4**, Roger Clemens, 1986
  Three consecutive games of 9 IP, most ....41**, Roger Clemens, 1986

BASES ON BALLS, most ....134, Mel Parnell, 1949
  Right-hander, most .... 121, Don Schwall, 1962; Mike Torrez, 1979

SHUTOUTS, most won ......10, Cy Young, 1904; Smokey Joe Wood, 1912
  Left-hander, most won .... 9, Babe Ruth, 1916

Most lost .... 8, Joe Harris, 1906
Most lost by 1–0 .... 5**, Bullet Joe Bush, 1918

HIT BATSMEN, most .... 20, Howard Ehmke, 1923
WILD PITCHES, most ....21, Earl Wilson, 1963
HOME RUNS, most ....34, Earl Wilson, 1964

SAVES, most.. 40, Jeff Reardon, 1991
Most, left-handed .... 24, Tom Burgmeier, 1980

*A.L. record
**Tied A.L. record
***Major-league record
****Tied major-league record

ROOKIE RECORDS

GAMES .... 162****, George Scott, 1966
AT-BATS .... 646, Tom Oliver, 1930
HITS.. 205, Johnny Pesky, 1942
SINGLES .... 165, Johnny Pesky, 1942
DOUBLES .... 47*, Fred Lynn, 1975
TRIPLES... 17, Russ Scarritt, 1929
HOME RUNS.. 34, Walt Dropo, 1950
TOTAL BASES.. 344, Ted Williams, 1939
RUNS .... 131, Ted Williams, 1939
RUNS BATTED IN .... 145***, Ted Williams, 1939
BATTING AVERAGE ....342 Pat Dougherty, 1902; .349, Wade Boggs,
                                                                                                  1982, 104G†
SLUGGING AVERAGE .... .609*, Ted Williams, 1939
BASES ON BALLS .... 107***, Ted Williams, 1939
MOST INTENTIONAL WALKS ....13, George Scott, 1966
STRIKEOUTS...152, George Scott, 1966
STOLEN BASES .... 35, Tris Speaker, 1909

*A.L. record
***Major-league record
****Tied major-league record
†Did not qualify for batting title but A.L. record, 100 games

INDIVIDUAL GAME AND INNING RECORDS

BATTING, GAME

Most Times Faced Pitcher ...... 8****, Clyde Vollmer, June 8, 1950, vs. St. L.

Most Times Faced Pitcher, No At-Bats .... 6**** (6 BB), Jimmie Foxx, June 16, 1938, at St. L.

Most Runs .... 6****, Johnny Pesky, May 8, 1946, vs. Chi.; Spike Owen, Aug. 21, 1986, at Clev.

Most Hits 6** (1 double, 5 singles) Jim Piersall, June 10, 1953, at St. L.; (1 double, 5 singles) Pete Runnels, Aug. 30, 1960, vs. Det.; (6 singles) Jerry Remy, Sept. 3–4, 1981, 20 innings vs. Sea.

Most Singles ....6 Jerry Remy, Sept. 3–4, 1981, 20 innings vs. Sea.

Most Doubles .... 4****, Billy Werber, July 17, 1935, 1st G. vs. Clev.; Al Zarilla, June 8, 1950, vs. St. L.; Orlando Cepeda, Aug. 8, 1973, at K.C.; Rick Miller, May 11, 1981, at Tor.

Most Consecutive Doubles ....4****, Billy Werber, July 17, 1935, 1st G. vs. Clev.

Most Triples .... 3****, Patsy Dougherty, Sept. 5, 1903, vs. Phil.

Most Home Runs .... 3, Jim Tabor, July 4, 1939 at Phil.; Ted Williams, July 14, 1946 (FP), 1st G. vs. Clev.; Bobby Doerr, June 8, 1950 (FP), vs. St. L.; Clyde Vollmer, July 26, 1951 (FP), vs. Chi.; Norm Zauchin, May 27, 1955 (FP), vs. Wash.; Ted Williams, May 8, 1957, at Chi.; Ted Williams, June 13, 1957, at Clev.; Ken Harrelson, June 14, 1968, at Clev.; Joe Lahoud, June 11, 1969, at Minn.; Fred Lynn, June 18, 1975, at Det.; Carl Yastrzemski, May 19, 1976, at Det.; Jim Rice, Aug. 29, 1977 (FP), vs. Oak.; Jim Rice, Aug. 29, 1983, 2nd G. at Tor.; Tom Brunansky, Sept. 29, 1990 (FP), vs. Tor.; Jack Clark, July 31, 1991 (FP), vs. Oak. (FP) = Fenway Park

Most Consecutive Home Runs .. 3, Ken Harrelson, June 14, 1968, at Clev.

Most Grand Slam Home Runs .... 2****, Jim Tabor, July 4, 1939, at Phil.; Rudy York, July 27, 1946, at St. L.

Most Total Bases .... 16**, Fred Lynn, June 18, 1975, at Det.

Most RBI .... 10, Rudy York, July 27, 1946, at St. L.; Norm Zauchin, May 27, 1955 vs. Wash.; Fred Lynn, June 18, 1975, at Det.

Batting in All Club's Runs (Most) 7, Ken Harrelson, June 14, 1968, at Clev.

Most Walks .... 6****, Jimmie Foxx, June 16, 1938, at St. L.

Most Intentional Walks .... 3, Carl Yastrzemski, April 17, 1968, vs. Chi.; Wade Boggs, April 10, 1990, vs. Det.

Most Strikeouts (9 innings) .... 5****, Ray Jarvis, April 20, 1969, vs. Clev.

Most Strikeouts (Extra innings) 6****, Cecil Cooper, June 14, 1974, at Calif.

Most Sacrifices .... 4****, Jack Barry, Aug. 21, 1916, vs. Clev.
Most Sacrifice Flies for RBI ...... 3****, Russ Nixon, Aug. 31, 1965, at Wash.

PITCHING, GAME

Shutout in First Major-League Game .... Done 9 times, last 3 Boo Ferriss,
                                                    April 29, 1945, at Phil.; Dave
                                                    Morehead, April 13, 1963, at Wash.;
                                                    Billy Rohr, April 14, 1967, at N.Y.
Least Hits Allowed First Game ...... 1****, Billy Rohr, April 14, 1967, at N.Y.
Most Balks................................4**, John Dopson, June 13, 1989, vs. Det.
Most Strikeouts .... 20***, Roger Clemens, April 29, 1986 (N), vs. Sea.
Most Consecutive Strikeouts.......... 8**, Roger Clemens, April 29, 1986 (N),
                                                    vs. Sea. (3 in 4th and 5th innings, 2 in 6th)
Most Innings .... 24**, Joe Harris, Sept. 1, 1906 (L 4–1), vs. Phil.
Most Innings in Relief .... 11, Ted Lewis, July 27, 1901 (L), at Chi.;
                                                    Babe Ruth, May 15, 1919 (W), at Chi.
Most Consecutive Scoreless .... 20*, Joe Harris, Sept. 1, 1906 (4th thru
                                                    23rd), vs. Phil.

BATTING, INNING

Most Times Faced Pitcher .... 3****, Ted Williams, July 4, 1948 (7th),
                                                    vs. Phil.; Sammy White, Gene Stephens, Tom
                                                    Umphlett, Johnny Lipon, George Kell, all on June
                                                    18, 1953 (7th), vs. Det.
Most Runs ....3****, Sammy White, June 18, 1953 (7th), vs. Det.
Most Hits .... 3****, Gene Stephens, June 18, 1953 (7th), vs. Det.
Most Pinch Hits .... 2****, Russ Nixon, May 4, 1962 (4th), vs. Chi.
Most Doubles .... 2****, Jody Reed, Sept. 8, 1991 (3rd), vs. Sea.
Most Home Runs ....2****, Bill Regan, June 16, 1928 (4th), at Chi.; Ellis
                                                    Burks, Aug. 27, 1990 (4th), at Clev.
Most RBI .... 6****, Tom McBride, Aug. 4, 1945 (4th inning, 2nd G.), at
                                                    Wash.; Carlos Quintana, July 30, 1991 (3rd), vs. Tex.
Home Run, First Major-League At-Bat ....Lefty LeFebvre, June 10, 1938,
                                                    vs. Chi.; Eddie Pellagrini, April 22,
                                                    1946, vs. Wash.

PITCHING, INNING

Most Batters Faced .... 16****, Merle Adkins, July 8, 1902 (6th), vs. Phil.;
Lefty O'Doul, July 7, 1923 (6th), vs. Clev.; Howard
Ehmke, Sept. 28, 1923 (6th), vs. N.Y.
Most Hits Allowed .... 12***, Merle Adkins, July 8, 1902 (6th), vs. Phil.
Most Runs Allowed .... 13***. Lefty O'Doul, July 7, 1923 (6th), vs. Clev.
Most Walks Allowed .... 6, Lefty O'Doul, July 7, 1923 (6th), vs. Clev.

*A.L. record
**Tied A.L. record
***Major-league record
****Tied major-league record

CLUB SEASON RECORDS

Most Players .... 48 in 1952
Fewest Players.. 18 in 1904
Most Games .... 163 in 1961, 1978, and 1985
Most Consecutive Games Without a Tie ....3,868*** (6/8/61 thru
7/30/85)
Most Extra-Inning Games Played in 1 Season .... 31 in 1943
Most At-Bats .... 5,720 in 1985 (163 games)
Most Runs .... 1,027 in 1950 (154 games)
Fewest Runs .... 463 in 1906 (154 games)
Most Hits... 1,665 in 1950 (154 games)
Fewest Hits .... 1,177 in 1905 (153 games)
Most Doubles .... 326 in 1989 (162 games)
Most Triples .... 113 in 1903 (141 games)
Most Home Runs .... 213 in 1977 (161 games)
Most Grand-Slam Home Runs ....9 in 1941, 1950, 1987
Most Home Runs by Pinch Hitters .... 6 in 1953
Most Times 5 or More Home Runs in 1 Game .... 8***, in 1977 (161 games)
Most Times 2 or More Consecutive Home Runs .... 16****, in 1977
(161 games)
Most Long Hits .... 538 in 1979 (160 games); 527 in 1977 (161 games)
Most Extra Bases on Long Hits .... 1,009 in 1977 (161 games)
Most Total Bases .. 2,560 in 1977 (161 games); 2,557 in 1950 (154 games)
Most Sacrifice Flies .... 59 in 1976 (152 games); 1977 (161 games);
1979 (160 games)

Most Stolen Bases .... 215 in 1909 (151 games)
Most Bases on Balls .... 835 in 1949 (155 games)
Most Strikeouts .... 1,020 in 1966 (162 games); 1967 (162 games)
Fewest Strikeouts .... 329 in 1921 (154 games)
Most Hit by Pitcher .... 66 in 1986 (161 games)
Fewest Hit by Pitcher .... 11 in 1934 (153 games)
Most Runs Batted In .... 974 in 1950 (154 games)
Highest Batting Average .... .302 in 1950 (154 games)
Lowest Batting Average .... .234 in 1905 (153 games); 1907 (155 games)
Highest Slugging Average .... .465 in 1977 (161 games)
Lowest Slugging Average .... .318 in 1916 (156 games); 1917 (157 games)
Most Grounded into Double plays .... 174***, in 1990 (162 games);
                                                                      169 in 1949 (155 games);
                                                                      1951 (154 games)
Fewest Grounded into Double plays .... 94 in 1942 (152 games)
Most Left on Base .... 1,308 in 1989 (162 games);
                                                                      1,304 in 1948 (155 games)
Fewest Left on Base .... 1,015 in 1929 (155 games)
Most .300 Hitters .... 9 in 1950
Most Players 100 Hits .... 9**** in 1984
Most Putouts .... 4,418 in 1978 (163 games)
Fewest Putouts .... 3,949 in 1938 (150 games)
Most Assists .... 2,195 in 1907 (155 games)
Fewest Assists.. 1,555 in 1964 (162 games)
Most Chances Accepted .... 6,425 in 1907 (155 games)
Fewest Chances Accepted .... 5,667 in 1938 (150 games)
Most Errors .... 373 in 1901 (137 games)
Fewest Errors.. 93 in 1988 (162 games)
Most Errorless Games .... 86 in 1971 (162 games); 1990 (162 games)
Most Consecutive Errorless Games .... 10 in 1986
Most Double plays .... 207 in 1949 (155 games)
Fewest Double plays .... 74 in 1913 (151 games)
Most Consecutive Games, 1 or More
    Double Plays ....25**** (38 double plays), 1951
Most DPs in Consecutive Games in
    Which DPs Were Made .... 38**** (25 games), 1951
Most Triple Plays ....3**** in 1979 (160 games)
Most Passed Balls .... 30 in 1987 (162 games)
Fewest Passed Balls .... 3 in 1975 (160 games); 1933 (149 games)
Highest Fielding Average .... .984 in 1988 (162 games)
Lowest Fielding Average .... .942 in 1901 (137 games)
Fewest Games Lost by 1 Run, Season .... 10*** in 1986 (won 24)
Most Games Won .... 105 in 1912

Most Games Won, Start of Season .... 6 in 1918
Most Games Won, Following All-Star Break .... 12 in 1988
Most Games Won, End of Season .... 8 in 1905; 1978
Most Games Lost .... 111 in 1932
Highest Percentage Games Won .... .691 in 1912 (won 105, lost 47)
Lowest Percentage Games Won .... .279 in 1932 (won 43, lost 111)
Games Won, league ....7,168 in 91 years
Games Lost, league ....6,872 in 91 years
Most Shutouts Won, Season .... 26 in 1918
Most Shutouts Lost, Season .... 28 in 1906
Most 1–0 Games Won .... 8 in 1918
Most 1–0 Games Lost .... 7 in 1909; 1914
Most Consecutive Games Won, Season .... 15 in 1946
Most Consecutive Games Lost, Season .... 20 in 1906
Most Consecutive Games Won, Home .... *24 in 1988
Most Times Finished First 12
Most Times Finished Second 14
Most Times Finished Last 10
Most Consecutive Games 1 or More
    Home Runs.. 14 (23 home runs) 1985

Note: Several records were set for some "fewest" categories in 1981; only 108
games in season.
*A.L. record
**Tied A.L. record
***Major-league record
****Tied major-league record

CLUB GAME, INNING RECORDS

BATTING, GAME

Most Times Faced Pitcher .... 64*, vs. St. L., June 8, 1950

Most Runs, One Club ....Boston 29**, St. Louis 4, June 8, 1950

Most Runs, Both Clubs ...... 36*, Boston 22, Philadelphia 14, June 29, 1950

Most Runs, Shutout .... Boston 19, Philadelphia 0, April 30, 1950

Most Runs by Opponent .... Cleveland 27, Boston 3, July 7, 1929

Most Runs, Shutout by Opponent .... Cleveland 19, Boston 0, May 18, 1955

Most Innings Scored, 9-Inning Game
(Scoring in every inning) ....8**, vs. Cleveland, Sept. 16, 1903
(did not bat in 9th)

Most Innings Scored, 9-Inning Game
(Scoring in every inning) by
Opponent .... 8**, by Chicago at Chi.,
May 11, 1949 (did not bat in 9th)

Most Runs to Overcome and Win .... 11 down, 1–12 vs. Clev.,
Aug. 28, 1950, won 15–14.

Most Spectacular Rally to Win .... down 5–12 vs. Wash., 1 on and 1 out
in 9th, June 18, 1961, won 13–12

Largest Lead Lost .... 10 runs up, vs. Tor., June 4, 1989, 10–0 after 6
innings, lost 13–11 in 12 innings

Most Hits, 1 Club ....28, vs. St. L., June 8, 1950

Most Hits, Both Clubs .... 45**, Phil. 27, Boston 18, July 8, 1902

Most Consecutive Hits, 1 Club ...... 10**, vs. Milw., June 2, 1901, 9th inning

Most Players 4 or More Hits .... 4**, vs. St. L., June 8, 1950

Most Singles, 1 Club .... 24****, vs. Det., June 18, 1953

Most Singles, Both Clubs .... 36****, Chicago 21, Boston 15, Aug. 15, 1922

Most Doubles, 1 Club .... 12*, at Det., July 29, 1990

Most Home Runs, 1 Club ....8, vs. Tor., July 4, 1977

Most HR, Season Opener, 1 Club .... 5****, vs. Wash. April 12, 1965

Most HR, Season Opener, Both Clubs .... 7****, vs. Wash. April 12, 1965

Most Players 2 or More HR, 1 Club .... 3****, vs. St. L., June 8, 1950

Most Players 1 or More HR, Both
Clubs ....9****, Min. 5, Boston 4, May 25, 1965;
Balt. 7, Boston 2, May 17, 1967; Boston 5, Milw. 4, May 22, 1977

Most HR Start of Game ....2**, vs. Minn., May 1, 1971 (Aparicio, Smith);
at Milw., June 20, 1973 (Miller, Smith); vs. N.Y.,
June 17, 1977 (Burleson, Lynn); vs. Clev.,
Sept. 5, 1985, 1st G. (Evans, Boggs)

Most HR, 9 Innings, None On ....7***, vs. Tor,, July 4, 1977

Most Grand Slams, 1 Club ....2****, vs. Chi., May 13, 1934 (Bucky
                                      Walters, Ed Morgan); vs. Phil., June 4, 1939
                                      (Jim Tabor 2); vs. St. L., July 27, 1946 (Rudy
                                      York 2); vs. Chi., May 10, 1960 (Vic Wertz,
                                      Rip Repulski); vs. Det., Aug. 7, 1984, G-1
                                      (Tony Armas, Bill Buckner); at Balt., June 10,
                                      1987 (Ellis Burks, Marty Barrett)

Most Runners Left on Base (9 Inning,
    SHO) ....14, vs. Oak., May 16, 1988
                                                              (L 3–0)
Most Total Bases ....60***, vs. St. L., June 8, 1950
Most Extra Base Hits ....17***, vs. St. L., June 8, 1950
Most RBI ....29***, vs. St. L., June 8, 1950
Most Strikeouts, 9 Innings ....19 vs. Calif., Aug. 12, 1974
Most Batters Walked, None Scored ....13 vs. Tex., May 18, 1986
Most Double plays Hit Into ....6*, vs. Minn., July 18, 1990
Most Triple Plays Hit Into .... 2***, vs. Minn., July 17, 1990

BATTING, INNING

Most Batters Facing Pitcher .... 23***, vs. Det., June 18, 1953 (7th)

Most Runs .... 17***, vs. Det., June 18, 1953 (7th)

Most Runs With 2 Out .... 11, at Clev., Aug. 21, 1986 (6th)

Most Runs With 2 Out, None On .... 9, vs. Milw., June 2, 1901 (9th)

Most Hits .... 14*, vs. Det., June 18, 1953 (7th)

Most Consecutive Hits .... 10****, vs. Milw., June 2, 1901 (9th)

Most Batters Reaching First Base, Consecutive .... 12, vs. Det., June 18, 1953 (7th)

Most Batters Reaching First Base .... 20***, vs. Det., June 18, 1953 (7th)

Most Triples .... 4, vs. Det., May 6, 1934 (4th)

Most Triples, Consecutive .... 4***, vs. Det., May 6, 1934 (4th)

Most Home Runs .... 4, vs. Phil., Sept. 24, 1940, G-1 (6th);
vs. Cleve., May 27, 1957 (6th);
at K.C., Aug. 26, 1957 (7th);
vs. N.Y., June 17, 1977 (1st);
vs. Tor., July 4, 1977 (8th);
vs. Milw., May 31, 1980 (4th)

Most Consecutive Home Runs .... 3, vs. Phil. Sept. 24, 1940, G-1 (6th); vs. Phil., April 19, 1948 (1st); vs. Det., June 6, 1948 (6th); vs. N.Y., Sept. 7, 1959 (7th); vs. Tor., July 4, 1977 (8th); vs. Sea., Aug. 13, 1977 (6th); vs. Milw., May 31, 1980 (4th)

Most Total Bases .... 25*, vs. Phil., Sept. 24, 1940, G-1 (6th)

Most Extra Base Hits .... 71****, vs. Phil., Sept. 24, 1940, G-1 (6th)

*A.L. record
**Tied A.L. record
***Major-league record
****Tied major-league record

YEARLY RESULTS

YEAR	PLACE	W–L	%	GAMES BEHIND OR AHEAD	ATTEN- DANCE	MANAGER	MULTI- MANAGER YEAR W–L
1901	2	79–59	.581	4	289,448	Jimmy Collins	
1902	3	77–60	.562	6.5	348,567	Jimmy Collins	
1903	1	91–47	.659	14.5	379,338	Jimmy Collins	
1904	1	95–59	.617	1.5	623,295*	Jimmy Collins	
1905	4	78–74	.513	16	466,828	Jimmy Collins	
1906	8	49–105	.318	45.5	410,209	Jimmy Collins,	44–92
						Chick Stahl	5–13
1907	7	59–90	.396	32.5	436,777	Cy Young,	3–4
						George Huff,	3–5
						Bob Unglaub,	8–20
						Deacon McGuire	45–61
1908	5	75–79	.487	15.5	473,048	Deacon McGuire,	53–62
						Fred Lake	22–17
1909	4	88–83	.583	9.5	668,965	Fred Lake	
1910	4	81–72	.529	22.5	584,619	Patsy Donovan	
1911	5	78–75	.510	24	503,961	Patsy Donovan	
1912	1	105–47	.691	14	597,096	Jake Stahl	
1913	4	79–71	.527	15.5	437,194	Jake Stahl,	39–41
						Bill Carrigan,	40–30
1914	2	91–62	.595	8.5	481,359*	Bill Carrigan	
1915	1	101–50	.669	2.5	539,885*	Bill Carrigan	
1916	1	91–63	.591	2	496,397	Bill Carrigan	
1917	2	90–62	.592	9	387,856	Jack Barry	
1918	1	75–51	.595	2.5	249,513	Ed Barrow	
1919	6	66–71	.482	20.5	417,291	Ed Barrow	
1920	5	72–81	.471	25.5	402,445	Ed Barrow	
1921	5	75–79	.487	23.5	279,273	Hugh Duffy	
1922	8	61–93	.396	33	259,184	Hugh Duffy	
1923	8	61–91	.401	37	229,668	Frank Chance	
1924	7	67–87	.436	25	448,556	Lee Fohl	
1925	8	47–105	.309	49.5	267,782	Lee Fohl	
1926	8	46–107	.301	44.5	285,155	Lee Fohl	

YEAR	PLACE	W–L	%	GAMES BEHIND OR AHEAD	ATTEN-DANCE	MANAGER	MULTI-MANAGER YEAR W–L
1927	8	51–103	.331	59	305,275	Bill Carrigan	
1928	8	57–96	.373	43.5	396,920	Bill Carrigan	
1929	8	58–96	.377	48	394,620	Bill Carrigan	
1930	8	52–102	.338	50	444,045	Heinie Wagner	
1931	6	62–90	.408	45	350,975	Shano Collins	
1932	8	43–111	.279	64	182,150	Shano Collins,	11–46
						Marty McManus	32–65
1933	7	63–86	.423	34.5	268,715	Marty McManus	
1934	4	76–76	.500	24	610,640	Bucky Harris	
1935	4	78–75	.516	16	558,568	Joe Cronin	
1936	6	74–80	.481	28.5	626,895	Joe Cronin	
1937	5	80–72	.526	21	559,659	Joe Cronin	
1938	2	88–61	.591	9.5	646,459	Joe Cronin	
1939	2	89–62	.589	17	573,070	Joe Cronin	
1940	4t	82–72	.532	8	716,234	Joe Cronin	
1941	2	84–70	.545	17	718,497	Joe Cronin	
1942	2	93–59	.612	9	730,340	Joe Cronin	
1943	7	68–84	.447	29	358,275	Joe Cronin	
1944	4	77–77	.500	12	506,975	Joe Cronin	
1945	7	71–83	.461	17.5	603,794	Joe Cronin	
1946	1	104–50	.675	12	1,416,944	Joe Cronin	
1947	3	83–71	.539	14	1,427,315	Joe Cronin	
1948	2***	96–59	.619	1	1,558,798	Joe McCarthy	
1949	2	96–58	.623	1	1,596,650	Joe McCarthy	
1950	3	94–60	.610	4	1,344,080	Joe McCarthy,	32–30
						Steve O'Neill	62–30
1951	3	87–67	.565	11	1,312,282	Steve O'Neill	
1952	6	76–78	.494	19	1,115,750	Lou Boudreau	
1953	4	84–69	.549	16	1,026,133	Lou Boudreau	
1954	4	69–85	.448	42	931,127	Lou Boudreau	
1955	4	84–70	.545	12	1,203,200	Pinky Higgins	
1956	4	84–70	.545	13	1,137,158	Pinky Higgins	
1957	3	82–72	.532	16	1,181,087	Pinky Higgins	
1958	3	79–75	.513	13	1,077,047	Pinky Higgins	

YEAR	PLACE	W–L	%	GAMES BEHIND OR AHEAD	ATTEN-DANCE	MANAGER	MULTI-MANAGER YEAR W–L
1959	5	75–79	.487	19	984,102	Pinky Higgins,	31–41
						Rudy York,	0–1
						Billy Jurges	44–38
1960	7	65–89	.422	32	1,129,866	Billy Jurges,	34–47
						Pinky Higgins	31–42
1961	6	76–86	.469	33	850,589	Pinky Higgins	
1962	8	76–84	.475	19	733,080	Pinky Higgins	
1963	7	76–85	.472	28	942,642	Johnny Pesky	
1964	8	72–90	.444	27	883,276	Johnny Pesky,	70–90
						Billy Herman	2–0
1965	9	62–100	.383	40	652,201	Billy Herman	
1966	9	72–90	.444	26	811,172	Billy Herman,	64–82
						Pete Runnels	8–8
1967	1	92–70	.568	1	1,727,832*	Dick Williams	
1968	4	86–76	.531	17	1,940,788	Dick Williams	
1969	3**	87–75	.537	22	1,833,246*	Dick Williams,	82–71
						Eddie Popowski	5–4
1970	3	87–75	.537	21	1,595,278*	Eddie Kasko	
1971	3	85–77	.525	18	1,678,732*	Eddie Kasko	
1972	2	85–70	.548	.5	1,441,718	Eddie Kasko	
1973	2	89–73	.549	8	1,481,002	Eddie Kasko	
1974	3	84–78	.519	7	1,566,411*	Darrell Johnson	
1975	1	95–65	.594	4.5	1,748,587*	Darrell Johnson	
1976	3	83–79	.512	15.5	1,895,846	Darrell Johnson,	41–45
						Don Zimmer	42–34
1977	2t	97–64	.602	2.5	2,074,549	Don Zimmer	
1978	2*	99–64	.607	1	2,320,643	Don Zimmer	
1979	3	91–69	.589	11.5	2,353,114	Don Zimmer	
1980	4	83–77	.519	19	1,956,092	Don Zimmer,	82–73
						Johnny Pesky	1–4
1981†	5	30–26	.536	4			
	2	29–23	.558	1.5	1,060,379	Ralph Houk	
1982	3	89–73	.549	6	1,950,124	Ralph Houk	
1983	6	78–84	.481	20	1,782,285	Ralph Houk	
1984	4	86–76	.531	18	1,661,618	Ralph Houk	
1985	5	81–81	.500	18.5	1,786,633	John McNamara	
1986	1	95–66	.590	5.5	2,147,641	John McNamara	

YEAR	PLACE	W–L	%	GAMES BEHIND OR AHEAD	ATTEN-DANCE	MANAGER	MULTI-MANAGER YEAR W–L
1987	5	78–84	.481	20	2,231,551	John McNamara	
1988	1	89–73	.549	1	2,464,851	John McNamara,	43–42
						Joe Morgan	46–31
1989	3	83–79	.512	6	2,510,012	Joe Morgan	
1990	1	88–74	.543	2	2,528,985	Joe Morgan	
1991	2t	84–78	.519	7	2,562,435	Joe Morgan	
1992	7	73–89	.451	23	2,468,574	Butch Hobson	

*Led league in attendance
**Beginning in 1969 the A.L. was split into two divisions with Boston in the Eastern Division
***Boston tied Cleveland for first but lost 1-game playoff
†1981 season split into first and second halves

YEARLY RESULTS

Manager Records (by wins)

		SEASONS	W–L	%
1.	Joe Cronin	13	1,071–916	.539
2.	Pinky Higgins	8	543–540	.501
3.	Bill Carrigan	6	489–500	.494
4.	Jimmy Collins	6	464–382	.562
5.	Don Zimmer	5	411–304	.575
6.	Eddie Kasko	4	346–295	.540
7.	Ralph Houk	4	312–282	.525
8.	Joe Morgan	3	301–262	.535
9.	John McNamara	4	297–273	.521
10.	Dick Williams	3	260–217	.545
11.	Lou Boudreau	3	229–227	.502
12.	Joe McCarthy	3	224–147	.604
13.	Darrell Johnson	3	220–188	.539
14.	Ed Barrow	3	213–203	.512
15.	Patsy Donovan	2	159–147	.520
16.	Lee Fohl	3	150–299	.334
17.	Steve O'Neill	2	149–97	.606
18.	Johnny Pesky	3	147–179	.451
19.	Jake Stahl	2	144–88	.621
20.	Hugh Duffy	2	136–172	.442
21.	Billy Herman	3	128–182	.413
22.	Fred Lake	2	110–100	.524
23.	Deacon McGuire	2	98–123	.443
24.	Marty McManus	2	95–151	.386
25.	Jack Barry	1	90–62	.592
26.	Billy Jurges	2	78–85	.479
27.	Bucky Harris	1	76–76	.500
28.	Butch Hobson	1	73–89	.451
29.	Shano Collins	2	73–136	.349
30.	Frank Chance	1	61–91	.401
31.	Heinie Wagner	1	52–102	.338
32.	Pete Runnels	1	8–8	.500
33.	Bob Unglaub	1	8–20	.286
34.	Eddie Popowski	1	5–4	.556
35.	Chick Stahl	1	5–13	.278
36.	Cy Young	1	3–4	.429

		SEASONS	W–L	%
37.	George Huff	1	3–5	.375
38.	Rudy York	1	0–1	.000

BOSTON RED SOX TOP 10 IN BATTING

GAMES

Carl Yastrzemski	3,308
Dwight Evans	2,505
Ted Williams	2,292
Jim Rice	2,089
Bobby Doerr	1,865
Harry Hooper	1,646
Wade Boggs	1,625
Rico Petrocelli	1,553
Dom DiMaggio	1,399
Frank Malzone	1,359

AT BATS

Carl Yastrzemski	11,988
Dwight Evans	8,726
Jim Rice	8,225
Ted Williams	7,706
Bobby Doerr	7,093
Harry Hooper	6,269
Wade Boggs	6,213
Dom DiMaggio	5,640
Rico Petrocelli	5,390
Frank Malzone	5,273

HITS

Carl Yastrzemski	3,419
Ted Williams	2,654
Jim Rice	2,452
Dwight Evans	2,373
Wade Boggs	2,098
Bobby Doerr	2,042
Harry Hooper	1,707
Dom DiMaggio	1,680
Frank Malzone	1,454
Rico Petrocelli	1,352

RUNS

Carl Yastrzemski	1,816
Ted Williams	1,798
Dwight Evans	1,435
Jim Rice	1,249
Bobby Doerr	1,094
Wade Boggs	1,067
Dom DiMaggio	1,046
Harry Hooper	988
Johnny Pesky	776
Jimmie Foxx	721

DOUBLES

Carl Yastrzemski	646
Ted Williams	525
Dwight Evans	474
Wade Boggs	422
Bobby Doerr	381
Jim Rice	373
Dom DiMaggio	308
Joe Cronin	270
Duffy Lewis	254
Billy Goodman	248

TRIPLES

Harry Hooper	130
Tris Speaker	106
Buck Freeman	91
Bobby Doerr	89
Larry Gardner	87
Jim Rice	79
Hobe Ferris	77
Dwight Evans	72
Ted Williams	71
Jimmy Collins	65

HOME RUNS

Ted Williams	521
Carl Yastrzemski	452
Jim Rice	382
Dwight Evans	379
Bobby Doerr	223
Jimmie Foxx	222
Rico Petrocelli	210
Jackie Jensen	170
Tony Conigliaro	162
Carlton Fisk	162

RBI

Carl Yastrzemski	1,844
Ted Williams	1,839
Jim Rice	1,451
Dwight Evans	1,346
Bobby Doerr	1,247
Jimmie Foxx	788
Rico Petrocelli	773
Joe Cronin	737
Jackie Jensen	733
Frank Malzone	716

BATTING AVERAGE (1,500 AT BATS)

Ted Williams	.344
Wade Boggs	.338
Tris Speaker	.337
Jimmie Foxx	.320
Pete Runnels	.320
Roy Johnson	.313
Johnny Pesky	.313
Mike Greenwell	.311
Fred Lynn	.308
Billy Goodman	.306

STOLEN BASES

Harry Hooper	300
Tris Speaker	266
Carl Yastrzemski	168
Heinie Wagner	141
Larry Gardner	134
Fred Parent	129
Tommy Harper	107
Billy Werber	107
Chick Stahl	105
Jimmy Collins	102
Duffy Lewis	102

BOSTON RED SOX TOP 10 PITCHING

GAMES

Bob Stanley	637
Ellis Kinder	365
Cy Young	327
Ike Delock	322
Bill Lee	321
Mel Parnell	289
Mike Fornieles	286
Dick Radatz	286
Luis Tiant	274
Roger Clemens	273

GAMES STARTED

Cy Young	297
Roger Clemens	272
Luis Tiant	238
Mel Parnell	232
Bill Monbouquette	228
Tom Brewer	217
Bruce Hurst	217
Joe Dobson	202
Frank Sullivan	201
Dennis Eckersley	191

COMPLETE GAMES

Cy Young	275
Bill Dinneen	156
George Winter	141
Smokey Joe Wood	121
Lefty Grove	119
Mel Parnell	113
Luis Tiant	113
Babe Ruth	105
Tex Hughson	99
Dutch Leonard	96

WINS

Cy Young	193
Roger Clemens	152
Mel Parnell	123
Luis Tiant	122
Smokey Joe Wood	116
Bob Stanley	115
Joe Dobson	106
Lefty Grove	105
Tex Hughson	96
Bill Monbouquette	96

LOSSES

Cy Young	112
Bob Stanley	97
Red Ruffing	96
George Winter	96
Jack Russell	94
Bill Monbouquette	91
Bill Dinneen	86
Tom Brewer	82
Luis Tiant	81
Frank Sullivan	80

WINNING PERCENTAGE
(100 DECISIONS)

Roger Clemens	.679
Smokey Joe Wood	.674
Babe Ruth	.659
Tex Hughson	.640
Cy Young	.633
Lefty Grove	.629
Ellis Kinder	.623
Mel Parnell	.621
Jesse Tannehill	.620
Wes Farrell	.608

INNINGS PITCHED

Cy Young	2,728
Roger Clemens	2,031
Luis Tiant	1,774
Mel Parnell	1,753
Bob Stanley	1,707
Bill Monbouquette	1,622
George Winter	1,600
Joe Dobson	1,544
Lefty Grove	1,540
Tom Brewer	1,509

SHUTOUTS

Cy Young	38
Roger Clemens	34
Smokey Joe Wood	28
Luis Tiant	26
Dutch Leonard	25
Mel Parnell	20
Ray Collins	19
Tex Hughson	19
Sad Sam Jones	18
Joe Dobson	17
Babe Ruth	17

STRIKEOUTS

Roger Clemens	1,873
Cy Young	1,341
Luis Tiant	1,075
Bruce Hurst	1,043
Smokey Joe Wood	990
Bill Monbouquette	969
Frank Sullivan	821
Ray Culp	794
Jim Lonborg	784
Dutch Leonard	771

WALKS

Mel Parnell	758
Tom Brewer	669
Joe Dobson	604
Jack Wilson	564
Roger Clemens	522
Willard Nixon	530
Ike Delock	514
Mickey McDermott	504
Luis Tiant	501
Fritz Ostermueller	491

ERA (1,000 IP)

Smokey Joe Wood	1.99
Cy Young	2.00
Dutch Leonard	2.11
Babe Ruth	2.19
Carl Mays	2.21
Ray Collins	2.51
Roger Clemens	2.80
Bill Dinneen	2.81
George Winter	2.91
Tex Hughson	2.94

SAVES

Bob Stanley	132
Dick Radatz	104
Ellis Kinder	91
Jeff Reardon	88
Sparky Lyle	69
Lee Smith	58
Bill Campbell	51
Mike Fornieles	48
Dick Drago	41
Tom Burgmeier	40

RED SOX YEARLY BASE-HIT LEADERS

YEAR	PLAYER	HITS	YEAR	PLAYER	HITS
1901	Jimmy Collins	185	1939	Ted Williams	185
1902	Buck Freeman	177	1940	Doc Cramer	*200
1903	Patsy Dougherty	*195	1941	Ted Williams	185
1904	Chick Stahl	173	1942	Johnny Pesky	*205
1905	Jesse Burkett	147	1943	Bobby Doerr	163
1906	Chick Stahl	170	1944	Bob Johnson	170
1907	Bunk Congalton	142	1945	Bob Johnson	148
1908	Harry Lord	145	1946	Johnny Pesky	*208
1909	Tris Speaker	168	1947	Johnny Pesky	*207
1910	Tris Speaker	183	1948	Ted Williams	188
1911	Tris Speaker	167	1949	Ted Williams	194
1912	Tris Speaker	222	1950	Dom DiMaggio	193
1913	Tris Speaker	190	1951	Dom DiMaggio	189
1914	Tris Speaker	*193	1952	Billy Goodman	157
1915	Tris Speaker	176	1953	Billy Goodman	161
1916	Harry Hooper	156	1954	Jackie Jensen	160
1917	Duffy Lewis	167	1955	Billy Goodman	176
1918	Harry Hooper	137	1956	Jackie Jensen	182
1919	Everett Scott	141	1957	Frank Malzone	185
1920	Harry Hooper	167	1958	Frank Malzone	185
1921	Stuffy McInnis	179	1959	Pete Runnels	176
1922	Del Pratt	183	1960	Pete Runnels	169
1923	George Burns	181	1961	Chuck Schilling	167
1924	Bill Wambsganss	174	1962	Carl Yastrzemski	191
1925	Ira Flagstead	160	1963	Carl Yastrzemski	*183
1926	Phil Todt	153	1964	Dick Stuart	168
1927	Buddy Myer	135	1965	Carl Yastrzemski	154
1928	Buddy Myer	168	1966	Carl Yastrzemski	165
1929	Russ Scarritt	159	1967	Carl Yastrzemski	*189
1930	Tom Oliver	189	1968	Carl Yastrzemski	162
1931	Earl Webb	196	1969	Reggie Smith	168
1932	Smead Jolley	164	1970	Carl Yastrzemski	186
1933	Roy Johnson	151	1971	Reggie Smith	175
1934	Billy Werber	200	1972	Tommy Harper	141
1935	Mel Almada	176	1973	Carl Yastrzemski	160
1936	Jimmie Foxx	198	1974	Carl Yastrzemski	155
1937	Joe Cronin	176	1975	Fred Lynn	175
1938	Joe Vosmik	*201	1976	Jim Rice	164

*Led league

YEAR	PLAYER	HITS	YEAR	PLAYER	HITS
1977	Jim Rice	206	1985	Wade Boggs	*240
1978	Jim Rice	*213	1986	Wade Boggs	207
1979	Jim Rice	201	1987	Wade Boggs	200
1980	Rick Burleson	179	1988	Wade Boggs	214
1981	Carney Lansford	134	1989	Wade Boggs	205
1982	Dwight Evans,		1990	Wade Boggs	187
	Jerry Remy	178	1991	Wade Boggs	181
1983	Wade Boggs	210	1992	Jody Reed	136
1984	Wade Boggs	203			

*Led league

RED SOX YEARLY LEADERS IN RUNS SCORED

YEAR	PLAYER	RUNS	YEAR	PLAYER	RUNS
1901	Jimmy Collins	109	1937	Jimmie Foxx	111
1902	Chick Stahl	92	1938	Jimmie Foxx	139
1903	Patsy Dougherty	*106	1939	Ted Williams	131
1904	Jimmy Collins,		1940	Ted Williams	*134
	Fred Parent	85	1941	Ted Williams	*135
1905	Jesse Burkett	78	1942	Ted Williams	*141
1906	Fred Parent	67	1943	Bobby Doerr	78
1907	Denny Sullivan	73	1944	Bob Johnson	106
1908	Amby McConnell	77	1945	Eddie Lake	81
1909	Harry Lord	86	1946	Ted Williams	*142
1910	Tris Speaker	92	1947	Ted Williams	*125
1911	Harry Hooper	93	1948	Dom DiMaggio	127
1912	Tris Speaker	136	1949	Ted Williams	*150
1913	Harry Hooper	100	1950	Dom DiMaggio	*131
1914	Tris Speaker	100	1951	Dom DiMaggio	*113
1915	Tris Speaker	108	1952	Dom DiMaggio	81
1916	Harry Hooper	75	1953	Jimmy Piersall	76
1917	Harry Hooper	89	1954	Ted Williams	93
1918	Harry Hooper	81	1955	Billy Goodman	100
1919	Babe Ruth	*103	1956	Billy Klaus,	
1920	Harry Hooper	91		Jimmy Piersall	91
1921	Nemo Leibold	88	1957	Jimmy Piersall	103
1922	Del Pratt	73	1958	Pete Runnels	103
1923	George Burns	91	1959	Jackie Jensen	101
1924	Ira Flagstead	106	1960	Pete Runnels	80
1925	Ira Flagstead	84	1961	Chuck Schilling	87
1926	Topper Rigney	71	1962	Carl Yastrzemski	99
1927	Ira Flagstead	63	1963	Carl Yastrzemski	91
1928	Ira Flagstead	84	1964	Eddie Bressoud	86
1929	Jack Rothrock	70	1965	Tony Conigliaro	82
1930	Tom Oliver	86	1966	Joe Foy	97
1931	Earl Webb	96	1967	Carl Yastrzemski	*112
1932	Roy Johnson	70	1968	Carl Yastrzemski	90
1933	Roy Johnson	88	1969	Carl Yastrzemski	96
1934	Billy Werber	129	1970	Carl Yastrzemski	*125
1935	Mel Almada	85	1971	Reggie Smith	85
1936	Jimmie Foxx	130	1972	Tommy Harper	92

*Led league

YEAR	PLAYER	RUNS	YEAR	PLAYER	RUNS
1973	Tommy Harper	92	1983	Wade Boggs	100
1974	Carl Yastrzemski	*93	1984	Dwight Evans	*121
1975	Fred Lynn	103	1985	Dwight Evans	110
1976	Carlton Fisk,		1986	Wade Boggs	107
	Fred Lynn	76	1987	Dwight Evans	109
1977	Carlton Fisk	106	1988	Wade Boggs	*128
1978	Jim Rice	121	1989	Wade Boggs	*113
1979	Jim Rice	117	1990	Wade Boggs,	
1980	Rick Burleson	89		Ellis Burks	89
1981	Dwight Evans	84	1991	Wade Boggs	93
1982	Dwight Evans	122	1992	Jody Reed	64

*Led league

RED SOX YEARLY LEADERS IN DOUBLES

YEAR	PLAYER	2B	YEAR	PLAYER	2B
1901	Jimmy Collins	42	1936	Eric McNair	36
1902	Buck Freeman	37	1937	Joe Cronin	40
1903	Buck Freeman	39	1938	Joe Cronin	*51
1904	Jimmy Collins	32	1939	Ted Williams	44
1905	Jimmy Collins	25	1940	Ted Williams	43
1906	Hobe Ferris	25	1941	Joe Cronin	38
1907	Hobe Ferris	25	1942	Dom DiMaggio	37
1908	Harry Lord	15	1943	Bobby Doerr	32
1909	Tris Speaker	26	1944	Bob Johnson	40
1910	Duffy Lewis	29	1945	Skeeter Newsome	30
1911	Tris Speaker	34	1946	Johnny Pesky	43
1912	Tris Speaker	*53	1947	Ted Williams	40
1913	Tris Speaker	35	1948	Ted Williams	*44
1914	Tris Speaker	*46	1949	Ted Williams	*39
1915	Duffy Lewis	31	1950	Vern Stephens	34
1916	Duffy Lewis,		1951	Dom DiMaggio	34
	Tilly Walker	29	1952	Billy Goodman	27
1917	Duffy Lewis	29	1953	George Kell	41
1918	Harry Hooper,		1954	Billy Goodman,	
	Babe Ruth	26		Jackie Jensen	25
1919	Babe Ruth	34	1955	Billy Goodman	31
1920	Harry Hooper	30	1956	Jimmy Piersall	*40
1921	Del Pratt	36	1957	Frank Malzone	31
1922	Del Pratt	44	1958	Pete Runnels	32
1923	George Burns	47	1959	Frank Malzone	34
1924	Bill Wambsganss	41	1960	Frank Malzone	30
1925	Ira Flagstead	38	1961	Carl Yastrzemski	31
1926	Baby Doll Jacobson	36	1962	Carl Yastrzemski	43
1927	Bill Regan	37	1963	Carl Yastrzemski	*40
1928	Ira Flagstead	41	1964	Eddie Bressoud	41
1929	Phil Todt	38	1965	Carl Yastrzemski	*45
1930	Bill Regan	35	1966	Carl Yastrzemski	*39
1931	Earl Webb	*67	1967	Carl Yastrzemski	31
1932	Urban Pickering	28	1968	Reggie Smith	*37
1933	Dusty Cooke	35	1969	Rico Petrocelli	32
1934	Roy Johnson	43	1970	Reggie Smith	32
1935	Joe Cronin	37	1971	Reggie Smith	*33

*Led league

YEAR	PLAYER	2B	YEAR	PLAYER	2B
1972	Tommy Harper	29	1983	Wade Boggs	44
1973	Orlando Cepeda,		1984	Dwight Evans	37
	Carl Yastrzemski	25	1985	Bill Buckner	46
1974	Carl Yastrzemski	25	1986	Wade Boggs	47
1975	Fred Lynn	*47	1987	Wade Boggs	40
1976	Dwight Evans	34	1988	Wade Boggs	*45
1977	Rick Burleson	36	1989	Wade Boggs	*51
1978	Carlton Fisk	39	1990	Jody Reed	*45
1979	Fred Lynn	42	1991	Jody Reed,	
1980	Dwight Evans	37		Wade Boggs	42
1981	Carney Lansford	23	1992	Tom Brunansky	31
1982	Dwight Evans	37			

*Led league

RED SOX YEARLY LEADERS IN TRIPLES

YEAR	PLAYER	3B	YEAR	PLAYER	3B
1901	Jimmy Collins,		1919	Babe Ruth	12
	Chick Stahl	16	1920	Harry Hooper	17
1902	Buck Freeman	20	1921	Shano Collins	12
1903	Buck Freeman	21	1922	Joe Harris	9
1904	Chick Stahl	*22	1923	Joe Harris	11
1905	Hobe Ferris	16	1924	Joe Harris,	
1906	Hobe Ferris	13		Bobby Veach	9
1907	Bob Unglaub	13	1925	Phil Todt	13
1908	Doc Gessler	14	1926	Phil Todt	12
1909	Tris Speaker	13	1927	Buddy Myer	11
1910	Jake Stahl	16	1928	Doug Taitt	14
1911	Tris Speaker	13	1929	Russ Scarritt	17
1912	Larry Gardner	18	1930	Bill Regan	10
1913	Tris Speaker	22	1931	Tom Oliver	5
1914	Larry Gardner	19	1932	Marv Olson	6
1915	Harry Hooper	13	1933	Dusty Cooke	10
1916	Harry Hooper,		1934	Roy Johnson,	
	Tilly Walker	11		Billy Werber	10
1917	Harry Hooper	11	1935	Joe Cronin	14
1918	Harry Hooper	13			

*Led league

YEAR	PLAYER	3B	YEAR	PLAYER	3B
1936	Jimmie Foxx,		1962	Lu Clinton	10
	Doc Cramer	8	1963	Lu Clinton	7
1937	Ben Chapman,		1964	Carl Yastrzemski	9
	Doc Cramer	11	1965	Lenny Green	6
1938	Jimmie Foxx	9	1966	Joe Foy	8
1939	Ted Williams	11	1967	George Scott	7
1940	Ted Williams	14	1968	Reggie Smith	5
1941	Lou Finney	10	1969	Reggie Smith	7
1942	Johnny Pesky	9	1970	Reggie Smith	7
1943	Tony Lupien	9	1971	John Kennedy	5
1944	Bobby Doerr	10	1972	Carlton Fisk	*9
1945	Bob Johnson,		1973	Rick Miller	7
	Tom McBride	7	1974	Dwight Evans	8
1946	Bobby Doerr	9	1975	Fred Lynn	7
1947	Bobby Doerr	10	1976	Fred Lynn,	
1948	Vern Stephens	8		Jim Rice	8
1949	Bobby Doerr	9	1977	Jim Rice	15
1950	Dom DiMaggio,		1978	Jim Rice	*15
	Bobby Doerr	*11	1979	Butch Hobson	7
1951	Johnny Pesky	6	1980	Jim Rice	6
1952	Hoot Evers,		1981	Dwight Evans	4
	Clyde Vollmer	4	1982	Dwight Evans	7
1953	Jimmy Piersall	9	1983	Wade Boggs	7
1954	Harry Agganis	8	1984	Dwight Evans	8
1955	Jackie Jensen	6	1985	Tony Armas,	
1956	Jackie Jensen	*11		Rich Gedman	5
1957	Frank Malzone,		1986	Tony Armas,	
	Jimmy Piersall	5		Marty Barrett	4
1958	Pete Runnells,		1987	Spike Owen	7
	Jimmy Piersall	5	1988	Mike Greenwell	8
1959	Pete Runnels	6	1989	Wade Boggs	7
1960	Don Buddin,		1990	Ellis Burks	8
	Lu Clinton	5	1991	Mike Greenwell	6
1961	Gary Geiger,		1992	Wade Boggs	4
	Carl Yastrzemski	6			

*Led league

RED SOX YEARLY LEADERS IN HOME RUNS

YEAR	PLAYER	HR	YEAR	PLAYER	HR
1901	Buck Freeman	12	1937	Jimmie Foxx	36
1902	Buck Freeman	11	1938	Jimmie Foxx	50
1903	Buck Freeman	*13	1939	Jimmie Foxx	*35
1904	Buck Freeman	7	1940	Jimmie Foxx	36
1905	Hobe Ferris	6	1941	Ted Williams	*37
1906	Chick Stahl	4	1942	Ted Williams	*36
1907	Hobe Ferris	4	1943	Bobby Doerr	16
1908	Doc Gessler	3	1944	Bob Johnson	17
1909	Tris Speaker	7	1945	Bob Johnson	12
1910	Jake Stahl	*10	1946	Ted Williams	38
1911	Tris Speaker	8	1947	Ted Williams	*32
1912	Tris Speaker	10	1948	Vern Stephens	29
1913	Harry Hooper	4	1949	Ted Williams	*43
1914	Tris Speaker	4	1950	Walt Dropo	34
1915	Babe Ruth	4	1951	Ted Williams	30
1916	Del Gainer,		1952	Dick Gernert	19
	Babe Ruth,		1953	Dick Gernert	21
	Tilly Walker	3	1954	Ted Williams	29
1917	Harry Hooper	3	1955	Ted Williams	28
1918	Babe Ruth	*11	1956	Ted Williams	24
1919	Babe Ruth	*29	1957	Ted Williams	38
1920	Harry Hooper	7	1958	Jackie Jensen	35
1921	Del Pratt	5	1959	Jackie Jensen	28
1922	George Burns	12	1960	Ted Williams	29
1923	Joe Harris	13	1961	Gary Geiger	18
1924	Ike Boone	13	1962	Frank Malzone	21
1925	Phil Todt	11	1963	Dick Stuart	42
1926	Phil Todt	7	1964	Dick Stuart	33
1927	Phil Todt	6	1965	Tony Conigliaro	*32
1928	Phil Todt	12	1966	Tony Conigliaro	28
1929	Jack Rothrock	6	1967	Carl Yastrzemski	*44
1930	Earl Webb	16	1968	Ken Harrelson	35
1931	Earl Webb	14	1969	Rico Petrocelli,	
1932	Smead Jolley	18		Carl Yastrzemski	40
1933	Roy Johnson	10	1970	Carl Yastrzemski	40
1934	Billy Werber	11	1971	Reggie Smith	30
1935	Billy Werber	14	1972	Carlton Fisk	22
1936	Jimmie Foxx	41	1973	Carlton Fisk	26

*Led league

YEAR	PLAYER	HR	YEAR	PLAYER	HR
1974	Rico Petrocelli,		1983	Jim Rice	*39
	Carl Yastrzemski	15	1984	Tony Armas	*43
1975	Jim Rice	22	1985	Dwight Evans	29
1976	Jim Rice	25	1986	Don Baylor	31
1977	Jim Rice	*39	1987	Dwight Evans	34
1978	Jim Rice	*46	1988	Rich Gedman,	
1979	Fred Lynn,			Mike Greenwell	22
	Jim Rice	39	1989	Nick Esasky	30
1980	Tony Perez	25	1990	Ellis Burks	21
1981	Dwight Evans	*22	1991	Jack Clark	28
1982	Dwight Evans	32	1992	Tom Brunansky	15

*Led league

RED SOX YEARLY LEADERS IN RBI

YEAR	PLAYER	RBI	YEAR	PLAYER	RBI
1901	Buck Freeman	114	1938	Jimmie Foxx	*175
1902	Buck Freeman	*121	1939	Ted Williams	*145
1903	Buck Freeman	*104	1940	Jimmie Foxx	119
1904	Buck Freeman	84	1941	Ted Williams	120
1905	Jimmy Collins	65	1942	Ted Williams	*137
1906	Chick Stahl	51	1943	Jim Tabor	85
1907	Bob Unglaub	62	1944	Bob Johnson	106
1908	Doc Gessler	63	1945	Bob Johnson	74
1909	Tris Speaker	77	1946	Ted Williams	123
1910	Jake Stahl	77	1947	Ted Williams	*114
1911	Duffy Lewis	86	1948	Vern Stephens	137
1912	Duffy Lewis	109	1949	Vern Stephens,	
1913	Duffy Lewis	90		Ted Williams	*159
1914	Tris Speaker	90	1950	Walt Dropo,	
1915	Duffy Lewis	76		Vern Stephens	*144
1916	Larry Gardner	62	1951	Ted Williams	126
1917	Duffy Lewis	65	1952	Dick Gernert	67
1918	Babe Ruth	66	1953	George Kell	73
1919	Babe Ruth	*114	1954	Jackie Jensen	117
1920	Jim Hendryx	73	1955	Jackie Jensen	*116
1921	Del Pratt	100	1956	Jackie Jensen	97
1922	Del Pratt	86	1957	Jackie Jensen,	
1923	George Burns	82		Frank Malzone	103
1924	Bobby Veach	99	1958	Jackie Jensen	*122
1925	Phil Todt	75	1959	Jackie Jensen	*112
1926	Baby Doll Jacobson,		1960	Vic Wertz	103
	Phil Todt	69	1961	Frank Malzone	87
1927	Ira Flagstead	69	1962	Frank Malzone	95
1928	Phil Todt	73	1963	Dick Stuart	*118
1929	Russ Scarritt	72	1964	Dick Stuart	114
1930	Earl Webb	66	1965	Felix Mantilla	92
1931	Earl Webb	103	1966	Tony Conigliaro	93
1932	Smead Jolley	99	1967	Carl Yastrzemski	*121
1933	Roy Johnson	95	1968	Ken Harrelson	109
1934	Roy Johnson	119	1969	Carl Yastrzemski	111
1935	Joe Cronin	95	1970	Tony Conigliaro	116
1936	Jimmie Foxx	143	1971	Reggie Smith	96
1937	Jimmie Foxx	127	1972	Rico Petrocelli	75

*Led league

YEAR	PLAYER	RBI	YEAR	PLAYER	RBI
1973	Carl Yastrzemski	95	1983	Jim Rice	126
1974	Carl Yastrzemski	79	1984	Tony Armas	*123
1975	Fred Lynn	105	1985	Bill Buckner	110
1976	Carl Yastrzemski	102	1986	Jim Rice	110
1977	Jim Rice	114	1987	Dwight Evans	123
1978	Jim Rice	*139	1988	Mike Greenwell	119
1979	Jim Rice	130	1989	Nick Esasky	108
1980	Tony Perez	105	1990	Ellis Burks	89
1981	Dwight Evans	71	1991	Mike Greenwell	83
1982	Dwight Evans	98	1992	Tom Brunansky	74

*Led league

RED SOX YEARLY LEADERS IN BATTING

YEAR	PLAYER	BA	YEAR	PLAYER	BA
1901	Buck Freeman	.346	1938	Jimmie Foxx	*.349
1902	Patsy Dougherty	.342	1939	Jimmie Foxx	.360
1903	Patsy Dougherty	.331	1940	Ted Williams	.344
1904	Chick Stahl	.294	1941	Ted Williams	*.406
1905	Jimmy Collins	.276	1942	Ted Williams	*.356
1906	Moose Grimshaw	.290	1943	Pete Fox	.288
1907	Bunk Congalton	.286	1944	Bobby Doerr	.325
1908	Doc Gessler	.308	1945	Johnny Lazor	.310
1909	Harry Lord	.311	1946	Ted Williams	.342
1910	Tris Speaker	.340	1947	Ted Williams	*.343
1911	Tris Speaker	.327	1948	Ted Williams	*.369
1912	Tris Speaker	.383	1949	Ted Williams	.343
1913	Tris Speaker	.365	1950	Billy Goodman	*.354
1914	Tris Speaker	.338	1951	Ted Williams	.318
1915	Tris Speaker	.322	1952	Billy Goodman	.306
1916	Larry Gardner	.308	1953	Billy Goodman	.313
1917	Duffy Lewis	.302	1954	Ted Williams	.345
1918	Harry Hooper	.289	1955	Billy Goodman	.294
1919	Babe Ruth	.322	1956	Ted Williams	.345
1920	Harry Hooper	.312	1957	Ted Williams	*.388
1921	Del Pratt	.324	1958	Ted Williams	*.328
1922	Joe Harris	.316	1959	Pete Runnels	.314
1923	Joe Harris	.339	1960	Pete Runnels	*.320
1924	Ike Boone	.333	1961	Frank Malzone,	
1925	Ike Boone	.330		Carl Yastrzemski	.266
1926	Ira Flagstead	.299	1962	Pete Runnels	*.326
1927	Buddy Myer	.288	1963	Carl Yastrzemski	*.321
1928	Buddy Myer	.313	1964	Eddie Bressoud	.293
1929	Jack Rothrock	.300	1965	Carl Yastrzemski	.312
1930	Earl Webb	.323	1966	Carl Yastrzemski	.278
1931	Earl Webb	.333	1967	Carl Yastrzemski	*.326
1932	Dale Alexander	*†.372	1968	Carl Yastrzemski	*.301
1933	Roy Johnson	.313	1969	Reggie Smith	.309
1934	Billy Werber	.321	1970	Carl Yastrzemski	.329
1935	Roy Johnson	.315	1971	Reggie Smith	.283
1936	Jimmie Foxx	.338	1972	Carlton Fisk	.293
1937	Ben Chapman	.307	1973	Carl Yastrzemski	.296

*Led league
†Alexander began season with Detroit; combined BA .367

YEAR	PLAYER	BA	YEAR	PLAYER	BA
1974	Carl Yastrzemski	.301	1984	Wade Boggs	.325
1975	Fred Lynn	.331	1985	Wade Boggs	*.368
1976	Fred Lynn	.314	1986	Wade Boggs	*.357
1977	Jim Rice	.320	1987	Wade Boggs	*.363
1978	Jim Rice	.315	1988	Wade Boggs	*.366
1979	Fred Lynn	*.333	1989	Wade Boggs	.330
1980	Jim Rice	.294	1990	Wade Boggs	.302
1981	Carney Lansford	*.336	1991	Wade Boggs	.332
1982	Jim Rice	.309	1992	Tom Brunansky	.266
1983	Wade Boggs	*.361			

*Led league

RED SOX YEARLY LEADERS IN STOLEN BASES

YEAR	PLAYER	SB	YEAR	PLAYER	SB
1901	Tommy Dowd	33	1936	Billy Werber	23
1902	Patsy Dougherty	20	1937	Ben Chapman	*†27
1903	Patsy Dougherty	35	1938	Ben Chapman	13
1904	Fred Parent	20	1939	Jim Tabor	16
1905	Fred Parent	25	1940	Jim Tabor	14
1906	Fred Parent	16	1941	Jim Tabor	17
1907	Heinie Wagner	20	1942	Dom DiMaggio	16
1908	Amby McConnell	31	1943	Pete Fox	22
1909	Harry Lord	36	1944	George Metkovich	13
1910	Harry Hooper	40	1945	George Metkovich	19
1911	Harry Hooper	38	1946	Dom DiMaggio	10
1912	Tris Speaker	52	1947	Johnny Pesky	12
1913	Tris Speaker	46	1948	Dom DiMaggio	10
1914	Tris Speaker	42	1949	Dom DiMaggio	9
1915	Tris Speaker	29	1950	Dom DiMaggio	*15
1916	Harry Hooper	27	1951	Billy Goodman	7
1917	Harry Hooper	21	1952	Faye Throneberry	16
1918	Harry Hooper	24	1953	Jimmy Piersall	11
1919	Harry Hooper	23	1954	Jackie Jensen	*22
1920	Mike Menosky	23	1955	Jackie Jensen	16
1921	Shano Collins	15	1956	Jackie Jensen	11
1922	Mike Menosky	9	1957	Jimmy Piersall	14
1923	Norm McMillan	13	1958	Jimmy Piersall	12
1924	Bill Wambsganss	14	1959	Jackie Jensen	20
1925	Homer Ezzell,		1960	Pete Runnels,	
	Doc Prothro	9		Gene Stephens	5
1926	Fred Haney	13	1961	Gary Geiger	16
1927	Ira Flagstead	12	1962	Gary Geiger	18
1928	Buddy Myer	*30	1963	Gary Geiger	9
1929	Jack Rothrock	23	1964	Dalton Jones,	
1930	Tom Oliver,			Carl Yastrzemski	6
	Bobby Reeves	6	1965	Lenny Green,	
1931	Jack Rothrock	31		Dalton Jones	8
1932	Roy Johnson	13	1966	Jose Tartabull	11
1933	Roy Johnson	13	1967	Reggie Smith	16
1934	Billy Werber	*40	1968	Joe Foy	26
1935	Billy Werber	*29	1969	Carl Yastrzemski	15

*Led league
†Chapman stole 8 bases with Washington

YEAR	PLAYER	SB
1970	Carl Yastrzemski	23
1971	Doug Griffin,	
	Reggie Smith	11
1972	Tommy Harper	25
1973	Tommy Harper	*54
1974	Tommy Harper	28
1975	Fred Lynn,	
	Jim Rice	10
1976	Rick Burleson,	
	Fred Lynn	14
1977	Rick Burleson	13
1978	Jerry Remy	30
1979	Jerry Remy	14

YEAR	PLAYER	SB
1980	Jerry Remy	14
1981	Carney Lansford	15
1982	Jerry Remy	16
1983	Jerry Remy	11
1984	Jackie Gutierrez	12
1985	Bill Buckner	18
1986	Marty Barrett	15
1987	Ellis Burks	27
1988	Ellis Burks	25
1989	Ellis Burks	21
1990	Ellis Burks	9
1991	Mike Greenwell	15
1992	Jody Reed	7

*Led league

RED SOX WIN LEADERS, YEAR BY YEAR

YEAR	PITCHER	W	YEAR	PITCHER	W
1901	Cy Young	*33	1937	Lefty Grove	17
1902	Cy Young	*32	1938	Jim Bagby,	
1903	Cy Young	*28		Jack Wilson	15
1904	Cy Young	26	1939	Lefty Grove	15
1905	Jesse Tannehill	22	1940	Joe Heving,	
1906	Jesse Tannehill,			Jack Wilson	12
	Cy Young	13	1941	Dick Newsome	19
1907	Cy Young	22	1942	Tex Hughson	*22
1908	Cy Young	21	1943	Tex Hughson	12
1909	Frank Arellanes	16	1944	Tex Hughson	18
1910	Eddie Cicotte	15	1945	Boo Ferriss	21
1911	Smokey Joe Wood	23	1946	Boo Ferriss	25
1912	Smokey Joe Wood	*34	1947	Joe Dobson	18
1913	Ray Collins	19	1948	Jack Kramer	18
1914	Ray Collins	20	1949	Mel Parnell	*25
1915	Rube Foster	20	1950	Mel Parnell	18
1916	Babe Ruth	23	1951	Mel Parnell	18
1917	Babe Ruth	24	1952	Mel Parnell	12
1918	Carl Mays	21	1953	Mel Parnell	21
1919	Herb Pennock	16	1954	Frank Sullivan	15
1920	Herb Pennock	16	1955	Frank Sullivan	*18
1921	Sad Sam Jones	23	1956	Tom Brewer	19
1922	Ray Collins	14	1957	Tom Brewer	16
1923	Howard Ehmke	20	1958	Ike Delock	14
1924	Howard Ehmke	19	1959	Jerry Casale	13
1925	Ted Wingfield	12	1960	Bill Monbouquette	14
1926	Ted Wingfield	11	1961	Don Schwall	15
1927	Slim Harriss	14	1962	Gene Conley,	
1928	Ed Morris	19		Bill Monbouquette	15
1929	Ed Morris	17	1963	Bill Monbouquette	20
1930	Milt Gaston	13	1964	Dick Radatz	16
1931	Danny MacFayden	16	1965	Earl Wilson	13
1932	Bob Kline	11	1966	Jose Santiago	12
1933	Gordon Rhodes	12	1967	Jim Lonborg	*22
1934	Wes Ferrell	14	1968	Ray Culp,	
1935	Wes Ferrell	*25		Dick Ellsworth	16
1936	Wes Ferrell	20	1969	Ray Culp	17

*Led league

YEAR	PITCHER	W		YEAR	PITCHER	W
1970	Ray Culp	17		1983	John Tudor	13
1971	Sonny Siebert	16		1984	Oil Can Boyd,	
1972	Marty Patton	17			Bruce Hurst,	
1973	Luis Tiant	20			Bob Ojeda	12
1974	Luis Tiant	22		1985	Oil Can Boyd	15
1975	Rick Wise	19		1986	Roger Clemens	*24
1976	Luis Tiant	21		1987	Roger Clemens	*20
1977	Bill Campbell	13		1988	Roger Clemens,	
1978	Dennis Eckersley	20			Bruce Hurst	18
1979	Dennis Eckersley	17		1989	Roger Clemens	17
1980	Dennis Eckersley	12		1990	Roger Clemens	21
1981	Bill Stanley,			1991	Roger Clemens	18
	Mike Torrez	10		1992	Roger Clemens	18
1982	Mark Clear	14				

*Led league

RED SOX LOSS LEADERS, YEAR BY YEAR

YEAR	PITCHER	L	YEAR	PITCHER	L
1901	Ted Lewis	16	1931	Jack Russell	18
1902	Bill Dinneen	*21	1932	Bob Weiland	16
1903	Bill Dinneen,		1933	Gordon Rhodes	15
	Norwood Gibson	11	1934	Johnny Welch	15
1904	Cy Young	16	1935	Wes Ferrell	14
1905	Cy Young	19	1936	Fritz Ostermueller	16
1906	Joe Harris,		1937	Johnny Marcum	11
	Cy Young	*21	1938	Jack Wilson	15
1907	George Winter	16	1939	Jack Wilson	11
1908	George Winter	14	1940	Jim Bagby	16
1909	Frank Arellanes	12	1941	Mickey Harris	14
1910	Smokey Joe Wood	13	1942	Charlie Wagner	11
1911	Smokey Joe Wood	17	1943	Tex Hughson	15
1912	Buck O'Brien	13	1944	Emmett O'Neill	11
1913	Dutch Leonard	16	1945	Emmett O'Neill	11
1914	Ray Collins	13	1946	Tex Hughson	11
1915	Rube Foster,		1947	Boo Ferriss,	
	Ernie Shore	8		Tex Hughson,	
1916	Carl Mays	13		Earl Johnson	11
1917	Dutch Leonard	17	1948	Joe Dobson	10
1918	Bullet Joe Bush	15		Mickey Harris	10
1919	Sad Sam Jones	20	1949	Joe Dobson	12
1920	Sad Sam Jones	16	1950	Ellis Kinder	12
1921	Sad Sam Jones	16	1951	Mel Parnell	11
1922	Herb Pennock	17	1952	Mel Parnell	12
1923	Howard Ehmke,		1953	Mickey McDermott	10
	Bill Piercy,		1954	Willard Nixon,	
	Jack Quinn	17		Frank Sullivan	12
1924	Howard Ehmke,		1955	Frank Sullivan	13
	Alex Ferguson	*17	1956	Bob Porterfield	12
1925	Howard Ehmke	20	1957	Tom Brewer,	
1926	Paul Zahniser	*18		Willard Nixon	13
1927	Slim Harriss	*21	1958	Tom Brewer	12
1928	Red Ruffing	*25	1959	Tom Brewer	12
1929	Red Ruffing	*22	1960	Frank Sullivan	16
1930	Milt Gaston,		1961	Gene Conley,	
	Jack Russell	*20		Bill Monbouquette	14

*Led league

YEAR	PITCHER	L	YEAR	PITCHER	L
1962	Don Schwall	15	1979	Mike Torrez	13
1963	Earl Wilson	16	1980	Mike Torrez	16
1964	Dave Morehead	15	1981	Frank Tanana	10
1965	Bill Monbouquette,		1982	Dennis Eckersley	13
	Dave Morehead	*18	1983	Dennis Eckersley	13
1966	Jose Santiago	13	1984	Oil Can Boyd,	
1967	Darrell Brandon	11		Bruce Hurst,	
1968	Gary Bell	11		Bob Ojeda	12
1969	Jim Lonborg	11	1985	Oil Can Boyd,	
1970	Ray Culp	14		Bruce Hurst	13
1971	Ray Culp	16	1986	Al Nipper	12
1972	Marty Pattin	13	1987	Bill Stanley	15
1973	Marty Pattin	15	1988	Roger Clemens	12
1974	Bill Lee	15	1989	Mike Smithson	14
1975	Luis Tiant	14	1990	Greg Harris,	
1976	Luis Tiant,			Dana Kiecker	9
	Jim Willoughby	12	1991	Greg Harris	12
1977	Ferguson Jenkins	10	1992	Frank Viola	12
1978	Mike Torrez	13			

*Led league

RED SOX COMPLETE GAMES LEADERS, YEAR BY YEAR

YEAR	PITCHER	CG	YEAR	PITCHER	CG
1901	Cy Young	38	1935	Wes Ferrell	*31
1902	Cy Young	*41	1936	Wes Ferrell	*28
1903	Cy Young	*34	1937	Lefty Grove	21
1904	Cy Young	40	1938	Lefty Grove	12
1905	Cy Young	32	1939	Lefty Grove	17
1906	Cy Young	28	1940	Lefty Grove,	
1907	Cy Young	33		Jack Wilson	9
1908	Cy Young	30	1941	Dick Newsome	17
1909	Frank Arellanes	17	1942	Tex Hughson	*22
1910	Eddie Cicotte	20	1943	Tex Hughson	*20
1911	Smokey Joe Wood	25	1944	Tex Hughson	19
1912	Smokey Joe Wood	*35	1945	Boo Ferriss	26
1913	Hugh Bedient,		1946	Boo Ferriss	26
	Ray Collins	19	1947	Joe Dobson	15
1914	Rube Foster,		1948	Joe Dobson,	
	Dutch Leonard	17		Mel Parnell	16
1915	Rube Foster	22	1949	Mel Parnell	*27
1916	Babe Ruth	23	1950	Mel Parnell	21
1917	Babe Ruth	*35	1951	Mel Parnell	11
1918	Carl Mays	*30	1952	Mel Parnell	15
1919	Sad Sam Jones	21	1953	Mel Parnell	12
1920	Sad Sam Jones	20	1954	Frank Sullivan	11
1921	Sad Sam Jones	25	1955	Frank Sullivan	16
1922	Jack Quinn	16	1956	Tom Brewer	15
1923	Howard Ehmke	28	1957	Tom Brewer	15
1924	Howard Ehmke	26	1958	Tom Brewer,	
1925	Howard Ehmke	22		Frank Sullivan	10
1926	Hal Wiltse,		1959	Tom Brewer	11
	Ted Wingfield	9	1960	Bill Monbouquette	12
1927	Hal Wiltse	13	1961	Bill Monbouquette	12
1928	Red Ruffing	*25	1962	Bill Monbouquette	11
1929	Milt Gaston	20	1963	Bill Monbouquette	13
1930	Milt Gaston	20	1964	Bill Monbouquette	7
1931	Danny MacFayden	17	1965	Bill Monbouquette	10
1932	Ivy Andrews	8	1966	Lee Stange	8
1933	Gordon Rhodes	14	1967	Jim Lonborg	15
1934	Wes Ferrell	17	1968	Jim Lonborg	22

*Led league

YEAR	PITCHER	CG	YEAR	PITCHER	CG
1969	Ray Culp	17	1981	Dennis Eckersley	8
1970	Ray Culp	15	1982	Dennis Eckersley	11
1971	Ray Culp,		1983	John Tudor	7
	Sonny Siebert	12	1984	Oil Can Boyd	10
1972	Marty Pattin	13	1985	Oil Can Boyd	13
1973	Luis Tiant	23	1986	Bruce Hurst	11
1974	Luis Tiant	25	1987	Roger Clemens	*18
1975	Luis Tiant	18	1988	Roger Clemens	*14
1976	Luis Tiant	19	1989	Roger Clemens	8
1977	Ferguson Jenkins	11	1990	Roger Clemens	7
1978	Dennis Eckersley	16	1991	Roger Clemens	13
1979	Dennis Eckersley	17	1992	Roger Clemens	11
1980	Dennis Eckersley	8			

*Led league

RED SOX SHUTOUT LEADERS, YEAR BY YEAR

YEAR	PITCHER	SH
1901	Cy Young	*5
1902	Cy Young	3
1903	Cy Young	*7
1904	Cy Young	*10
1905	Jesse Tannehill	6
1906	Jesse Tannehill	2
1907	Cy Young	6
1908	Cy Young	3
1909	Smokey Joe Wood	4
1910	Ray Collins	4
1911	Smokey Joe Wood	5
1912	Smokey Joe Wood	*10
1913	Ray Collins, Earl Moseley	3
1914	Ray Collins, Dutch Leonard	7
1915	Rube Foster	5
1916	Babe Ruth	*9
1917	Babe Ruth	6
1918	Carl Mays	*8
1919	Sad Sam Jones, Herb Pennock	5
1920	Herb Pennock	4
1921	Sad Sam Jones	*5
1922	Jack Quinn	4
1923	Howard Ehmke	2
1924	Howard Ehmke	4
1925	Red Ruffing	3
1926	Howard Ehmke, Slim Harris, Tony Welzer, Hal Wiltse, Ted Wingfield, Paul Zahniser	1
1927	Del Lundgren	2
1928	Jack Russell	2
1929	Danny MacFayden	4

YEAR	PITCHER	SH
1930	Milt Gaston	2
1931	Ed Durham	2
1932	Bob Kline, Johnny Welch	1
1933	Lloyd Brown, George Pipgras	2
1934	Wes Ferrell	3
1935	Wes Ferrell	3
1936	Lefty Grove	*6
1937	Lefty Grove	2
1938	Jack Wilson	3
1939	Lefty Grove	2
1940	Jim Bagby, Lefty Grove, Herb Hash	1
1941	Charlie Wagner	3
1942	Tex Hughson	4
1943	Tex Hughson	4
1944	Tex Hughson	2
1945	Boo Ferriss	5
1946	Boo Ferriss, Tex Hughson	6
1947	Denny Galehouse, Tex Hughson, Earl Johnson	3
1948	Joe Dobson	5
1949	Ellis Kinder	*6
1950	Mel Parnell	2
1951	Mel Parnell	3
1952	Mel Parnell	3
1953	Mel Parnell	5
1954	Frank Sullivan	3
1955	Willard Nixon, Frank Sullivan	3
1956	Tom Brewer	4
1957	Frank Sullivan	3
1958	Frank Sullivan	2

*Led league

YEAR	PITCHER	SH	YEAR	PITCHER	SH
1959	Tom Brewer,		1976	Rick Wise	4
	Jerry Casale	3	1977	Luis Tiant	3
1960	Bill Monbouquette	3	1978	Luis Tiant	5
1961	Gene Conley,		1979	Bill Stanley	4
	Don Schwall	2	1980	Chuck Rainey,	
1962	Bill Monbouquette	4		Bill Stanley,	
1963	Earl Wilson	3		Mike Torrez	1
1964	Bill Monbouquette	5	1981	Dennis Eckersley	2
1965	Bill Monbouquette,		1982	Dennis Eckersley	3
	Dave Morehead	2		Chuck Rainey	3
1966	Darrell Brandon,		1983	Bruce Hurst	2
	Lee Stange	2		John Tudor	2
1967	Jim Lonborg	2	1984	Bob Ojeda	5
	Lee Stange	2	1985	Oil Can Boyd	3
1968	Ray Culp	6	1986	Bruce Hurst	4
1969	Ray Culp	2	1987	Roger Clemens	*7
1970	Gary Peters	4	1988	Roger Clemens	*8
1971	Sonny Siebert	4	1989	Roger Clemens	3
1972	Luis Tiant	6	1990	Roger Clemens	*4
1973	John Curtis	4	1991	Roger Clemens	*4
1974	Luis Tiant	*7	1992	Roger Clemens	*5
1975	Bill Lee	4			

*Led league

RED SOX ERA LEADERS, YEAR BY YEAR

YEAR	PITCHER	ERA	YEAR	PITCHER	ERA
1901	Cy Young	*1.63	1939	Lefty Grove	*2.54
1902	Cy Young	2.15	1940	Lefty Grove	4.00
1903	Cy Young	2.08	1941	Charlie Wagner	3.08
1904	Cy Young	1.97	1942	Tex Hughson	2.59
1905	Cy Young	1.82	1943	Tex Hughson	2.64
1906	Bill Dinneen	2.92	1944	Tex Hughson	2.26
1907	Cy Morgan	1.97	1945	Boo Ferriss	2.95
1908	Cy Young	1.26	1946	Tex Hughson	2.75
1909	Eddie Cicotte	1.97	1947	Joe Dobson	2.95
1910	Ray Collins	1.62	1948	Mel Parnell	3.14
1911	Smokey Joe Wood	2.02	1949	Mel Parnell	*2.78
1912	Smokey Joe Wood	1.91	1950	Mel Parnell	3.61
1913	Smokey Joe Wood	2.29	1951	Mel Parnell	3.26
1914	Dutch Leonard	*1.00	1952	Mel Parnell	3.62
1915	Smokey Joe Wood	*1.49	1953	Mickey McDermott	3.01
1916	Babe Ruth	*1.75	1954	Frank Sullivan	3.15
1917	Carl Mays	1.74	1955	Frank Sullivan	2.91
1918	Bullet Joe Bush	2.11	1956	Frank Sullivan	3.42
1919	Carl Mays	2.48	1957	Frank Sullivan	2.73
1920	Harry Harper	2.13	1958	Ike Delock	3.38
1921	Sad Sam Jones	3.22	1959	Tom Brewer	3.77
1922	Jack Quinn	3.48	1960	Bill Monbouquette	3.64
1923	Bill Piercy	3.42	1961	Don Schwall	3.32
1924	Jack Quinn	3.26	1962	Bill Monbouquette	3.33
1925	Howard Ehmke	3.69	1963	Earl Wilson	3.75
1926	Hal Wiltse	4.22	1964	Bill Monbouquette	4.04
1927	Slim Harriss	4.17	1965	Bill Monbouquette	3.69
1928	Ed Morris	3.52	1966	Jose Santiago	3.66
1929	Danny MacFayden	3.62	1967	Lee Stange	2.77
1930	Milt Gaston	3.92	1968	Ray Culp	2.92
1931	Wilcy Moore	3.89	1969	Mike Nagy	3.11
1932	Ivy Andrews	3.80	1970	Ray Culp	3.05
1933	Bob Weiland	3.87	1971	Sonny Siebert	2.91
1934	Fritz Ostermueller	3.48	1972	Luis Tiant	*1.91
1935	Lefty Grove	*2.70	1973	Bill Lee	2.75
1936	Lefty Grove	*2.81	1974	Luis Tiant	2.92
1937	Lefty Grove	3.02	1975	Bill Lee,	
1938	Lefty Grove	*3.07		Rick Wise	3.95

*Led league

YEAR	PITCHER	ERA	YEAR	PITCHER	ERA
1976	Luis Tiant	3.06	1985	Oil Can Boyd	3.70
1977	Ferguson Jenkins	3.68	1986	Roger Clemens	*2.48
1978	Dennis Eckersley	2.99	1987	Roger Clemens	2.97
1979	Dennis Eckersley	2.99	1988	Roger Clemens	2.93
1980	Bill Stanley	3.39	1989	Roger Clemens	3.13
1981	Mike Torrez	3.69	1990	Roger Clemens	*1.93
1982	Bill Stanley	3.10	1991	Roger Clemens	*2.62
1983	Bob Ojeda	4.04	1992	Roger Clemens	*2.41
1984	Bruce Hurst	3.92			

*Led league

RED SOX SAVES LEADERS, YEAR BY YEAR

YEAR	PITCHER	SAVES	YEAR	PITCHER	SAVES
1901	Ted Lewis	1	1928	Ed Morris	5
1902	Nick Altrock	1	1929	Milt Gaston	2
1903	Cy Young	2	1930	Milt Gaston,	
1904	Cy Young	1		Danny MacFayden	2
1905	George Winter	3	1931	Wilcy Moore	*10
1906	Joe Harris,		1932	Wilcy Moore	4
	George Winter,		1933	Bob Kline	4
	Cy Young	2	1934	Fritz Ostermueller	3
1907	Tex Pruiett,		1935	Rube Walberg	3
	Cy Young	3	1936	Jack Wilson	3
1908	Eddie Cicotte,		1937	Jack Wilson	7
	Cy Morgan,		1938	Archie McKain	6
	Cy Young	2	1939	Joe Heving	7
1909	Frank Arellanes	*8	1940	Jack Wilson	5
1910	Charlie Hall	5	1941	Mike Ryba	6
1911	Charlie Hall,		1942	Mace Brown	6
	Smokey Joe Wood	5	1943	Mace Brown	9
1912	Hugh Bedient	3	1944	Frank Barrett	8
1913	Hugh Bedient,		1945	Frank Barrett	3
	Charlie Hall	5	1946	Bob Klinger	*9
1914	Dutch Leonard	*4	1947	Earl Johnson	8
1915	Carl Mays	*6	1948	Earl Johnson	5
1916	Dutch Leonard	5	1949	Ellis Kinder,	
1917	Babe Ruth	2		Walt Masterson	4
1918	Bullet Joe Bush	2	1950	Ellis Kinder	9
1919	Allen Russell	†*4	1951	Ellis Kinder	*14
1920	Herb Pennock	2	1952	Al Benton	6
1921	Allen Russell	3	1953	Ellis Kinder	*27
1922	Alex Ferguson,		1954	Ellis Kinder	15
	Allen Russell	2	1955	Ellis Kinder	18
1923	Jack Quinn	7	1956	Ike Delock	9
1924	Jack Quinn	7	1957	Ike Delock	11
1925	Ted Wingfield	2	1958	Leo Kiely	12
1926	Ted Wingfield	3	1959	Mike Fornieles	11
1927	Danny MacFayden,		1960	Mike Fornieles	*14
	Red Ruffing	2	1961	Mike Fornieles	15

*Led league
†2 more saves with New York

YEAR	PITCHER	SAVES	YEAR	PITCHER	SAVES
1962	Dick Radatz	*24	1978	Bill Stanley	10
1963	Dick Radatz	25	1979	Dick Drago	13
1964	Dick Radatz	*29	1980	Tom Burgmeier	24
1965	Dick Radatz	22	1981	Bill Campbell	7
1966	Don McMahon	9	1982	Mark Clear,	
1967	John Wyatt	20		Bill Stanley	14
1968	Lee Stange	12	1983	Bill Stanley	33
1969	Sparky Lyle	17	1984	Bill Stanley	22
1970	Sparky Lyle	20	1985	Steve Crawford	12
1971	Sparky Lyle	16	1986	Bill Stanley	16
1972	Bob Bolin,		1987	Wes Gardner	10
	Bill Lee	5	1988	Lee Smith	29
1973	Bob Bolin	15	1989	Lee Smith	25
1974	Diego Segui	10	1990	Jeff Reardon	21
1975	Dick Drago	15	1991	Jeff Reardon	40
1976	Jim Willoughby	10	1992	Jeff Reardon	‡27
1977	Bill Campbell	*31			

*Led league
‡3 more saves with Atlanta (N.L.)

5
ALL-TIME RED SOX ROSTER

ALL-TIME RED SOX ROSTER—BATTERS

NAME	YEARS	POSITION	AB	HITS	HR	BA
Adair, Jerry	1967–1968	SS-2B	524	137	5	.261
Agganis, Harry	1954–1955	1B	517	135	11	.261
Agnew, Sam	1916–1918	C	526	101	0	.192
Alexander, Dale	1932–1933	1B	689	228	13	.331
Allenson, Gary	1979–1984	C	1,027	231	19	.225
Almada, Mel	1933–1937	OF	1,171	319	6	.272
Alvarado, Luis	1968–1970	SS	234	47	1	.201
Anderson, Brady	1988	OF	148	34	0	.230
Andres, Ernie	1946	3B	41	4	0	.098
Andrew, Kim	1975	2B	2	1	0	.500
Andrews, Mike	1966–1970	2B	2,101	563	47	.268
Aparicio, Luis	1971–1973	SS	1,426	361	7	.253
Armas, Tony	1983–1986	OF	2,023	510	113	.252
Armbruster, Charlie	1905–1907	C	352	53	0	.151
Asbjornson, Casper	1928–1929	C	45	6	0	.133
Aspromonte, Ken	1957–1958	2B	94	23	0	.245
Aulds, Doyle	1947	C	4	1	0	.250
Avila, Bobby	1959	2B	45	11	3	.244
Aviles, Ramon	1977	2B	1	0	0	.000
Azcue, Joe	1969	C	51	11	0	.216
Bailey, Bob	1977–1978	DH	96	18	4	.188
Bailey, Gene	1920	OF	135	31	0	.230
Baker, Floyd	1953–1954	3B	192	51	0	.266
Baker, Jack	1976–1977	1B	26	3	1	.115
Baker, Tracy	1911	1B	1	0	0	.000
Ball, Neal	1912–1913	2B	103	19	0	.184
Barbare, Walter	1918	3B	29	5	0	.172
Barna, Babe	1943	OF	112	19	2	.170
Barrett, Bill	1929–1930	OF	388	103	3	.265
Barrett, Bob	1929	3B	126	34	0	.270
Barrett, Jimmy	1907–1908	OF	398	96	1	.241
Barrett, Marty	1982–1990	2B	3,362	935	17	.278
Barrett, Tommy	1992	2B	3	0	0	.000
Barry, Jack	1915–1917, 1919	2B	1,074	241	2	.224
Batts, Matt	1947–1951	C	558	152	9	.272
Baylor, Don	1986–1987	DH	924	220	47	.238
Beniquez, Juan	1971–1975	OF	799	219	8	.274
Benzinger, Todd	1987–1988	OF	628	165	21	.263

NAME	YEAR(S)	POSITION	AB	HITS	HR	BA
Berberet, Lou	1958	C	167	35	2	.210
Berg, Moe	1935–1939	C	409	107	3	.262
Berger, Boze	1939	SS	30	9	0	.300
Berry, Charlie	1928–1932	C	1,029	277	14	.269
Bevan, Hal	1952	3B	1	0	0	.000
Bigelow, Elliot	1929	OF	211	60	1	.284
Bischoff, John	1925–1926	C	260	70	1	.269
Bishop, Max	1934–1935	2B	375	94	2	.251
Blackwell, Tim	1974–1975	C	254	56	0	.220
Bluhm, Red	1918	PH	1	0	0	.000
Boggs, Wade	1982–1992	3B	6,213	2,098	85	.338
Bolling, Milt	1952–1957	SS	853	211	15	.247
Boone, Ike	1923–1925	OF	978	325	22	.332
Boone, Ray	1960	1B	78	16	1	.205
Boudreau, Lou	1951–1952	SS	275	73	5	.265
Bowen, Sam	1977–1980	OF	22	3	1	.136
Bradley, Hugh	1910–1912	1B	261	53	2	.203
Brady, Cliff	1920	2B	180	41	0	.228
Bratschi, Fred	1926–1927	OF	168	46	0	.274
Bressoud, Ed	1962–1965	SS	1,958	528	57	.270
Brohamer, Jack	1978–1980	3B-2B	493	126	3	.256
Brumley, Mike	1991–1992	SS-3B	119	25	0	.210
Brunansky, Tom	1990–1992	OF	1,378	350	46	.254
Bucher, Jim	1944–1945	3B	428	110	4	.257
Buckner, Bill	1984–1987, 1990	1B	2,070	577	48	.279
Buddin, Don	1956–1961	SS	2,126	519	39	.244
Burda, Bob	1972	1B	73	12	2	.164
Burkett, Jesse	1905	OF	573	147	4	.257
Burks, Ellis	1987–1992	OF	2,794	785	93	.281
Burleson, Rick	1974–1980	SS	4,064	1,114	38	.274
Burns, George	1922–1923	1B	1,109	352	19	.317
Busby, Jim	1959–1960	OF	102	23	1	.225
Cady, Hick	1912–1917	C	803	196	0	.244
Camilli, Dolph	1945	1B	198	42	2	.212
Campbell, Paul	1941–1942, 1946	1B-OF	41	4	0	.098
Carbo, Bernie	1974–1978	OF	986	257	45	.261
Carey, Tom	1939–1942, 1946	2B-SS	250	65	0	.260
Carlisle, Walter	1908	OF	10	1	0	.100
Carlstrom, Swede	1911	SS	6	1	0	.167

NAME	YEAR(S)	POSITION	AB	HITS	HR	BA
Carlyle, Cleo	1927	OF	278	65	1	.234
Carlyle, Roy	1925–1926	OF	441	137	9	.311
Carrigan, Bill	1906, 1908–1916	C	1,970	506	6	.257
Cater, Danny	1972–1974	1B	638	167	14	.262
Cepeda, Orlando	1973	DH	550	159	20	.289
Cerone, Rick	1988–1989	C	560	143	7	.255
Chadbourne, Chet	1906–1907	2B-OF	81	24	0	.296
Chaplin, Ed	1920–1922	C	76	14	0	.184
Chapman, Ben	1937–1938	OF	903	293	13	.324
Christopher, Joe	1966	OF	13	1	0	.077
Christopher, Loyd	1945	OF	14	4	0	.286
Cicero, Joe	1929–1930	OF	62	15	0	.242
Cissell, Bill	1934	2B	416	111	4	.267
Clark, Danny	1924	3B	325	90	2	.277
Clark, Jack	1991–1992	DH	738	174	33	.236
Clinton, Lu	1960–1964	OF	1,427	359	49	.252
Cochran, George	1918	3B	60	7	0	.117
Coffey, Jack	1918	3B	44	7	1	.159
Coleman, Dave	1977	OF	12	0	0	.000
Collins, Jimmy	1901–1907	3B	2,972	881	25	.296
Collins, Shano	1921–1925	OF	1,599	433	5	.271
Combs, Merrill	1947, 1949–1950	3B	92	20	1	.217
Congalton, Bunk	1907	OF	496	142	2	.286
Conigliaro, Billy	1969–1971	OF	829	223	33	.269
Conigliaro, Tony	1964–1970, 1975	OF	2,955	790	162	.267
Connally, Bud	1925	SS	107	28	0	.262
Connolly, Ed	1929–1932	C	371	66	0	.178
Connolly, Joe	1924	OF	10	1	0	.100
Conroy, Bill	1942–1944	C	386	76	5	.197
Consolo, Billy	1953–1959	SS-2B	618	140	6	.227
Cooke, Dusty	1933–1936	OF	1,257	357	15	.284
Cooney, Jimmy	1917	2B	26	8	0	.222
Cooper, Cecil	1971–1976	1B	1,330	377	40	.283
Cooper, Scott	1990–1992	3B	373	109	5	.292
Correll, Vic	1972	C	4	2	0	.500
Coughtry, Marlan	1960	2B	19	3	0	.158
Cox, Ted	1977	DH	58	21	1	.362
Cramer, Doc	1936–1940	OF	3,111	940	1	.302
Cravath, Gavvy	1908	OF	277	71	1	.256

NAME	YEAR(S)	POSITION	AB	HITS	HR	BA
Creeden, Pat	1931	2B	8	0	0	.000
Criger, Lou	1901–1908	C	1,943	405	6	.208
Cronin, Joe	1935–1945	SS	3,892	1,168	119	.300
Culberson, Leon	1943–1947	OF	1,188	319	14	.269
Dahlgren, Babe	1935–1936	1B	582	154	10	.265
Daley, Pete	1955–1959	C	653	160	11	.245
Dallessandro, Dom	1937	OF	46	5	0	.109
Danzig, Babe	1909	1B	13	2	0	.154
Darwin, Bobby	1976–1977	OF	115	21	3	.183
Daughters, Bob	1937	PR	0	0	0	—
Demeter, Don	1966–1967	OF	269	78	10	.290
Dente, Sam	1947	3B	168	39	0	.232
Derrick, Mike	1970	OF-1B	33	7	0	.212
Desautels, Gene	1937–1940	C	1,086	276	2	.254
Devine, Mickey	1920	C	12	2	0	.167
DeVormer, Al	1923	C	209	54	0	.258
Diaz, Bo	1977	C	1	0	0	.000
Dickey, George	1935–1936	C	34	1	0	.029
Didier, Bob	1974	C	14	1	0	.071
Dillard, Steve	1975–1977	2B	313	82	2	.262
DiMaggio, Dom	1940–1942, 1946–1953	OF	5,640	1,680	87	.298
DiPietro, Bob	1951	OF	11	1	0	.091
Dodson, Pat	1986–1988	1B	99	20	4	.202
Doerr, Bobby	1937–1944, 1946–1951	2B	7,093	2,042	223	.288
Donahue, John	1923	OF	36	10	1	.278
Donahue, Pat	1908–1910	C	266	59	3	.222
Doran, Tom	1904–1906	C	38	4	0	.105
Dougherty, Patsy	1902–1904	OF	1,223	398	4	.325
Dowd, Tommy	1901	OF	594	159	3	.268
Doyle, Danny	1943	C	43	9	0	.209
Doyle, Denny	1975–1977	2B	1,197	313	6	.261
Dropo, Walt	1949–1952	1B	1,092	307	51	.281
Duffy, Frank	1978–1979	3B-SS-2B	107	27	0	.252
Dugan, Joe	1922	3B	341	98	3	.287
Durst, Cedric	1930	OF	302	74	1	.245
Dwyer, Jim	1979–1980	OF	373	104	11	.279
Easler, Mike	1984–1985	DH	1,169	337	43	.288
Eggert, Elmer	1927	2B	3	0	0	.000
Eibel, Hack	1920	OF-P	43	8	0	.186
Engle, Clyde	1910–1914	1B-3B	1,680	445	6	.265

NAME	YEAR(S)	POSITION	AB	HITS	HR	BA
Esasky, Nick	1989	1B	564	156	30	.277
Evans, Al	1951	C	24	3	0	.125
Evans, Dwight	1972–1990	OF	8,726	2,373	379	.272
Evers, Hoot	1952–1954	OF	709	177	25	.250
Ezzell, Homer	1924–1925	3B	463	128	0	.276
Fanzone, Carmen	1970	3B	15	3	0	.200
Farrell, Doc	1935	2B	7	2	0	.286
Farrell, Duke	1903–1905	C	271	69	0	.255
Ferrell, Rick	1933–1937	C	1,791	541	16	.302
Ferris, Hobe	1901–1907	2B	3,689	876	34	.237
Fewster, Chick	1922–1923	2B-SS-3B	367	91	0	.248
Finney, Lou	1939–1942, 1944–1945	OF-1B	1,930	580	13	.301
Fiore, Mike	1970–1971	1B	112	18	1	.161
Fisk, Carlton	1969, 1971–1980	C	3,860	1,097	162	.284
Fitzgerald, Howie	1926	OF	97	25	0	.258
Flagstead, Ira	1923–1929	OF	2,941	867	27	.295
Flaherty, John	1992	C	66	13	0	.197
Flair, Al	1941	1B	30	6	0	.200
Foster, Eddie	1920–1922	3B	907	240	0	.265
Fothergill, Bob	1933	OF	32	11	0	.344
Fowler, Boob	1926	3B	8	1	0	.125
Fox, Pete	1941–1945	OF	1,717	496	6	.289
Foxx, Jimmie	1936–1942	1B	3,288	1,051	222	.320
Foy, Joe	1966–1968	3B	1,515	373	41	.246
Freeman, Buck	1901–1907	OF-1B	3,077	879	48	.286
Freeman, John	1927	OF	2	0	0	.000
French, Charlie	1909–1910	2B-SS	207	50	0	.242
Friberg, Bernie	1933	2B-3B	41	13	0	.317
Friend, Owen	1955	SS	42	11	0	.262
Fuller, Frank	1923	2B	21	5	0	.238
Gaffke, Fabian	1936–1939	OF	250	61	7	.244
Gagliano, Phil	1971–1972	OF-3B-SS	150	43	0	.287
Gainor, Del	1914–1917, 1919	1B	716	196	8	.274
Gallagher, Bob	1972	PH	5	0	0	.000
Galvin, Jim	1930	PH	2	0	0	.000
Garbark, Bob	1945	C	199	52	0	.261
Gardner, Billy	1962–1963	2B	283	70	0	.247
Gardner, Larry	1908–1917	3B	3,919	1,106	16	.282
Garrison, Ford	1943–1944	OF	178	48	1	.270

NAME	YEAR(S)	POSITION	AB	HITS	HR	BA
Gaston, Alex	1926, 1929	C	417	93	2	.223
Gedman, Rich	1980–1990	C	2,856	741	83	.259
Geiger, Gary	1959–1965	OF	2,002	507	71	.253
Gelbert, Charlie	1940	3B	91	18	0	.198
Gerber, Wally	1928–1929	SS	391	79	0	.202
Gernert, Dick	1952–1959	1B	2,255	568	101	.252
Gessler, Doc	1908–1909	OF	831	249	3	.300
Geygan, Chappie	1924–1926	SS	103	26	0	.252
Giannini, Joe	1911	SS	2	1	0	.500
Gibson, Russ	1967–1969	C	656	152	7	.232
Gilbert, Andy	1942, 1946	OF	12	1	0	.083
Gile, Don	1959–1962	C	120	18	3	.150
Gilhooley, Frank	1919	OF	112	27	0	.241
Gillis, Grant	1929	2B	73	18	0	.247
Ginsberg, Joe	1961	C	24	6	0	.250
Gleason, Harry	1901–1903	3B-OF	254	57	2	.224
Glenn, Joe	1940	C	47	6	0	.128
Godwin, John	1905–1906	3B-OF-SS	236	50	0	.212
Goggin, Chuck	1974	2B	1	0	0	.000
Gonzales, Eusebio	1918	SS	5	2	0	.400
Gooch, Johnny	1933	C	77	14	0	.182
Goodman, Billy	1947–1957	2B-1B	4,399	1,344	14	.306
Gosger, Jim	1963, 1965–1966	OF	466	116	14	.249
Graham, Charlie	1906	C	90	21	1	.233
Graham, Lee	1983	OF	6	0	0	.000
Graham, Skinny	1934–1935	OF	57	14	0	.246
Green, Lenny	1965–1966	OF	506	135	8	.267
Green, Pumpsie	1959–1962	2B-SS	742	181	12	.244
Greenwell, Mike	1985–1992	OF	2,980	912	84	.306
Griffin, Doug	1971–1977	2B	2,081	517	7	.248
Grimes, Ray	1920	1B	4	1	0	.250
Grimshaw, Moose	1905–1907	1B	894	229	4	.256
Gross, Turkey	1925	SS	32	3	0	.094
Guerra, Mike	1951	C	32	5	0	.156
Guerrero, Mario	1973–1974	SS	503	121	0	.241
Guindon, Bobby	1964	1B-OF	8	1	0	.125
Gunning, Hy	1911	1B	9	1	0	.111
Gutierrez, Jackie	1983–1985	SS	734	181	4	.247
Gutteridge, Don	1946–1947	2B-3B	178	33	3	.185
Hale, Odell	1941	3B	24	5	1	.208
Haley, Ray	1915–1916	C	8	1	0	.125

NAME	YEAR(S)	POSITION	AB	HITS	HR	BA
Hancock, Garry	1978, 1980–1982	OF	254	58	4	.228
Haney, Fred	1926–1927	3B	578	134	3	.232
Hardy, Carroll	1960–1962	OF	788	186	13	.236
Harper, Tommy	1972–1974	OF	1,565	405	36	.259
Harrell, Billy	1961	3B-SS	37	6	0	.162
Harrelson, Ken	1967–1969	OF	661	173	41	.262
Harris, Joe	1922–1925	OF-1B	1,401	442	23	.315
Hartley, Grover	1927	C	244	67	1	.275
Hatcher, Billy	1992	OF	315	75	1	.238
Hatfield, Fred	1950–1952	3B	200	39	3	.195
Hatton, Grady	1954–1956	3B	687	180	9	.262
Hayden, Jack	1906	OF	322	80	1	.248
Hayes, Frankie	1947	C	13	2	0	.154
Hearn, Ed	1910	SS	2	0	0	.000
Heep, Danny	1989–1990	OF	389	108	5	.278
Heise, Bob	1975–1976	3B	182	42	0	.231
Helms, Tommy	1977	DH	59	16	1	.271
Hemphill, Charlie	1901	OF	545	142	3	.261
Henderson, Dave	1986–1987	OF	235	53	9	.226
Hendryx, Tim	1920–1921	OF	500	152	0	.304
Henriksen, Olaf	1911–1917	OF	487	131	1	.269
Herrera, Mike	1925–1926	2B	276	76	0	.275
Heving, Johnny	1924–1925, 1928–1930	C	794	213	0	.268
Hickman, Charley	1902	OF	108	32	3	.296
Higgins, Pinky	1937–1938, 1946	3B	1,294	386	16	.298
Hiller, Hob	1920–1921	3B-SS	30	5	0	.167
Hinkle, Gordie	1934	C	75	13	0	.173
Hinson, Paul	1928	PR	0	0	0	—
Hitchcock, Billy	1948–1949	1B-2B	271	67	1	.247
Hoblitzell, Doc	1914–1918	1B	1,534	413	3	.269
Hobson, Butch	1975–1980	3B	2,230	561	94	.252
Hodapp, Johnny	1933	2B	413	129	3	.312
Hoderlein, Mel	1951	2B-3B	14	5	0	.357
Hoey, Jack	1906–1908	OF	500	116	0	.232
Hoffman, Glenn	1980–1987	SS	1,927	473	22	.245
Hofmann, Fred	1927–1928	C	416	104	0	.250
Holm, Billy	1945	C	135	25	0	.185
Hooper, Harry	1909–1920	OF	6,270	1,707	30	.272
Horn, Sam	1987–1989	1B	273	61	16	.223

NAME	YEAR(S)	POSITION	AB	HITS	HR	BA
Horton, Tony	1964–1967	1B	350	91	1	.260
Housie, Wayne	1991	OF	8	2	0	.250
Howard, Elston	1967–1968	C	319	66	6	.207
Howard, Paul	1909	OF	15	3	0	.200
Hughes, Terry	1974	3B	69	14	1	.203
Hunter, Buddy	1971, 1973, 1975	2B	17	5	0	.294
Hunter, Herb	1920	OF	12	1	0	.083
Jackson, Ron	1960	1B	31	7	0	.226
Jacobson, Baby Doll	1926–1927	OF	549	158	6	.288
Janvrin, Hal	1911, 1913–1917	SS-2B	1,548	357	4	.231
Jenkins, Tom	1925–1926	OF	114	28	0	.246
Jensen, Jackie	1954–1959, 1961	OF	3,857	1,089	170	.282
Johnson, Bob	1944–1945	OF	1,054	318	29	.302
Johnson, Deron	1974–1976	1B	73	14	1	.192
Johnson, Roy	1932–1935	OF	1,954	611	31	.313
Jolley, Smead	1932–1933	OF	942	280	27	.297
Jones, Charlie	1901	OF	41	6	0	.146
Jones, Dalton	1964–1969	2B-3B	1,842	447	26	.243
Jones, Jake	1947–1948	1B	509	116	17	.228
Joost, Eddie	1955	SS-2B	119	23	5	.193
Josephson, Duane	1971–1972	C	388	97	11	.250
Judge, Joe	1933–1934	1B	123	37	0	.301
Jurak, Ed	1982–1985	SS-3B-1B	259	70	1	.270
Karow, Marty	1927	SS-3B	10	2	0	.200
Kasko, Eddie	1966	SS	136	29	1	.213
Kell, George	1952–1954	3B	829	253	18	.305
Kellett, Red	1934	SS	9	0	0	.000
Keltner, Ken	1950	3B	28	9	0	.321
Kendall, Fred	1978	1B	41	8	0	.195
Kennedy, John	1970–1974	2B-3B-SS	783	190	13	.243
Keough, Marty	1956–1960	OF	493	114	9	.231
Klaus, Billy	1955–1958	SS-3B	1,626	428	25	.263
Kleinow, Red	1910–1911	C	161	25	1	.155
Knight, John	1907	3B	360	78	2	.217
Kosco, Andy	1972	OF	47	10	3	.213
Kroner, John	1935–1936	2B-3B-SS	302	88	4	.291
Krug, Marty	1912	SS	39	12	0	.308
Kutcher, Randy	1988–1990	OF	246	55	3	.224
LaChance, Candy	1902–1905	1B	1,677	421	8	.251

NAME	YEAR(S)	POSITION	AB	HITS	HR	BA
LaForest, Ty	1945	3B	204	51	2	.250
LaFrancois, Roger	1982	C	10	4	0	.400
Lahoud, Joe	1968–1971	OF	601	123	26	.205
Lake, Eddie	1943–1945	SS	815	201	14	.247
Lamar, Bill	1919	OF	148	43	0	.291
Lancellotti, Rick	1990	1B	8	0	0	.000
Landis, Jim	1967	OF	7	1	1	.143
Langford, Sam	1926	PH	1	0	0	.000
Lansford, Carney	1981–1982	3B	881	279	15	.317
LaPorte, Frank	1908	2B	156	37	0	.237
Lary, Lyn	1934	SS	419	101	2	.241
Lazor, Johnny	1943–1946	OF	596	157	6	.263
Lee, Dud	1924–1926	SS	550	131	0	.238
Legett, Lou	1933–1935	C	43	12	0	.279
Lehner, Paul	1952	OF	3	2	0	.667
Leibold, Nemo	1921–1923	OF	756	215	1	.284
Lenhardt, Don	1952, 1954	OF	171	49	10	.287
Lepcio, Ted	1952–1959	2B	1,622	401	53	.247
Lerchen, Dutch	1910	SS	15	0	0	.000
Lewis, Duffy	1910–1917	OF	4,325	1,248	27	.289
Lewis, Jack	1911	2B	59	16	0	.271
Lickert, John	1981	C	0	0	0	—
Lipon, Johnny	1952–1953	SS	379	79	0	.208
Lock, Don	1969	OF	58	13	1	.224
Loepp, George	1928	OF	51	9	3	.176
Lonergan, Walt	1911	2B	26	7	0	.269
Lord, Harry	1907–1910	3B	1,420	389	3	.274
Lucas, Johnny	1931–1932	OF	3	0	0	.000
Lupien, Tony	1940, 1942–1943	1B	1,090	294	7	.270
Lynch, Walt	1922	C	2	1	0	.500
Lynn, Fred	1974–1980	OF	3,062	944	124	.308
Lyons, Steve	1985–1986, 1991–1992	OF	735	187	10	.254
Madden, Tom	1909–1911	C	67	20	0	.299
Mahoney, Jim	1959	SS	23	3	1	.130
Mallett, Jerry	1959	OF	15	4	0	.267
Malzone, Frank	1955–1965	3B	5,273	1,454	131	.276
Mantilla, Felix	1963–1965	2B-OF	1,137	326	54	.287
Manush, Heinie	1936	OF	313	91	0	.291
Marquardt, Ollie	1931	2B	39	7	0	.179
Marshall, Bill	1931	PR	0	0	0	—

NAME	YEAR(S)	POSITION	AB	HITS	HR	BA
Marshall, Mike	1990–1991	DH	174	50	5	.287
Martin, Babe	1948–1949	C	6	2	0	.333
Marzano, John	1987–1992	C	462	107	6	.232
Matchick, Tommy	1970	3B	14	1	0	.071
Mauch, Gene	1956–1957	2B	247	68	2	.275
Maxwell, Charlie	1950–1952, 1954	OF	207	42	3	.203
Mayer, Wally	1917–1918	C	61	13	0	.213
Maynard, Chick	1922	SS	24	3	0	.125
McAuliffe, Dick	1974–1975	2B-3B	287	59	5	.206
McBride, Tom	1943–1947	OF	814	228	1	.280
McCann, Emmett	1926	SS-3B	3	0	0	.000
McCarver, Tim	1974–1975	C	49	15	0	.306
McConnell, Amby	1908–1910	2B	990	254	2	.257
McFarland, Ed	1908	C	48	10	0	.208
McGah, Ed	1946–1947	C	51	8	0	.157
McGovern, Art	1905	C	44	5	0	.114
McGuire, Deacon	1907–1908	PH	5	3	1	.600
McHale, Jim	1908	OF	67	15	0	.224
McInnis, Stuffy	1918–1921	1B	2,006	594	3	.296
McLean, Larry	1901	1B	19	4	0	.211
McManus, Marty	1931–1933	3B-2B	730	193	9	.264
McMillan, Norm	1923	3B-2B-SS	459	116	0	.253
McNair, Eric	1936–1938	2B-SS	1,045	289	16	.277
McNally, Mike	1915–1920	2B-3B-SS	592	137	0	.231
McNeil, Norm	1919	C	9	3	0	.333
McWilliams, Bill	1931	PH	2	0	0	.000
Mejias, Roman	1963–1964	OF	458	105	13	.229
Mele, Sam	1947–1949, 1954–1955	OF	842	234	21	.278
Melillo, Oscar	1935–1937	2B	783	192	1	.245
Menosky, Mike	1920–1923	OF	1,603	459	9	.286
Merchant, Andy	1975–1976	C	6	2	0	.333
Merson, Jack	1953	2B	4	0	0	.000
Metkovich, Catfish	1943–1946	OF	1,690	440	23	.260
Miles, Dee	1943	OF	121	26	0	.215
Miller, Bing	1935–1936	OF	185	56	4	.303
Miller, Elmer	1922	OF	147	28	4	.190
Miller, Hack	1918	OF	29	8	0	.276
Miller, Otto	1930–1932	3B	761	212	0	.279
Miller, Rick	1971–1977, 1981–1985	OF	2,573	683	23	.265

NAME	YEAR(S)	POSITION	AB	HITS	HR	BA
Mills, Buster	1937	OF	505	149	7	.295
Mitchell, Johnny	1922–1923	SS	550	129	1	.235
Moncewicz, Freddie	1928	SS	1	0	0	.000
Montgomery, Bob	1970–1979	C	1,185	306	23	.258
Moore, Bill	1926–1927	C	87	18	0	.207
Morgan, Eddie	1934	1B	528	141	3	.267
Morgan, Red	1906	3B	307	66	1	.215
Morton, Guy	1954	PH	1	0	0	.000
Moses, Jerry	1965, 1968–1970	C	472	131	13	.278
Moses, Wally	1946–1948	OF	619	155	6	.250
Moskiman, Doc	1910	1B	9	1	0	.111
Moss, Les	1951	C	202	40	3	.198
Mulleavy, Greg	1933	PR	0	0	0	—
Muller, Freddie	1933–1934	2B	49	9	0	.184
Mundy, Bill	1913	1B	47	12	0	.255
Muser, Tony	1969	1B	9	1	0	.111
Myer, Buddy	1927–1928	3B-SS	1,005	303	3	.301
Myers, Hap	1910–1911	1B-OF	44	16	0	.364
Naehring, Tim	1990–1992	SS/2B	326	72	5	.221
Narleski, Bill	1929–1930	SS-3B-2B	358	95	0	.265
Neitzke, Ernie	1921	OF	25	6	0	.240
Newman, Jeff	1983–1984	C	195	39	4	.200
Newsome, Skeeter	1941–1945	SS-2B	1,681	437	4	.260
Niarhos, Gus	1952–1953	C	93	13	0	.140
Nichols, Reid	1980–1985	OF	759	203	15	.267
Niemiec, Al	1934	2B	32	7	0	.219
Niles, Harry	1908–1910	OF	635	154	3	.243
Nixon, Russ	1960–1965, 1968	C	1,337	358	13	.268
Nonnenkamp, Red	1938–1940	OF	262	69	0	.263
Nunamaker, Les	1911–1914	C	356	88	0	.247
O'Berry, Mike	1979	C	59	10	1	.169
O'Brien, Jack	1903	OF	338	71	3	.210
O'Brien, Syd	1969	3B	263	64	9	.243
O'Brien, Tommy	1949–1950	OF	156	32	3	.205
Oglivie, Ben	1971–1973	OF	438	103	10	.235
Okrie, Len	1952	C	1	0	0	.000
Oliver, Gene	1968	C	35	5	0	.143
Oliver, Tom	1930–1933	OF	1,931	534	0	.277
Olson, Karl	1951, 1953–1955	OF	342	79	2	.231

NAME	YEAR(S)	POSITION	AB	HITS	HR	BA
Olson, Marv	1931–1933	2B	457	110	0	.241
O'Neill, Bill	1904	OF	51	10	0	.196
O'Neill, Steve	1924	C	307	73	0	.238
Orme, George	1920	OF	6	2	0	.333
O'Rourke, Frank	1922	SS	216	57	1	.264
Ostdiek, Harry	1908	C	3	0	0	.000
Ostrowski, John	1948	PH	1	0	0	.000
Owen, Marv	1940	3B-1B	57	12	0	.211
Owen, Mickey	1954	C	68	16	1	.235
Owen, Spike	1986–1988	SS	820	200	8	.244
Owens, Frank	1905	C	2	0	0	.000
Pagliaroni, Jim	1955, 1960–1962	C	698	177	92	.254
Pankovits, Jim	1990	2B	0	0	0	—
Papi, Stan	1979–1980	2B	117	22	1	.188
Parent, Fred	1901–1907	SS	3,846	1,051	19	.273
Parrish, Larry	1988	DH	158	41	7	.259
Partee, Roy	1943–1944, 1946–1947	C	859	226	2	.263
Paschal, Ben	1920	OF	28	10	0	.357
Patterson, Hank	1932	C	1	0	0	.000
Pavletich, Don	1970–1971	C-1B	92	16	1	.174
Peacock, Johnny	1937–1944	C	1,297	355	1	.274
Pellagrini, Eddie	1946–1947	3B-SS	302	62	6	.205
Pena, Tony	1990–1992	C	1,365	335	13	.245
Perez, Tony	1980–1982	1B	1,087	289	40	.266
Perrin, John	1921	OF	13	3	0	.231
Pesky, Johnny	1942, 1946–1952	SS-3B	4,085	1,277	13	.313
Peterson, Bob	1906–1907	C	131	25	1	.191
Petrocelli, Rico	1963, 1965–1976	SS-3B	5,390	1,352	210	.251
Philley, Dave	1962	OF	42	6	0	.143
Picinich, Val	1923–1925	C	680	182	4	.268
Pickering, Urbane	1931–1932	3B	798	205	11	.257
Piersall, Jimmy	1950, 1952–1958	OF	3,369	919	66	.273
Pittinger, Pinky	1921–1923	3B	454	104	0	.229
Plantier, Phil	1990–1992	OF	512	137	18	.268
Plews, Herb	1959	2B	12	1	0	.083
Polly, Nick	1945	3B	7	1	0	.143
Pond, Ralph	1910	OF	4	1	0	.250

NAME	YEAR(S)	POSITION	AB	HITS	HR	BA
Poquette, Tom	1979, 1981	OF	156	51	2	.327
Porter, Dick	1934	OF	265	80	0	.302
Poulsen, Ken	1967	3B-SS	5	1	0	.200
Pratt, Del	1921–1922	2B	1,128	352	11	.312
Pratt, Larry	1914	C	4	0	0	.000
Prothro, Doc	1925	3B	415	130	0	.313
Purtell, Billy	1910–1911	3B	250	58	1	.232
Pytlak, Frankie	1941, 1945–1946	C	367	95	2	.259
Quinones, Rey	1986	SS	190	45	2	.237
Quintana, Carlos	1988–1991	1B	1,073	306	18	.285
Rader, Dave	1980	C	137	45	3	.328
Reder, Johnny	1932	1B	37	5	0	.135
Reed, Jody	1987–1992	2B-SS	2,658	743	17	.280
Reeves, Bobby	1929–1931	3B	816	187	4	.229
Regan, Bill	1926–1930	2B	2,260	611	17	.270
Rehg, Wally	1913–1915	OF	257	62	0	.241
Reichle, Dick	1922–1923	OF	385	99	1	.257
Remy, Jerry	1978–1984	2B	2,809	802	2	.286
Renna, Bill	1958–1959	OF	78	17	4	.218
Repulski, Rip	1960–1961	OF	161	40	3	.248
Reynolds, Carl	1934–1935	OF	657	191	10	.291
Rhyne, Hal	1929–1932	SS	1414	348	0	.246
Rice, Jim	1974–1989	OF	8,225	2,452	382	.298
Richter, Al	1951, 1953	SS	66	11	0	.167
Riggert, Joe	1911	OF	146	31	2	.212
Rigney, Topper	1926–1927	SS	543	144	4	.265
Rising, Pop	1905	OF	29	3	0	.103
Rivera, Luis	1989–1992	SS	1,371	330	20	.241
Robidoux, Billy Jo	1990	1B	44	8	1	.182
Robinson, Aaron	1951	C	74	15	2	.203
Robinson, Floyd	1968	OF	24	3	0	.125
Rodgers, Bill	1915	2B	6	0	0	.000
Rogell, Billy	1925, 1927–1928	2B-SS-3B	672	157	2	.234
Rollings, Red	1927–1928	3B-1B	232	60	0	.259
Romero, Ed	1986–1989	SS-3B-2B	656	155	2	.236
Romine, Kevin	1985–1991	OF	630	158	5	.251
Rosar, Buddy	1950–1951	C	254	64	2	.252
Rosenthal, Si	1925–1926	OF	357	95	4	.266
Roth, Braggo	1919	OF	227	58	0	.256
Rothrock, Jack	1925–1932	OF-SS-2B	1,905	529	14	.278

NAME	YEAR(S)	POSITION	AB	HITS	HR	BA
Rudi, Joe	1981	DH	122	22	6	.180
Ruel, Muddy	1921–1922, 1931	C	802	216	1	.269
Runnels, Pete	1958–1962	2B-1B	2,578	825	29	.320
Russell, Rip	1946–1947	3B	326	65	7	.199
Ruth, Babe	1914–1919	P-OF	1,110	342	49	.308
Ryan, Jack	1929	OF	3	0	0	.000
Ryan, Mike	1964–1967	C	705	142	7	.201
Rye, Gene	1931	OF	39	7	0	.179
Sadowski, Eddie	1960	C	93	20	3	.215
Satriano, Tom	1969–1970	C	292	63	3	.216
Sax, Dave	1985–1987	C	50	16	1	.320
Scarritt, Russ	1929–1931	OF	1,026	294	3	.287
Schang, Wally	1918–1920	C	942	274	4	.291
Scherbarth, Bob	1950	C	0	0	0	—
Schilling, Chuck	1961–1965	2B	1,969	470	23	.239
Schlesinger, Rudy	1965	PH	1	0	0	.000
Schmees, George	1952	OF	64	13	0	.203
Schmidt, Dave	1981	C	42	10	2	.238
Schofield, Dick	1969–1970	2B	365	84	3	.230
Schreckengost, Ossee	1901	C	280	85	0	.304
Scott, Everett	1914–1921	SS	3,887	956	7	.246
Scott, George	1966–1971, 1977–1979	1B	4,234	1,088	154	.257
Seeds, Bob	1933–1934	1B-OF	236	57	0	.242
Selbach, Kip	1904–1906	OF	1,022	248	4	.243
Shaner, Wally	1926–1927	OF	597	165	3	.276
Shanks, Howard	1923–1924	3B-SS-2B	657	168	3	.256
Shannon, Red	1919	2B	290	75	0	.259
Shaw, Al	1909	C	41	4	0	.098
Shea, Merv	1933	C	56	8	0	.143
Sheaffer, Danny	1987	C	66	8	1	.121
Shean, Dave	1918–1919	2B	525	126	0	.240
Sheridan, Neill	1948	PH	1	0	0	.000
Shofner, Strick	1947	3B	13	2	0	.154
Shorten, Chick	1915–1917	OF	294	66	0	.224
Siebern, Norm	1967–1968	1B	74	11	0	.149
Simmons, Al	1943	OF	133	27	1	.203
Sizemore, Ted	1979–1980	2B	111	28	1	.252
Skinner, Camp	1923	OF	13	3	0	.231
Slattery, Jack	1901	C	3	1	0	.333
Small, Charlie	1930	OF	18	3	0	.167

NAME	YEAR(S)	POSITION	AB	HITS	HR	BA
Smith, Al	1964	3B	51	11	2	.216
Smith, Broadway Aleck	1903	C	33	10	0	.303
Smith, Elmer	1922	OF	231	66	6	.286
Smith, George	1966	2B	403	86	8	.213
Smith, John	1931	1B	15	2	0	.133
Smith, Paddy	1920	C	2	0	0	.000
Smith, Reggie	1966–1973	OF	3,780	1,064	149	.281
Snell, Wally	1913	C	8	3	0	.375
Solters, Moose	1934–1935	OF	444	128	7	.288
Speaker, Tris	1907–1915	OF	3,947	1,327	39	.336
Spence, Stan	1940–1941, 1948–1949	OF	682	161	16	.236
Spencer, Tubby	1909	C	74	12	0	.162
Spognardi, Andy	1932	2B	34	10	0	.294
Stahl, Chick	1901–1906	OF	3,004	871	17	.290
Stahl, Jake	1903, 1908–1910, 1912–1913	1B	1,648	456	21	.277
Standeart, Jerry	1929	1B	18	3	0	.167
Stansbury, Jack	1918	3B	47	6	0	.128
Stapleton, Dave	1980–1986	1B-2B	2,028	550	41	.271
Statz, Jigger	1920	OF	3	0	0	.000
Steiner, Ben	1945–1946	2B	308	79	3	.256
Steiner, Red	1945	C	59	12	0	.203
Stenhouse, Mike	1986	OF-1B	21	2	0	.095
Stephens, Gene	1952–1953, 1955–1960	OF	1,316	325	24	.247
Stephens, Vern	1948–1952	SS-3B	2,545	721	122	.283
Stokes, Al	1925–1926	C	138	25	0	.181
Stone, George	1903	PH	2	0	0	.000
Stone, Jeff	1989–1990	OF	17	4	0	.235
Storie, Howie	1931–1932	C	25	5	0	.200
Stringer, Lou	1948–1950	2B	69	17	2	.246
Strunk, Amos	1918–1919	OF	597	156	0	.261
Stuart, Dick	1963–1964	1B	1,215	328	75	.270
Stumpf, George	1931–1933	OF	238	55	1	.231
Sullivan, Denny	1907–1908	OF	904	220	1	.243
Sullivan, Haywood	1955, 1957, 1959–1960	C	133	20	3	.150
Sullivan, Marc	1982, 1984–1987	C	360	67	5	.186
Sumner, Carl	1928	OF	29	8	0	.276

NAME	YEAR(S)	POSITION	AB	HITS	HR	BA
Swanson, Bill	1914	2B	20	4	0	.200
Sweeney, Bill	1930–1931	1B	741	222	5	.300
Tabor, Jim	1938–1944	3B	3,074	838	90	.273
Taitt, Doug	1928–1929	OF	547	162	3	.296
Tarbert, Arlie	1927–1928	OF	86	16	0	.186
Tartabull, Jose	1966–1968	OF	581	148	0	.255
Tarver, La Schelle	1986	OF	25	3	0	.120
Tasby, Willie	1960	OF	385	108	7	.281
Tate, Bennie	1932	C	273	67	2	.245
Tebbetts, Birdie	1947–1950	C	1,408	404	19	.287
Thomas, Fred	1918	3B	144	37	1	.257
Thomas, George	1966–1971	OF	435	115	9	.264
Thomas, Lee	1964–1965	1B-OF	922	244	35	.265
Thomas, Pinch	1912–1917	C	872	210	2	.241
Thomson, Bobby	1960	OF	114	30	5	.263
Thoney, Jack	1908–1909, 1911	OF	476	116	2	.244
Throneberry, Faye	1952, 1955–1957	OF	505	128	12	.253
Tillman, Bob	1962–1967	C	1,617	382	49	.236
Tobin, Jack	1926–1927	OF	583	173	3	.297
Tobin, Jackie	1945	3B	278	70	0	.252
Todt, Phil	1924–1930	1B	3,218	832	52	.259
Tonneman, Tony	1911	C	5	1	0	.200
Truesdale, Frank	1918	2B	36	10	0	.278
Umphlett, Tommy	1953	OF	495	140	3	.283
Unglaub, Bob	1904–1905, 1907–1908	1B-3B	944	237	2	.251
Vache, Tex	1925	OF	252	79	3	.313
Valdez, Julio	1980–1983	SS	87	18	1	.207
Valentin, John	1992	SS	185	51	5	.276
Van Camp, Al	1931–1932	OF-1B	427	112	0	.262
Vaughn, Mo	1991–1992	1B	574	140	17	.244
Veach, Bobby	1924–1925	OF	524	154	5	.294
Vernon, Mickey	1956–1957	1B	673	190	22	.282
Vick, Sammy	1921	OF	77	20	0	.260
Vitt, Ossie	1919–1921	3B	997	223	1	.224
Vollmer, Clyde	1950–1953	OF	805	211	40	.262
Vosmik, Joe	1938–1939	OF	1,175	354	16	.301
Wagner, Hal	1944, 1946–1947	C	658	174	7	.264
Wagner, Heinie	1906–1916, 1918	SS	3,277	822	10	.251

NAME	YEAR(S)	POSITION	AB	HITS	HR	BA
Walker, Chico	1980–1981, 1983–1984	2B	81	20	1	.247
Walker, Tilly	1916–1917	OF	804	207	5	.257
Walsh, Jimmy	1916–1917	OF	202	52	0	.257
Walters, Bucky	1933–1934	3B	283	69	8	.244
Walters, Fred	1945	C	93	16	0	.172
Walters, Roxy	1919–1923	C	764	156	0	.204
Wambsganss, Bill	1924–1925	2B	992	257	1	.259
Wanninger, Pee-Wee	1927	SS	60	12	0	.200
Warner, John	1902	C	222	52	0	.234
Warstler, Rabbit	1930–1933	SS	1,053	226	2	.215
Watson, Bob	1979	1B	312	105	13	.337
Watwood, Johnny	1932–1933	OF	296	70	0	.236
Webb, Earl	1930–1932	OF	1,230	395	35	.321
Webster, Ray	1960	2B	3	0	0	.000
Wedge, Eric	1991–1992	DH	69	18	5	.261
Welch, Frank	1927	OF	28	5	0	.179
Welch, Herb	1925	SS	38	11	0	.289
Werber, Bill	1933–1936	3B	2,045	575	38	.281
Wertz, Vic	1959–1961	1B	1,007	276	37	.274
White, Sammy	1951–1959	C	3,342	881	63	.264
Whiteman, George	1907, 1918	OF	226	59	1	.261
Whitt, Ernie	1976	C	18	4	1	.222
Wilber, Del	1952–1954	C	308	71	11	.231
Wilhoit, Joe	1919	OF	18	6	0	.333
Williams, Dana	1989	DH	5	1	0	.200
Williams, Denny	1924–1925, 1928	OF	321	85	0	.265
Williams, Dib	1935	3B-2B	251	63	3	.251
Williams, Dick	1963–1964	1B-3B	205	46	7	.224
Williams, Ken	1928–1929	OF	601	188	11	.313
Williams, Rip	1911	1B-C	284	68	0	.239
Williams, Ted	1939–1942, 1946–1960	OF	7,706	2,654	521	.344
Wilson, Archie	1952	OF	38	10	0	.263
Wilson, Gary	1902	2B	8	1	0	.125
Wilson, Les	1911	OF	7	0	0	.000
Wilson, Squanto	1914	1B	0	0	0	—
Winningham, Herm	1992	OF	234	55	1	.235
Winsett, Tom	1930–1931, 1933	OF	89	16	1	.180
Wolfe, Larry	1979–1980	2B-3B	101	22	4	.218
Wolter, Harry	1909	1B-P-OF	122	30	2	.246

NAME	YEAR(S)	POSITION	AB	HITS	HR	BA
Wood, Ken	1952	OF	20	2	0	.100
Wright, Tom	1948–1951	OF	176	50	1	.284
Yastrzemski, Carl	1961–1983	OF-1B	11,988	3,419	452	.285
Yerkes, Steve	1909, 1911–1914	2B-SS	1,808	467	3	.258
York, Rudy	1946–1947	1B	763	199	23	.261
Zarilla, Al	1949–1950, 1952–1953	OF	1,072	310	20	.289
Zauchin, Norm	1951, 1955–1957	1B	664	158	32	.238
Zupcic, Bob	1991–1992	OF	417	112	4	.269

ALL-TIME RED SOX ROSTER—PITCHERS

NAME	YEARS	WINS	LOSSES	PCT.	SAVES
Aase, Don	1977	6	2	.750	0
Adams, Bob	1925	0	0	—	0
Adkins, Doc	1902	1	1	.500	0
Altrock, Nick	1902–1903	0	3	.000	1
Anderson, Fred	1909, 1913	0	6	.000	0
Anderson, Larry	1990	0	0	—	1
Andrews, Ivy	1932–1933	15	19	.441	1
Aponte, Luis	1980–1983	8	6	.571	7
Appleton, Pete	1932	0	3	.000	0
Arellanes, Frank	1908–1910	24	22	.522	8
Atkins, Jim	1950, 1952	0	1	.000	0
Auker, Eldon	1939	9	10	.474	0
Bader, King	1917–1918	3	3	.500	1
Bagby, Jim	1938–1940, 1946	37	38	.493	4
Baker, Al	1939	0	0	—	0
Barberich, Frank	1910	0	0	—	0
Barr, Steve	1974–1975	1	1	.500	0
Barrett, Frank	1944–1945	12	10	.545	11
Barry, Ed	1905–1907	1	6	.143	0
Baumann, Frank	1955–1959	13	8	.619	1
Bayne, Bill	1929–1930	5	5	.500	0
Bedient, Hugh	1912–1914	43	35	.551	9
Bell, Gary	1967–1968	23	19	.523	4
Bennett, Dennis	1965–1967	12	13	.480	0
Bennett, Frank	1927–1928	0	1	.000	0
Benton, Al	1952	4	3	.571	6
Beville, Ben	1901	0	2	.000	0
Billingham, Jack	1980	1	3	.250	0
Bird, Doug	1983	1	4	.200	1
Black, Dave	1923	0	0	—	0
Blethen, Clarence	1923	0	0	—	0
Boddicker, Mike	1988–1990	39	22	.639	0
Boerner, Larry	1932	0	4	.000	0
Bolin, Bobby	1970–1973	10	8	.556	0
Bolton, Tom	1987–1992	21	23	.477	1
Borland, Tom	1960–1961	0	4	.000	3
Bowers, Stew	1935–1936	2	1	.667	0
Bowman, Joe	1944–1945	12	10	.545	0

NAME	YEARS	WINS	LOSSES	PCT.	SAVES
Bowsfield, Ted	1958–1960	5	5	.500	2
Boyd, Oil Can	1982–1989	60	56	.517	0
Bradley, Herb	1927–1929	1	4	.200	0
Brady, King	1908	1	0	1.000	0
Brandon, Darrell	1966–1968	13	19	.406	5
Brett, Ken	1967, 1969–1971	10	15	.400	3
Brewer, Tom	1954–1961	91	82	.526	3
Brickner, Ralph	1952	3	1	.750	1
Brillheart, Jim	1931	0	0	—	0
Brodowski, Dick	1952, 1955	6	5	.545	0
Brown, Hal	1953–1955	13	14	.481	0
Brown, Lloyd	1933	8	11	.421	1
Brown, Mace	1942–1943, 1946	18	10	.643	16
Brown, Mike	1982–1986	12	18	.400	0
Burchell, Fred	1907–1909	13	12	.520	0
Burgmeier, Tom	1978–1982	21	12	.636	40
Burton, Jim	1975, 1977	1	2	.333	1
Bush, Joe	1918–1921	46	39	.541	4
Bushelman, Jack	1911–1912	1	1	.500	0
Bushey, Frank	1927, 1930	0	1	.000	0
Butland, Bill	1940, 1942, 1946–1947	9	3	.750	1
Byerly, Bud	1958	1	2	.333	0
Caldwell, Earl	1948	1	1	.500	0
Caldwell, Ray	1919	7	4	.636	0
Campbell, Bill	1977–1981	28	19	.596	0
Carroll, Ed	1929	1	0	1.000	0
Casale, Jerry	1958–1960	15	17	.469	0
Cascarella, Joe	1935–1936	0	5	.000	0
Cecil, Rex	1944–1945	6	10	.375	0
Chakales, Bob	1957	0	2	.000	3
Chaney, Esty	1913	0	0	—	0
Charton, Pete	1964	0	2	.000	0
Chase, Ken	1942–1943	5	5	.500	0
Chech, Charlie	1909	7	5	.583	0
Chesbro, Jack	1909	0	1	.000	0
Chittum, Nels	1959–1960	3	0	1.000	0
Cicotte, Ed	1908–1912	51	46	.526	4

NAME	YEARS	WINS	LOSSES	PCT.	SAVES
Cisco, Galen	1961–1962, 1967	6	12	.333	1
Clark, Otie	1945	4	4	.500	0
Clear, Mark	1981–1985	35	23	.603	38
Clemens, Roger	1984–1992	152	72	.679	0
Clemons, Lance	1974	1	0	1.000	0
Cleveland, Reggie	1974–1978	46	41	.529	4
Clevenger, Tex	1954	2	4	.333	0
Clowers, Bill	1926	0	0	—	0
Collins, Ray	1909–1915	84	62	.575	4
Collins, Rip	1922	14	11	.560	0
Comstock, Ralph	1915	1	0	1.000	0
Conley, Gene	1961–1963	29	32	.475	2
Connolly, Ed	1964	4	11	.267	0
Cooper, Guy	1914–1915	1	1	.500	0
Coumbe, Fritz	1914	1	2	.333	1
Cramer, Doc	1938	0	0	—	0
Crawford, Steve	1980–1987	19	16	.543	17
Cremins, Bob	1927	0	0	—	0
Crouch, Zack	1988	0	0	—	0
Culp, Ray	1968–1973	71	58	.550	0
Cuppy, Nig	1901	4	6	.400	0
Curry, Steve	1988	0	1	.000	0
Curtis, Jack	1970–1973	26	23	.531	0
Darwin, Danny	1991–1992	12	15	.444	3
Deal, Cot	1947–1948	1	1	.500	0
Deininger, Pep	1902	0	0	—	0
Delock, Ike	1952–1953, 1955–1963	83	72	.535	31
Denman, Brian	1982	3	4	.429	0
Deutsch, Mel	1946	0	0	—	0
Deviney, Hal	1920	0	0	—	0
Dickman, Emerson	1936, 1938–1941	22	15	.595	8
Dinneen, Bill	1902–1907	85	86	.497	1
Dobens, Ray	1929	0	0	—	0
Dobson, Joe	1941–1943, 1946–1950, 1954	106	72	.596	9
Dodge, Sam	1921–1922	0	0	—	0

NAME	YEARS	WINS	LOSSES	PCT.	SAVES
Donohue, Pete	1932	0	1	.000	0
Dopson, John	1989–1992	19	19	.500	0
Dorish, Harry	1947–1949, 1956	7	11	.389	2
Dorsey, Jim	1984–1985	0	1	.000	0
Drago, Dick	1974–1975, 1978–1980	30	29	.508	41
Dreisewerd, Clem	1944–1946	6	6	.500	0
Dubuc, Jean	1918	0	1	.000	0
Duliba, Bob	1965	4	2	.667	1
Dumont, George	1919	0	4	—	0
Durham, Ed	1929–1932	19	38	.333	1
Earley, Arnie	1960–1965	10	19	.345	14
Eckersley, Dennis	1978–1984	84	70	.545	0
Ehmke, Howard	1923–1926	51	64	.443	8
Eibel, Hack	1920	0	0	—	0
Ellsworth, Dick	1968–1969	16	7	.696	0
Ellsworth, Steve	1988	1	6	.143	0
Evans, Bill	1951	0	0	—	0
Ferguson, Alex	1922–1925	32	48	.400	5
Ferrell, Wes	1934–1937	62	40	.608	1
Ferriss, Boo	1945–1950	65	30	.684	8
Finch, Joel	1979	0	3	.000	0
Fine, Tommy	1947	1	2	.333	0
Fischer, Hank	1966–1967	3	5	.375	1
Fleming, Bill	1940–1941	2	3	.400	1
Flowers, Ben	1951, 1953	1	4	.200	3
Foreman, Frank	1901	0	1	.000	0
Foreman, Happy	1926	0	0	—	0
Fornieles, Mike	1957–1963	39	35	.527	46
Fortune, Gary	1920	0	2	.000	0
Fossas, Tony	1991–1992	4	4	.500	3
Foster, Rube	1913–1917	58	34	.630	3
Foxx, Jimmie	1939	0	0	—	0
Francis, Ray	1925	0	2	.000	0
Freeman, Hersh	1952–1953, 1955	2	4	.333	0
Fuhr, Oscar	1924–1925	3	12	.200	0
Fullerton, Curt	1921–1925, 1933	10	37	.213	3
Gale, Rich	1984	2	3	.400	0

NAME	YEARS	WINS	LOSSES	PCT.	SAVES
Galehouse, Denny	1939–1940, 1947–1949	34	31	.523	3
Gallagher, Ed	1932	0	3	.000	0
Gardiner, Mike	1991–1992	13	20	.394	0
Gardner, Wes	1986–1990	17	26	.395	12
Garman, Mike	1969, 1971–1973	2	2	.500	0
Garrison, Cliff	1928	0	0	—	0
Gaston, Milt	1929–1931	27	52	.342	4
Gibson, Norwood	1903–1906	34	32	.515	0
Gillespie, Bob	1950	0	0	—	0
Glaze, Ralph	1906–1908	15	21	.417	0
Gonzales, Joe	1937	1	2	.333	0
Gray, Dave	1964	0	0	—	0
Gray, Jeff	1990–1991	4	7	.364	10
Gregg, Vean	1914–1916	9	11	.450	3
Griffin, Marty	1928	0	3	.000	0
Grilli, Guido	1966	0	1	.000	0
Grissom, Marv	1953	2	6	.250	0
Grove, Lefty	1934–1941	105	62	.629	4
Gumpert, Randy	1952	1	0	1.000	1
Hageman, Casey	1911–1912	0	2	.000	0
Hall, Sea Lion	1909–1913	45	32	.584	11
Harper, Harry	1920	5	14	.263	0
Harris, Bill	1938	5	5	.500	1
Harris, Greg	1989–1992	30	32	.484	6
Harris, Joe	1905–1907	3	30	.091	3
Harris, Mickey	1940–1941, 1946–1949	43	42	.506	1
Harriss, Slim	1926–1928	28	42	.400	2
Harshman, Jack	1959	2	3	.400	0
Hartenstein, Chuck	1970	0	3	.000	1
Hartman, Charlie	1908	0	0	—	0
Hash, Herb	1940–1941	8	7	.533	4
Hassler, Andy	1978–1979	3	3	.500	1
Hausmann, Clem	1944–1945	9	14	.391	4
Heep, Danny	1990	0	0	—	0
Heffner, Bob	1963–1965	11	20	.355	6
Heflin, Randy	1945–1946	4	11	.267	0
Heimach, Fred	1926	2	9	.182	0
Henry, Bill	1952–1955	15	20	.429	1

NAME	YEARS	WINS	LOSSES	PCT.	SAVES
Henry, Jim	1936–1937	6	1	.857	0
Hernandez, Ramon	1977	0	1	.000	1
Herrin, Tom	1954	1	2	.333	0
Hesketh, Joe	1990–1992	20	17	.541	1
Hetzel, Eric	1989–1990	3	7	.300	0
Heving, Joe	1938–1940	31	11	.738	12
Hillman, Dave	1960–1961	3	5	.375	0
Hinrichs, Paul	1951	0	0	—	0
Hisner, Harley	1951	0	1	.000	0
Hockette, George	1934–1935	4	4	.500	0
Hoeft, Billy	1959	0	3	.000	0
Holcombe, Ken	1953	1	0	1.000	1
Hooper, Harry	1913	0	0	—	0
House, Tom	1976–1977	2	3	.400	4
Howe, Les	1923–1924	2	0	1.000	0
Hoy, Pete	1992	0	0	—	0
Hoyt, Waite	1919–1920	10	12	.455	1
Hudson, Sid	1952–1954	16	22	.421	7
Hughes, Ed	1905–1906	3	2	.600	0
Hughes, Tom	1902–1903	23	10	.697	0
Hughson, Tex	1941–1944, 1946–1949	96	54	.640	17
Humphrey, Bill	1938	0	0	—	0
Hunt, Ben	1910	2	3	.400	0
Hurd, Tom	1954–1956	13	10	.565	11
Hurst, Bruce	1980–1988	88	73	.547	0
Husting, Bert	1902	0	1	.000	0
Irvine, Daryl	1990–1992	4	5	.444	0
Jacobson, Beany	1907	0	0	—	0
Jamerson, Charley	1924	0	0	—	0
James, Bill	1919	3	5	.375	0
Jarvis, Ray	1969–1970	5	7	.417	1
Jenkins, Ferguson	1976–1977	22	21	.512	0
Johnson, Earl	1940–1941, 1946–1950	40	32	.556	17
Johnson, Hank	1933–1935	16	15	.516	3
Johnson, John Henry	1983–1984	4	4	.500	2
Johnson, Rankin	1914	4	9	.308	0
Johnson, Vic	1944–1945	6	7	.462	2
Jones, Rick	1976	5	3	.625	0
Jones, Sad Sam	1916–1921	64	59	.520	4

NAME	YEARS	WINS	LOSSES	PCT.	SAVES
Judd, Oscar	1941–1945	20	18	.526	3
Kallio, Rudy	1925	1	4	.200	0
Karger, Ed	1909–1911	21	17	.553	1
Karl, Andy	1943	1	1	.500	1
Karr, Benn	1920–1922	16	27	.372	2
Kellett, Al	1924	0	0	—	0
Kellum, Win	1901	2	3	.400	0
Kelly, Ed	1914	0	0	—	0
Kemmerer, Russ	1954–1955, 1957	6	4	.600	0
Kennedy, Bill	1953	0	0	—	2
Kiecker, Dana	1990–1991	10	12	.455	0
Kiefer, Joe	1925–1926	0	4	.000	0
Kiely, Leo	1951, 1954–1956, 1958–1959	25	25	.500	28
Killilay, Jack	1911	4	2	.667	0
Kinder, Ellis	1948–1955	86	52	.623	91
Kinney, Walt	1918	0	0	—	0
Kison, Bruce	1985	5	3	.625	1
Kline, Bob	1930–1933	23	26	.469	6
Kline, Ron	1969	0	1	.000	1
Klinger, Bob	1946–1947	4	3	.571	14
Kolstad, Hal	1962–1963	0	4	.000	2
Koonce, Cal	1970–1971	3	5	.375	2
Kramer, Jack	1948–1949	24	13	.649	1
Krausse, Lew	1972	1	3	.250	1
Kreuger, Rick	1975–1977	2	2	.500	0
Kroh, Rube	1906–1907	2	4	.333	0
Lake, Eddie	1944	0	0	—	0
Lamabe, Jack	1963–1965	16	20	.444	7
Lamp, Dennis	1988–1991	20	16	.556	2
Landis, Bill	1967–1969	9	8	.529	4
LaRose, John	1978	0	0	—	0
Lee, Bill	1969–1978	94	68	.580	13
LeFebvre, Bill	1938–1939	1	1	.500	0
Leheny, Regis	1932	0	0	—	0
Leister, John	1987, 1990	0	2	.000	0
Leonard, Dutch	1913–1918	90	63	.588	11
LeRoy, Louis	1910	0	0	—	0
Lewis, Duffy	1913	0	0	—	0

NAME	YEARS	WINS	LOSSES	PCT.	SAVES
Lewis, Ted	1901	16	17	.485	1
Lisenbee, Hod	1929–1932	15	33	.313	0
Littlefield, Dick	1950	2	2	.500	1
Lockwood, Skip	1980	3	1	.750	2
Lollar, Tim	1985–1986	7	5	.583	1
Lonborg, Jim	1965–1971	68	65	.511	2
Lucey, Joe	1925	0	1	.000	0
Lucier, Lou	1943–1944	3	4	.429	0
Lundgren, Carl	1926–1927	5	14	.263	0
Lyle, Sparky	1967–1971	22	17	.564	69
Lyons, Steve	1991	0	0	—	0
MacFayden, Danny	1926–1932	52	78	.400	4
MacLeod, Bill	1962	0	1	.000	0
MacWhorter, Keith	1980	0	3	.000	0
Magrini, Pete	1966	0	1	.000	0
Mahoney, Chris	1910	0	1	.000	1
Maloy, Paul	1913	0	0	—	0
Manzanillo, Josias	1991	0	0	—	0
Marchildon, Phil	1950	0	0	—	0
Marcum, Johnny	1936–1938	26	30	.464	4
Marichal, Juan	1974	5	1	.833	0
Masterson, Walt	1949–1952	15	11	.577	7
Matthews, Bill	1909	0	0	—	0
Mays, Carl	1915–1919	72	51	.585	12
McCabe, Dick	1918	0	1	.000	0
McCall, Windy	1948–1949	0	1	.000	0
McCarthy, Tom	1985	0	0	—	0
McDermott, Mickey	1948–1953	48	34	.585	8
McDonald, Jim	1950	1	0	1.000	0
McGlothen, Lynn	1972–1973	9	9	.500	0
McGraw, Bob	1919	0	2	.000	0
McHale, Marty	1910–1911, 1916	0	3	.000	0
McKain, Archie	1937–1938	13	12	.520	8
McLaughlin, Jud	1931–1933	0	0	—	0
McMahon, Doc	1908	1	0	1.000	0
McMahon, Don	1966–1967	9	9	.500	11
McNaughton, Gordon	1932	0	1	.000	0
Meola, Mike	1933, 1936	0	2	.000	1
Merena, Spike	1934	1	2	.333	0
Meyer, Russ	1957	0	0	—	0

NAME	YEARS	WINS	LOSSES	PCT.	SAVES
Michaels, John	1932	1	6	.143	0
Midkiff, Dick	1938	1	1	.500	0
Mills, Dick	1970	0	0	—	0
Mitchell, Charlie	1984–1985	0	0	—	0
Mitchell, Fred	1901–1902	6	7	.462	0
Moford, Herb	1959	0	2	.000	0
Molyneaux, Vince	1918	1	0	1.000	0
Monbouquette, Bill	1958–1965	96	91	.513	1
Moore, Wilcy	1931–1932	15	23	.395	1
Morehead, Dave	1963–1968	35	56	.385	0
Moret, Roger	1970–1975	41	18	.695	6
Morgan, Cy	1907–1909	22	25	.468	2
Morris, Ed	1928–1931	42	45	.483	6
Morrissey, Deacon	1901	0	0	—	0
Morton, Kevin	1991	6	5	.545	0
Moseley, Earl	1913	9	5	.643	0
Moser, Walter	1911	0	1	.000	0
Mueller, Gordy	1950	0	0	—	0
Muffett, Billy	1960–1962	9	15	.375	2
Mulligan, Joe	1934	1	0	1.000	0
Mulroney, Frank	1930	0	1	.000	0
Murphy, Johnny	1947	0	0	—	3
Murphy, Rob	1989–1990	5	13	.278	16
Murphy, Tom	1976–1977	4	6	.400	8
Murphy, Walter	1931	0	0	—	0
Murray, George	1923–1924	9	20	.310	0
Musser, Paul	1919	0	2	.000	0
Mustaikis, Alex	1940	0	1	.000	0
Myers, Elmer	1920–1922	17	14	.548	0
Nagle, Judge	1911	1	1	.500	0
Nagy, Mike	1969–1972	19	10	.655	0
Neitzke, Ernie	1921	0	0	—	0
Neubauer, Hal	1925	1	0	1.000	0
Newhauser, Don	1972–1974	4	3	.571	5
Newsom, Bobo	1937	13	10	.565	0
Newsome, Dick	1941–1943	35	33	.515	0
Nichols, Chet	1960–1963	5	8	.385	6
Nipper, Al	1983–1987	42	43	.494	0
Nippert, Merlin	1962	0	0	—	0
Nixon, Willard	1950–1958	69	72	.489	3
Nourse, Chet	1909	0	0	—	0

NAME	YEARS	WINS	LOSSES	PCT.	SAVES
Oberlin, Frank	1906–1907	2	8	.200	0
O'Brien, Buck	1911–1913	29	23	.558	0
O'Doul, Lefty	1923	1	1	.500	0
Ojeda, Bob	1980–1985	44	39	.530	1
Olmsted, Hank	1905	1	2	.333	0
Olson, Ted	1936–1938	1	1	.500	0
O'Neill, Emmett	1943–1945	15	26	.366	0
Osinski, Dan	1966–1967	7	5	.583	4
Ostermueller, Fritz	1934–1940	59	65	.476	13
Palm, Mike	1948	0	0	—	0
Papai, Al	1950	4	2	.667	2
Pape, Larry	1909, 1911–1912	13	9	.591	3
Parnell, Mel	1947–1956	123	75	.621	10
Partenheimer, Stan	1944	0	0	—	0
Patten, Casey	1908	0	1	.000	0
Pattin, Marty	1972–1973	32	28	.533	1
Paxton, Mike	1977	10	5	.667	0
Pennock, Herb	1915–1917, 1919–1922, 1934	61	59	.508	6
Pertica, Bill	1918	0	0	—	0
Peters, Gary	1970–1972	33	25	.569	2
Petry, Dan	1991	0	0	—	1
Phillips, Ed	1970	0	2	.000	0
Piercy, Bill	1922–1924	16	33	.327	0
Pipgras, George	1933–1935	9	9	.500	1
Pizarro, Juan	1968–1969	6	9	.400	4
Plympton, Jeff	1991	0	0	—	0
Poindexter, Jennings	1936	0	2	.000	0
Pole, Dick	1973–1976	14	14	.500	1
Porterfield, Bob	1956–1958	7	16	.304	1
Potter, Nels	1941	2	0	1.000	0
Prentiss, George	1901–1902	3	2	.600	0
Price, Joe	1989	2	5	.286	0
Pruiett, Tex	1907–1908	4	18	.182	5
Quantrill, Paul	1992	2	3	.400	1
Quinn, Frank	1949–1950	0	0	—	0
Quinn, Jack	1922–1925	45	54	.455	14
Radatz, Dick	1962–1966	49	34	.590	104
Rainey, Chuck	1979–1982	23	14	.622	1

NAME	YEARS	WINS	LOSSES	PCT.	SAVES
Reardon, Jeff	1990–1992	8	9	.471	88
Reed, Jerry	1990	2	1	.667	2
Reeves, Bobby	1931	0	0	—	0
Remmerswaal, Win	1979–1980	3	1	.750	0
Renko, Steve	1979–1980	20	18	.526	0
Rhodes, Gordon	1932–1935	27	45	.375	4
Rich, Woody	1939–1941	5	3	.625	1
Ripley, Allen	1978–1979	5	6	.455	1
Ripley, Walt	1935	0	0	—	0
Ritchie, Jay	1964–1965	2	3	.400	2
Robinson, Jack	1949	0	0	—	0
Rochford, Mike	1988–1990	0	1	.000	0
Rogers, Lee	1938	1	1	.500	0
Roggenburk, Garry	1966, 1968–1969	0	1	.000	0
Rohr, Billy	1967	2	3	.400	0
Romo, Vicente	1969–1970	14	12	.538	1
Ross, Buster	1924–1926	7	12	.368	1
Rothrock, Jack	1928	0	0	—	0
Ruffing, Red	1924–1930	34	96	.262	8
Russell, Allan	1919–1922	28	28	.500	10
Russell, Jack	1926–1932, 1936	41	94	.304	0
Ruth, Babe	1914–1919	89	46	.659	4
Ryan, Jack	1909	4	3	.571	0
Ryan, Ken	1992	0	0	—	1
Ryba, Mike	1941–1946	36	25	.590	16
Sadowski, Bob	1966	1	1	.500	0
Sambito, Joe	1986–1987	4	6	.400	0
Sanders, Ken	1966	3	6	.333	2
Santiago, Jose	1966–1970	33	23	.589	8
Sayles, Bill	1939	0	0	—	0
Scarborough, Ray	1951–1952	13	14	.481	4
Schanz, Charley	1950	3	2	.600	0
Schiraldi, Calvin	1986–1987	12	7	.632	15
Schlitzer, Biff	1909	4	4	.500	1
Schmees, George	1952	0	0	—	0
Schmitz, Johnny	1956	0	0	—	0
Schroll, Al	1958–1959	1	4	.200	0
Schwall, Don	1961–1962	24	22	.522	0
Seaver, Tom	1986	5	7	.417	0

NAME	YEARS	WINS	LOSSES	PCT.	SAVES
Segui, Diego	1974–1975	8	13	.381	0
Sellers, Jeff	1985–1988	13	22	.371	0
Settlemire, Merle	1928	0	6	.000	0
Shea, John	1928	0	0	—	0
Sheldon, Rollie	1966	1	6	.143	0
Shields, Ben	1930	0	0	—	0
Shore, Ernie	1914–1917	58	32	.644	3
Short, Bill	1966	0	0	—	0
Siebert, Sonny	1969–1973	57	41	.582	5
Simmons, Pat	1928–1929	0	2	.000	2
Sisler, Dave	1956–1959	24	25	.490	4
Skok, Craig	1973	0	1	.000	1
Slayton, Steve	1928	0	0	—	0
Smith, Bob	1955	0	0	—	0
Smith, Charlie	1909–1911	14	6	.700	1
Smith, Doug	1912	0	0	—	0
Smith, Eddie	1947	1	3	.250	0
Smith, Frank	1910–1911	1	2	.333	0
Smith, George	1930	1	2	.333	0
Smith, Lee	1988–1990	12	7	.632	58
Smith, Pete	1962–1963	0	1	.000	0
Smith, Riverboat	1958	4	3	.571	0
Smithson, Mike	1988–1989	16	20	.444	2
Sommers, Rudy	1926–1927	0	0	—	0
Sothoron, Allen	1921	0	2	.000	0
Spanswick, Bill	1964	2	3	.400	0
Sparks, Tully	1902	7	9	.438	0
Speaker, Tris	1914	0	0	—	0
Spring, Jack	1957	0	0	—	0
Sprowl, Bobby	1978	0	2	.000	0
Stallard, Tracy	1960–1962	2	7	.222	2
Stange, Lee	1966–1969	28	35	.444	18
Stanley, Bob	1977–1989	115	97	.542	132
Steele, Elmer	1907–1909	9	12	.429	1
Stephenson, Jerry	1963, 1965–1968	8	19	.296	1
Stewart, Sammy	1986	4	1	.800	0
Stigman, Dick	1966	2	1	.667	0
Stimson, Carl	1923	0	0	—	0
Stobbs, Chuck	1947–1951	33	23	.589	1
Stone, Dean	1957	1	3	.250	1

NAME	YEARS	WINS	LOSSES	PCT.	SAVES
Sturdivant, Tom	1960	3	3	.500	1
Suchecki, Jim	1950	0	0	—	0
Sullivan, Frank	1953–1960	90	80	.529	6
Susce, George	1955–1958	18	14	.563	2
Swormstedt, Len	1906	1	1	.500	0
Taitt, Doug	1928	0	0	—	0
Tanana, Frank	1981	4	10	.286	0
Tannehill, Jesse	1904–1908	62	38	.620	1
Tatum, Ken	1971–1973	2	6	.250	0
Taylor, Harry	1950–1952	7	9	.438	2
Taylor, Scott	1992	1	1	.500	0
Terry, Yank	1940, 1942–1945	20	28	.417	2
Thielman, Jake	1908	0	0	—	0
Thomas, Blaine	1911	0	0	—	0
Thomas, Tommy	1937	0	2	.000	0
Thormahlen, Hank	1921	1	7	.125	0
Tiant, Luis	1971–1978	122	81	.584	3
Torrez, Mike	1978–1982	60	54	.526	0
Trautwein, John	1988	0	1	.000	0
Trimble, Joe	1955	0	0	—	0
Trout, Dizzy	1952	9	8	.529	1
Trujillo, Mike	1985–1986	4	4	.500	1
Tudor, John	1979–1983	39	32	.549	1
Turley, Bob	1963	1	4	.200	0
Van Dyke, Ben	1912	0	0	—	0
Vandenberg, Hy	1935	0	0	—	0
Veale, Bob	1972–1974	4	4	.500	15
Viola, Frank	1992	13	12	.520	0
Volz, Jake	1901	1	0	1.000	0
Wade, Jake	1939	1	4	.200	0
Wagner, Charlie	1938–1942, 1946	32	23	.582	0
Wagner, Gary	1969–1970	4	4	.500	7
Walberg, Rube	1934–1937	21	27	.438	5
Wall, Murray	1957–1959	13	14	.481	14
Waslewski, Gary	1967–1968	6	9	.400	2
Weaver, Monte	1939	1	0	1.000	1
Weiland, Bob	1932–1934	15	35	.300	4
Welch, Johnny	1932–1936	33	40	.452	5
Welzer, Tony	1926–1927	10	14	.417	1

NAME	YEARS	WINS	LOSSES	PCT.	SAVES
Wenz, Fred	1968–1969	1	0	1.000	0
Werle, Bill	1953–1954	0	2	.000	0
Widmar, Al	1947	0	0	—	0
Wight, Bill	1951–1952	9	8	.529	0
Williams, Dave	1902	0	0	—	0
Williams, Stan	1972	0	0	—	0
Williams, Ted	1940	0	0	—	0
Willoughby, Jim	1975–1977	14	16	.467	20
Wills, Ted	1959–1962	6	9	.400	1
Wilson, Duane	1958	0	0	—	0
Wilson, Earl	1959–1960, 1962–1966	56	58	.491	0
Wilson, Jack	1935–1941	67	67	.500	20
Wilson, Jim	1945–1946	6	8	.429	0
Wilson, John	1927–1928	0	2	.000	0
Wiltse, Hal	1926–1928	18	35	.340	1
Wingfield, Ted	1924–1927	24	44	.353	5
Winn, George	1919	0	0	—	0
Winter, George	1901–1908	82	96	.461	3
Winters, Clarence	1924	0	1	.000	0
Wise, Rick	1974–1977	47	32	.595	0
Wittig, Johnnie	1949	0	0	—	0
Wolter, Harry	1909	4	4	.500	0
Wood, Joe	1944	0	1	.000	0
Wood, Smokey Joe	1908–1915	116	56	.674	9
Wood, Wilbur	1961–1964	0	5	.000	0
Woods, John	1924	0	0	—	0
Woods, Pinky	1943–1945	13	21	.382	3
Woodward, Bob	1985–1988	4	4	.500	0
Workman, Hoge	1924	0	0	—	0
Worthington, Al	1960	0	1	.000	0
Wright, Jim	1978–1979	9	4	.692	0
Wyatt, John	1966–1968	14	13	.519	28
Wyckoff, John	1916–1918	0	0	—	1
Young, Cy	1901–1908	192	112	.632	9
Young, Matt	1991–1992	3	11	.214	0
Zahniser, Paul	1925–1926	11	30	.268	1
Zeiser, Matt	1914	0	0	—	0
Zuber, Bill	1946–1947	6	1	.857	0